T0322659

CHINA INCORPORATED

CHINA INCORPORATED

The Politics of a World Where China is Number One

Kerry Brown

BLOOMSBURY ACADEMIC
LONDON · NEW YORK · OXFORD · NEW DELHI · SYDNEY

BLOOMSBURY ACADEMIC
Bloomsbury Publishing Plc
50 Bedford Square, London, WC1B 3DP, UK
1385 Broadway, New York, NY 10018, USA
29 Earlsfort Terrace, Dublin 2, Ireland

BLOOMSBURY, BLOOMSBURY ACADEMIC and the Diana logo are
trademarks of Bloomsbury Publishing Plc

First published in Great Britain 2023

Cover design by Namkwan Cho
Cover image © nakornkhai/Adobe Stock

A catalogue record for this book is available from the British Library.

Library of Congress Cataloging-in-Publication Data

Names: Brown, Kerry, 1967– author.
Title: China incorporated : the politics of a world where China
is number one / Kerry Brown.
Description: London ; New York : Bloomsbury Academic, 2023. |
Includes bibliographical references and index.
Identifiers: LCCN 2022053434 (print) | LCCN 2022053435 (ebook) |
ISBN 9781350267244 (hardback) | ISBN 9781350267251 (epub) |
ISBN 9781350267268 (pdf) | ISBN 9781350267275
Subjects: LCSH: China–Foreign relations–21st century. |
China–Foreign relations–Western countries. | Western countries–Foreign
relations–China. | World politics–1989–
Classification: LCC DS779.47 .B76 2023 (print) | LCC DS779.47 (ebook) |
DDC 327.510182/1—dc23/eng/20230111
LC record available at https://lccn.loc.gov/2022053434
LC ebook record available at https://lccn.loc.gov/2022053435

ISBN: HB: 978-1-3502-6724-4
       ePDF: 978-1-3502-6726-8
       eBook: 978-1-3502-6725-1

Typeset by RefineCatch Limited, Bungay, Suffolk
Printed and bound in India

To find out more about our authors and books visit www.bloomsbury.com
and sign up for our newsletters.

CONTENTS

AN IMPORTANT NOTE ON TERMINOLOGY

This is a book about China and the world. A lot of the time, however, when I talk about that world outside China I am referring more specifically to the part of the world which economically, ideologically, geopolitically and militarily has been dominant at least since the Second World War. One term for this is 'the West'. Another is 'the developed world'. Sometimes one can say 'America and its allies'. None of these terms is ideal. In this work, I have sometimes used 'the West' and sometimes 'the Enlightenment West'. This latter captures the important fact that we are talking about a world of ideas, not just a geographical place. The 'Enlightenment West' while currently headquartered in Washington, embraces contemporary Europe (this includes the European Union, and countries in Western, Central and Eastern Europe that are not part of the EU), but also Australia, New Zealand, and stretches to treaty allies of the US and democracies like Japan. The 'Enlightenment West' refers to a commitment to a set of political and social ideas, and to a cultural outlook, which originated in seventeenth-century Europe, and is best expressed by Immanuel Kant's 'What is the Enlightenment?' with a strong stress on personal conscience and the freedom of the individual. I am aware of the debate and controversy around just how coherent both the set of ideas called Enlightenment ones are, and how varied those supposedly subscribing to these are. But for the purposes of this book, I have accepted this as the clearest label against which contemporary China stands in contrast. For China, while things are a little easier, I am referring at least since 1949 to the People's Republic of China, with its capital in Beijing, and ruled over by a Communist Party enjoying a monopoly on power. At times, when referring to Chinas that existed before this, in dynastic history, I try to offer more precision by directly using the specific dynasty, such as the Ming, or the Qing. I am aware that like the West, China is a plural term. I am also aware that 'China' is far more than its current political system, and that there are many in China who do not subscribe to that system, even though they have little choice but to live under it. But for the high level of argument pursued in this book, I did not want to dilute my central points at the risk of coming down to distracting levels of detail. I do not believe that has negated from the validity of my argument.

INTRODUCTION

Round about the end of December 2019 in the central Chinese city of Wuhan, doctors began noticing a new, unpleasant cough with flu symptoms that was starting to appear in patients checking into hospitals. The Chinese health care system has no primary care facilities. When people fall ill, they must go to hospitals to have triage of their problems. That gives these places a sometimes chaotic, disturbing feel, throwing together a super-busy doctor's surgery with an Accident and Emergency department. On an online WeChat forum, some of the doctors started to speculate that this cold looked similar to that symptomatic of the SARS virus (sever acute respiratory syndrome) that had engulfed the country, and part of the region, almost two decades before.

Since that outbreak in 2003, sporadic outbursts of avian and other viruses transmitted to humans by animals were always met by swift, decisive action. In Xi Jinping's China, however, anti-corruption purges and demands for greater accountability from officials was part of the new ethos since his rise to power in late 2012. While popular with the public who had grown weary of over-mighty officials forever being on the take and who enjoyed seeing the once seemingly omnipotent humbled by punishments, jail terms, and, in the worst cases, even more draconian treatment, by 2019 the campaigns had resulted in a culture of fear and cautiousness amongst officials. No one wanted to deliver bad news to the big leaders at the centre in Beijing – and specifically the Big Leader, Xi. For a short but critical period, local officials in the city tried to keep a lid on things and manage the situation, hoping against hope it would go away. But by the final days of the year, things were already spiralling out of control. A local pandemic was emerging. The central government had to be informed. Things rapidly deteriorated. The World Health Organisation (WHO) was formally told of a new virus on the 31 December.

The immediate consequences were largely in China. Within a little over a month, Jiang Chaolian, Communist Party head of Hubei province where Wuhan was situated, and Ma Guoqiang, his counterpart in the city itself, were dismissed. They were the initial scapegoats. Li Wenliang, the local eye doctor who had first alerted officials of the new disease, died on 7 February of COVID-19, the name given to the virus. News of his warnings, and the attempted coverup by panicky local officials a few weeks earlier had already started to spread more widely. Fang Fang, a local writer, in her 'Wuhan Diary', also broadcast later that year to the outside world in an English translation, described the sense of panic and incompetence. 'In the Same Breath', by filmmaker Nanfu Wang, and 'Days and Nights in Wuhan' by Cao Jinling both contained copious filmed material showing the physical and psychological impact of the disease as it spread. Over the first few months of 2020, China went into various stages of lockdown. Whole cities were closed. People wore face masks. The world watched as Xi Jinping himself seemed to disappear from public view for a couple of weeks at the end of January. American journalist Walter Russell Mead in an article in the *Wall Street Journal* on 3 February called China 'the real sick man of Asia'. 'The mighty Chinese juggernaut has been humbled this week, apparently by a species-hopping bat virus,' Mead wrote. 'While Chinese authorities struggle to control the epidemic and restart their economy, a world that has grown accustomed to contemplating China's inexorable rise was reminded that nothing, not even Beijing's power, can be taken for granted.'[1]

The article aroused the full fury of the Chinese government. Wall Street journalists were expelled from the country in vengeful retaliation (though also prompted by the expulsion of Chinese journalists from the US because of the claims they were spies working undercover). Netizens from China online went into angry melt-down. Meanwhile, in the rest of the world, the commentariat and other public figures readied themselves in expectation of a replay of the events around SARS over 2003. That had been a largely regional, and mostly a greater China problem.[2] For many it had underlined how autocratic systems such as that of the People's Republic from Beijing were simply unable to function properly in preventing, and then dealing, with an issue like this. The disaster bringing to an end this egregious, non-democratic and, in their eyes, illegitimate system was finally coming, they said. Jamil Anderlini, a seasoned Beijing based journalist for the respected *Financial Times* called this 'China's Chernobyl moment', referring to the nuclear plant disaster in the former Soviet Union in 1986. This was widely interpreted by historians as a key landmark prefiguring the ultimate demise of that regime, something which happened five years later.[3]

Fatefully, within weeks, the whole story changed. COVID-19 spread to Europe, the US and elsewhere. Governments were all consumed by the same sense of panic and afflicted by indecision and division. In the UK, prime minister Boris Johnson was seen to be blithely shaking hands in a hospital with patients, underplaying the infectiousness of the disease. But by 27 March he had contracted it himself, and within a few weeks was in intensive care in hospital. Donald Trump of the United States was also flippant early on before contracting it, with disastrous impacts in his re-election campaign, later in the year. Countries that prided themselves as bastions of personal liberty and freedom imposed measures every bit as draconian as those that China had used. In Italy, Germany, the UK and France, people were forbidden to leave their homes except to shop for food and undertake essential tasks. By April, the globe was in a full-blown pandemic, the first since a century before when Spanish Flu had killed up to fifty million people.

By the time of writing (January 2022), COVID-19 had claimed 5 million lives across the globe. Despite the creation of numerous successful vaccines, over a quarter of a billion people had contracted the disease. The anomaly was that the numbers both of deaths and infections was far higher in North America or Europe than in China. As of January 2022, the US had had 55 million infections, and 830,000 deaths. China in the same time had posted figures of 104,000 and 4,600 respectively. COVID-19 had flattened the geopolitics of the world. No one had emerged looking wholly competent – China for being the place where the outbreak started, and the rest of the world for failing to deal with it well when it came for them. China, the US, France, the UK, Australia, even New Zealand, had all had to use exceptional measures. None have emerged unscathed. Events in Wuhan which were still being argued about two years later had changed things dramatically.

A pandemic is a most unfortunate event to happen for many reasons. One however is more about symbolism than the tragedies of human suffering and death. That is simply the way in which the spread of COVID-19 has created new and dramatic geopolitical sentiments towards its most populous country, and one that stands ready to be the world's largest economy in the next decade or so. China and the outside world now regard each other and speak to each other in a different way. Where there was once at worst ambiguity, there is now much more clarity. The US was already becoming more vocal about its dislike both of the system China governs itself under, and what it does in the wider world, but by mid-2020, the incumbent in the White House was calling the disease 'the China Virus'. In China, all pretence at a restrained, measured counter-response was thrown to the wind. Trained diplomats, in person and online, spoke with such ferocity about the claims made about their nation and its government that they were branded 'Wolf Warriors'. This was after a highly jingoistic Chinese propaganda film of the same name where Chinese soldiers, Rambo-like, take on foreigners and violently beat them in war. In Europe, politicians in France, Italy, Germany and the UK started to speak about China as the major geopolitical problem of its time, waking up to an issue that had been around for decades as though it were something that had just dropped from a clear blue sky. As never before, China with its huge economy, its massive military, its rising global reach, was a threat, a problem for these people. Some of this language hovered on the edges of xenophobia. One book grandly referred to China's 'hidden hand', spreading across the landscape of the world, physically and virtually dipping into the politics of others, manipulating things to accord with its own aims.[4]

A virus, like some modern plague, brought to the surface for others divisions, and mutual antipathy, that had long simmered. For a broad coalition of figures in the West (here meaning North America, Europe, Australasia and their main security allies – see note at start), it represented everything they feared and disliked about the communist China they saw rearing up before them. Right at the beginning of the pandemic, in one of the final public events I took part in, I remember debating at the Oxford Union whether there should be a new Cold War with China. Ranged against my side there was a self-professed informal adviser to Trump, a former Canadian beauty queen and human rights activist who had been born in China, and a vocal student. Despite the heartfelt, emotionally fraught stories from the beauty queen about the predatory evil emanating across the world from Beijing, and the solemn declarations from the American about how China was coming and that we had better throw up our defences and go beat it back, our side, speaking against the motion, and in support of pragmatism and engagement, won – just about. It is unlikely we would be able to duplicate our success again today, so much has public opinion, for the moment at least, shifted.

The pandemic has made feelings of mutual distrust and mutual dislike palpable. In that context, this book seeks to take no sides. There are no heroes or good guys in the story I am about to try to tell. For all the appalling statements made in places across the US and Europe, and elsewhere, by public figures operating in democracies, Chinese actors, in government, and online, have been every bit as bad. The nadir of this was the moment on Twitter (a platform long banned in China) when an

American official posted a racist comment about Chinese people, only for a Chinese journalist to respond with the single word comment 'Bitch'! No one in this chaotic game came out looking good. COVID-19 exposed levels of vitriol as never before – all of it amply performed in public on social media so that only the most accomplished at avoiding unpleasant sights managed not to see it.

I had my own limited experience of this. Sometime halfway through that fateful year 2020, increasingly amazed at the amount of fury and anger aimed at Chinese, and China itself, I put out a piece on a website.[5] This simply argued that, with its current political confusions and the very odd behaviour of elected figures like Trump and the UK's prime minister Johnson, along with the ineptness of the West's own response to the pandemic, was it any wonder that even the most neutral citizen of the People's Republic would start to see their own system in a slightly less negative light. Better the vaguely competent devil you know that the shambolic, incompetent devil you don't – especially if they spent half the time railing at you that you're wrong. My main target was the fervent assumption creeping into almost everything about China in media, think tank reports and a slew of new books that the government running the huge country was existentially evil. These gave the impression that its leaders from Xi downwards leaped out of bed each day with a fiendish look on their faces and a vow in their heart to inflict more suffering on their people and the rest of the world. The default on almost every issue brought to attention that involved China in some parts of this media and think tank community and elsewhere was therefore that it was going to be guilty of the worse actions for the worst reasons.[6] That seemed to be both unjust, and untrue. It also meant that on areas where China might be criticized and held to account, the whole point was muted and made irrelevant because of the sense that nothing it did or could try to do would ever be any good because it was guilty even before it opened its mouth on everything.

Underneath this complex, far longer-term factors than the pandemic were in play. Rising fear by the US and its allies of China succeeding under a one-party system against their own predictions and convictions was one. That was an ideological or political issue, and one that will be discussed later in this book in detail. But beneath this were darker themes. Trump's 'China Virus' meme captured it, stirring up a rise in anti-Asian hate crimes in the US. The jumpiness of some in the West derived not so much from China being communist than from the idea that for the first time in the modern era the world was going to see an Asian country have a chance of rising to be the world's largest economy.

Mindsets seemed to be geared towards either refusing to accept this or doing everything they could to pretend this moment was never going to happen. Now was the time for a fightback. Resentments were rising. My piece about the ways in which moralizing from the West, and assuming that we had superior social and political values and therefore could lecture China and tell it what to do were doomed to failure, was met by what counted, at least for me, as a tsunami of online abuse and criticism.

For twenty-four hours, and for the first and last time, I engaged. It was grim work. Weird figures with online profiles that conveyed the minimum, or nothing, about who they were, levelled abuse, saying that I was an apologist for a genocidal actor. The Chinese government's behaviour in Xinjiang became a particular point of attack, even though I had written about that critically elsewhere, and was not addressing it specifically in my piece. One lobbyist in the UK who did have a name and public profile leaped in with the tired old line of how they loved the Chinese people and wanted to deliver them from the evil of their government. My sarcastic response that one could say the same things about the British were one an opponent of the current governing regime was rewarded by hot air and rhetoric. Just a little deployment of imagination made me wonder how on earth I would feel were I for instance a Chinese student or a non-political Chinese citizen in the face of all this. These people probably had critical views of their government. But faced by ill focussed, wide ranging and deep antipathy towards aspects of their country, it would probably put them off liberal western values if they led to crude, unkind behaviour like this. Once the US was accused of 'losing China' in the 1950s when it cut all links with Mao's newly established People's Republic. These days, there were many in the West that under the guise of 'saving China' were doing precisely the same thing.

I haven't engaged that deeply with online debates since. Dextrous muting of a few of the loudest and most ill-informed voices (never block, that just gives figures a reason to crow about their victory) has at least saved me from most of the online sledging. But the broader point I learned that day has not gone away. As this book shall argue, we are clearly living through one of the most complex and difficult moments humankind has ever faced, at least in modern history. It is clearer, day by day, that we need a different, more suitable vocabulary to deal with this situation. Polarized discourse, characterized by either/or, them or us, and stark binaries are not going to work. And yet, a large and influential group working in government, think tanks, even academia, seem to want to continue dividing the world neatly between the good and the bad, and seeing China as the ultimate representative of the latter. This suits the distorted and distorting ecosystem of Twitter. It has almost zero relevance to the real world we live in.

To add to the frustration many of these figures, in my experience, at least in private are aware of the complexities. But the public discourse condemns them to using these simple binary terms. It is as though one were ordered to describe quantum physics using purely pre-Newtonian terms and concepts. In the world of material science and physics we can have relativity. But apparently that is not the case in politics or international relations where absolutes preside with monolithic certainty. The 'evil' Xi Jinping, and the 'bad' Communist Party of China, oppressing the 'good' enslaved people of their nation, is a far easier trope to broadcast on media in print, online or on screen. And yet, alas, this, as this book hopes to show, is a fairy story. It is, however, a fairy story that impacts through its simplification and distortion on the real world and is becoming increasingly dangerous to deal with. It has, in essence, become something akin to a mass delusion.

This new China delusion is a problem for a number of reasons. First of all, it downplays the very thing that is most problematic and worrying about what we are confronting – its complexity. Were this purely a struggle between good and bad, where the West with its preferential and more just values was seeking to prevail over a China which represented things which were overtly harmful, then we would all be able to queue up in the right place to make ourselves available for the great looming battle. However, as I will argue later, China offers something far more difficult to pin down. A power marching with renewed confidence and vigour towards us in order to change our minds, upend and reform our systems, to broadly make us become more like it – in effect a new global colonizer or imperialist power – would be terrifying but at least offer clarity. China however is far less easy to categorize. Is it really in the business of creating the world to be just like itself? Does it believe that America, Europe, and other powers will ultimately embrace a sinified Marxist-Leninist one-party system, underpinned by hybrid Confucian, Daoist and Buddhist values? It is hard to see this as being what is happening. China has local issues and limited matters it is keen to get either global assent, or passive compliance with – the status of Taiwan, control of Hong Kong, and of the South and East China Sea, and its own internal affairs being the most prominent of these. Beyond that, the Chinese global vision remains as vexed and elusive, I suspect to itself as well as to others. In 2022, more clearly than in 2020, we can say only one thing – that more than ever before, if China is in the business of promoting its model and system of governance and administration for others, it has never looked less attractive, and more off-putting. Its critics should be pleased with its evident failure. They should not be so perpetually wound up by their conviction that in fact it is winning the image wars despite all the evidence.

Secondly, having simple binary narratives about China and its current and future global role means ironically that policymakers and businesses often over-privilege its power in the world. Tellingly, in a book about existential issues facing humanity by Oxford academic Toby Ord written in 2019, while he makes compelling cases for pandemics, climate change, nuclear war or accidents, artificial intelligence, and even the globe being struck by an asteroid, showing how these if they ever occurred or got out of hand would prove catastrophic to humanity, China and the threat it poses figures barely at all. As the world's largest nuclear power at the moment, America for instance is more of a threat to itself through potential accidents or wrong deployment of weapons than any outside actor. The USSR proved this with the tragic Chernobyl accident in 1986 which caused more internal damage than it did to the outside world, being credited with contributing to the demise of the Soviet Union five years later. Seeing the 'China Threat' as one that overshadows everything else, with an almost obsessive worry and concern means that a manageable problem immediately becomes unmanageable because of nothing more than the way we think about it and the elevated priority we give it. Though attitudes and decisions held by outsiders with no real link to the reality of the place and the meaning of its global role, China becomes a colossus rather than one amongst a series of other far greater issues which it must be seen alongside to be assessed more coherently and with proportion. In fact, on the existential issues listed above, for climate change, and nuclear accidents, China is more an ally than a foe. And on artificial intelligence, the issue that Ord judges the most immediate and pressing of all those he writes of, China's more freewheeling and entrepreneurial research environment in this area may well be the one that throws up, for Chinese people and the government, the very issues that Europe and the US have worried about and tried to put pre-emptive measures in place to avoid. Seeing China as no problem and no challenge is clearly naïve. But so too is seeing it as the greatest threat and the greatest challenge. Simple binary 'good / evil' labels towards China achieve precisely that latter distortion.

Finally, painting China in oversimplistic terms, and seeing the problems it poses as merely a replay of the Cold War era when the good West was ranged against the evil Soviet Union, means that even for those with worries and concerns about the problems China poses, they have the worst possible tools to try to mitigate or deal with these. Seeing Xi Jinping for instance as some all-consuming, all-powerful new oriental despot is one case in point. This does not recognize the complex nexus of power and interest groups that his style of leadership sits in, along with the ways in which it is the result of agreement, consensus and negotiation between these, rather than about a particular individual. That means that the vast, complex ecosystem this sort of Leadership (here spelt with a capital 'L' to stress its almost corporate nature) relies on is simply missed, ignored, swept away without any proper attention. It is as though one produced a history of civilization by only focussing on famous humans, thinking their story is the sole one that matters. Xi's power, its dominance and autocracy, are the result of varied social, ideological, political and domestic forces – and the interface between these and the outside world. All contribute to what we witness today. The role of the Communist Party as an organization and how best to understand that, and of significant figures such as Wang Huning, China's current chief ideologue, and those working in the cultural and ideological sphere, stretching back decades, all need to be factored in. Daydreaming about the time when Xi is felled and Chinese start streaming into the streets, liberated and happy to finally be lifted from oppression, are simply that – daydreams. Xi may well be a politician deeply interested in power – but that is about as informative as saying that a footballer is interested in kicking a ball around a pitch. The important questions are about how he operates, what context he operates in, who he needs to operate with, what aims are set, and how spectators and an audience get factored in. Power after all is useless without something or someone to be powerful over. It is relational. The Chinese political context is saturated in complex interlinkages and groups. And yet the simple story of Xi the all-consuming despot and autocrat is one that occurs almost every day, across non-Chinese language media.[7]

As never before, China in the last decade or so has been in the business of creating narratives and stories. The China Dream, the Belt and Road Initiative (BRI), the centennial goals domestically, and the march of the country toward rejuvenation are examples of these. The outside world however is stuck with stories about China which in their broad outline and binary nature reach back decades. They are in urgent need of revision, and, in some cases, outright rejection now. China has changed. So too must our most fundamental ideas about the place. This book is principally concerned with the business of what sort of new story might work best about China for the rest of the world, and China's role in that world. If we use the current dominant mindsets, at least as they are manifested in public discourse in Europe and America, we will end up with an insoluble problem, because we will not be responding to reality but to our own fantasies. If, for instance, we accept that genocidal actions are crimes against humanity, and that in Xinjiang in particular China has engaged in genocidal measures, then it is hard to justify any relationship or cooperation. And yet, in trade, on climate change, for reasons ranging from the good of humanity to self-interest for those involved, engagement continues, and in some places has deepened. This is an incoherent position. It is one that will be discussed at more length later in this book. But it is importantly symptomatic of how adopting absolute positions in one area then dictates how one should act in others in ways which, currently, are neither happening, nor, more seriously, can even be tenable or possible. It is through situations like this that we urgently learn we need a new story. The one about the 'evil Communist Party of China' and its bad leaders no longer helps, or works, any more than falling for their supreme goodness and faultlessness – the story that state propagandists in Beijing put out themselves. We have few ways of dealing with the huge challenges China poses for itself, and for the outside world, as it rises to a more dominant global position. But using fresh ways of thinking, updating and revising our own positions, and adapting our mindsets is one of them. I believe that it is the most crucial. This book, in however small a way, will hopefully contribute to that task.

Chapter One

THE THREE KEY THINGS ABOUT CHINA FOR THE MODERN WORLD

Sir John Barrow, First Baronet, a geographer, civil servant and administrator, was one of the great representatives of the British Empire during their proactive phase in the late eighteenth and early nineteenth century when his country was the world's greatest industrializing and trading nation. With a navy that had technologically already left the rest of its competitors behind, Britain was in the business of seeking new opportunities, new goods, new markets – and new places to send migrants to. America had slipped from the hands of the emerging British empire in 1776. But with the remarkable East India Company, an extraordinary non-government force run from plain offices with few personnel in the city of London, and yet furnished with its own army, bureaucracy and quasi-state powers abroad, the nation was unperturbed. An embassy was sent to the Qing court in 1793 led by Lord George Macartney. It trod paths which had already been proceeded along by Portuguese and Dutch emissaries over the previous century or so. But this one was in the business of hammering deals to open up what was expected to be the vast potential of the Chinese world.

Much had been imagined about this potential. Writers in the Enlightenment period from Voltaire and Leibniz in France and Germany respectively had, going from material found in sources largely written by Jesuits who had visited and lived in China in the century and a half before, built up the vision of a place which had a powerful appeal to the imagination. Chinoiserie had started to appear in British, French and other European cultures. The first contours of an idea of the Far East as 'exotic' started to appear. With its imperial bureaucratic system, staffed by Confucian scholars, and its remote, all-powerful emperor, a certain image of China appeared in literature and the writings of figures as diverse as Samuel Johnson and the poet S. T. Coleridge. Merchants were now trying to operate from one of the few places open to the outside world for trade in the country – Canton (today's Guangdong). But the opportunities were too limited. The Macartney embassy was one of a number over this period that tried to at least change this (the Dutch, for instance, sent a number, the last of which was only two years after the Macartney one).

John Barrow is important because of the account he left of his own impressions while a young man on the delegation. While clearly impressed and interested in what he saw attending the imperial court in China, the sense of an ossified, stagnant system which had collapsed in on itself is never far from his mind. 'The general character and complexion of the court is, as Lord Macartney has justly observed,' Barrow wrote in his account, was

> 'a singular mixture of ostentatious hospitality and inbred suspicion, ceremonious civility and real rudeness, shadowy complaisance and substantial perverseness; and this prevails through all the departments connected with the Court, although somewhat modified by the personal disposition of those at their head; but as to that genuine politeness, which distinguishes our manners, it cannot be expected in Orientals, considering among other things the light in which they are accustomed to regard the female part of society.' Whether the great ministers of state, who have daily intercourse in the different tribunals, sometimes relax from the stiff and formal deportment observed towards each other in public, I am not able to say, but when at Court they invariably observe certain stated forms and expression as studied and ceremonious as if they had never met before.[1]

Barrow did not return to China after that visit, but his views on a country and administration which had largely been left behind in time by changes in the outside world carried weight. Later in his life he was to serve in important roles in the British government system. Historians in more recent times like the American Kenneth Pomerantz have coined the pithy phrase, 'The Great Divergence' to refer to the ways from the start of the nineteenth century the Qing economy and its levels of development were superseded by those of Western Europe in particular.[2] There were no single, easy reasons for this. That the Qing China was an important global player before this period has been supported by data about economic size assembled by, amongst others, economist Angus Maddison. His argument that until around 1820, in gross terms at least, Qing China's economic size was the largest in the world, has had wide discussion and debate. Larger or not, imperial China had a global role before the nineteenth century. After that, it was perpetually marginalized and diminished.[3]

Barrow's views were supplemented by a whole host of different western narratives about the demise of the Qing, and the fragmentation and turmoil of Chinese history in the twentieth century. China as 'the sick man of Asia' as it was called in the 1930s, as a place successively carved up by colonizing powers from Britain to Germany and Japan, is now embedded as part of global history. Few would dispute that between the First Opium Wars from 1839, to the end of the Civil War between the Nationalist and the Communists in 1949 which resulted in the latter's victory and the establishment of the People's Republic, China, either as the Qing till 1911, or under the Republican administration, thereafter, was in a period of painful transition. There were points in this phase when the sustainability and survival of China as a sovereign entity were in question. Weakness, victimization and suffering pervade this story, not just as it is told externally, but within the country too, in the patriotic tales of humiliation that have been favoured as part of education since the 1990s in Chinese schools.

That mindset amongst non-Chinese continues to this day. China is often figured as a place about to collapse, because of its unwieldly, out of date governance system. Its economic implosion, for many critics adopting the guise of fortune tellers has been on the horizon for years. Some soothsayers have made predicting catastrophe a fundamental core of their career. Gordan Chang, a US-based writer, has been peering into the tea leaves and forecasting woe since 2001.[4] On the principle of even a stopped clock being correct two times a day, perhaps Mr Chang hopes that through constant repetition, one day his bold prediction will be said so often it comes true. The only change is the timeline by which this happens, extending increasingly far into the future. Even when authors themselves are not predicting imminent implosion, their headline writers are. American academic David Shambaugh wrote a piece in the *Wall Street Journal* dissecting weaknesses and incoherence in the Chinese political system. He made plenty of valid points. But the newspaper plastered 'The Coming Crackup' across the top of the piece, giving readers a wholly different expectation before they'd even looked at his arguments. Struggling, vexed, conflicted, unstable China has been a staple of external discourse, and some internal ones too, for many years.[5]

All we can be sure about is that as of the time of writing (November 2021) the one thing that has been consistent about large predictions of China's future in the last five decades has been their wrongness. Roger Irvine in a study of these in the economic, political and social realm issued in 2016 assembles many of these and shows in a sobering fashion how awry they were. After the death of Mao Zedong in 1976, for instance, most observers forecast the continuation of a more leftist, radical group in the leadership in power – people around Jiang Qing, Mao's widow, and the so-called Gang of Four (a phrase Mao himself used only a couple of times according to the most detailed records of his life, but which became heavily deployed since). Of those based in Beijing at the embassies there, only Stephen Fitzgerald of Australia foresaw possible changes that might make China follow the development path of Japan, Taiwan and others and use export-led growth and fast industrialization by opening up to the outside world. His was a lone voice. Not a single prominent economist saw what was about to happen from late 1978 onwards – acceptance of foreign capital, investment, allowance of a domestic market, and toleration of entrepreneurs.[6]

Even when a large part of this story was clarified, and it was clear China was undergoing unexpected changes and reforms a few years later, this new narrative was rarely read accurately. I recall discussion at the time (I was a student then at Cambridge) where people felt that the uprising in 1989 was a clear sign of the ultimate end of the one-party system in the country. That did not happen. Nor too did the expected withdrawal of China into itself in the aftermath – Deng Xiaoping's Southern Tour, as paramount leader, in early 1992, corrected that misperception, with its renewed commitment to continuing economic changes. China's reform of its state-owned enterprises, and its entry to the World Trade Organisation (WTO) a decade later were also portends of imminent dramatic changes for some. Leaders like Hu Jintao once they emerged were seen as potential liberals. Forces like the religious group the Falungong and the China Democracy Party in the late 1990s were interpreted as categorical and clear signs that the winds of change were blowing, and that the Communist Party was going to have to dramatically adapt and change, and that it needed to face up to the fact that the end of history and the ultimate victory of liberal, multi-party democratic models was going to sweep it up as much as anyone else that stood in the way. Even now, Xi Jinping's own era of ascent and confidence is followed by the outside world, looking perpetually for clues of internal dissent, opposition and even potential coups which might portend the demise of the system he leads. He too was seen by some at the start as a leader who would not be able to hold the vast political and economic complexity of his country together. Things would need to change, many said. The problem was that while change indeed happened, it was almost always vastly different from what had been expected by the pundits.

As someone who has been involved in this story and observed and commented on it for over thirty years, I am as culpable as anyone else in this sobering record of misprediction. In the late 2000s after doing a project travelling around different places in China looking at foreign support for democratization, I too felt convinced that the system would have to change. There was too much fractiousness, inequality was going through the roof, society was in ferment, even the national leaders were talking about unsustainability of their growth model, and at times of its governance. It seemed all that they could do was use vast levels of violence and surveillance to keep a lid on things. Listening to Hu Jintao and his clunky, robotic statements, I wondered how the political elite in the country had ended up so remote and out of touch with their own people. I confess it openly, here and now: over that period, I really did sincerely believe that with just a little openness to new political models, with more participation in decision making, with a roadmap to political reform, the country would be on a healthier and more feasible long-term path. I also confess that I believed that path had to lead to a place where the government looked not dissimilar to the multi-party system of the UK, or the US. We were better at governing ourselves, I thought. This dim view of China as it was was reinforced by memorable encounters with somewhat jaded and careworn foreigners I had come across in the previous two decades while there. One especially stayed with me – an American of Chinese heritage who I bumped into very early one morning coming off an all-night train journey arriving at Beijing Station. Faced with chaos at the ticket barriers to leave the platform, when the American and I wearily made our way through and were standing recovering outside, she sighed. 'Well, look on the bright side,' she said, 'At least we can get out of this place. These suckers are stuck here.' And with that she cast a half contemptuous, half pitying look at the sea of Chinese around us and marched off.

So much of what has happened in the People's Republic in the last few decades has been unexpected. In 2022 I am much humbler and more cautious when engaged in tea leaf reading these days. Change in China will continue to happen, and we all have to make educated guesses about where the larger story is going. But while doing so we need to be careful and circumspect. In economic and social areas, but less in political ones, just as China has changed vastly in the last decades, it will continue to do so in the future. The one lesson we can truly learn from the past is how often the country transformed in ways that defied expectations, negatively and positively. It is likely to do so in the future.

There is something else we need to be clear about, which relates more to the way this story is told rather than its content. Any new narrative about our understanding and engagement with China we want to tell needs to be preceded with an honest acceptance that this is, and always has been, a tale profoundly shaped as much by us, the tellers of it, as what it is about. There is no neat subject- object division here. In the global era, there is no longer a China story we can grant ourselves the luxury of being apart from and relating from the outside. It includes us and is partly about us, both its good and its bad parts. We need to improve our understanding of the role our own thinking and assumptions play before we start getting into the business of claiming absolute objectivity. We need a better awareness of how easily we have taken our own hopes and desires as an intrinsic part of China itself and dressed them up as facts, dictating what kind of China there might need to be to fulfil these. In essence, we need to see China, and ourselves, as they are, rather than as we wish they would be.

To start achieving this, I would propose that there are broadly three fundamental areas where we need to focus on – three things that have changed which run against many former expectations, and which need to be factored into our new mindsets and the revised and dynamic stories we will need to start devising. They each involve aspects of how we understand and conceptualize China's powers. Knocking away the story of China as weak and marginal and a kind of runner-up to the West is the first. Thinking about China as a more complete actor, with sea as well as land capacity is the second. And accepting and then working out what a world where Chinese values are as important as western, or Enlightenment ones, is the third. These are the huge new factors that we need to get our heads around. Once we do that, we have the chance of having a better, more durable, and workable model of what China is for us, and a more accurate idea of what it is in itself.

Strong China

Weak, unstable China, perpetually on the verge of cracking up, saddled with a governance system that is doomed to fail, it only being a question of when and how badly rather than if – this is a place anyone who reads just a fraction of the commentary on the modern country knows well. Weak China, where poverty rules, and marginalization is the norm, has figured in the imagination of foreign politicians, commentators and policy makers for much of the last seventy plus years since the People's

Republic was founded in 1949. Over that time, in the early decades, it is true the country gave every indication of fitting the definition of a state on the edge of failing, being riven by internal struggles, economically dysfunctional and largely inactive of the world stage. Who would have looked at the news seeping out of the country during the Maoist era with reports of widespread famines in the early 1960s, and then the chaos of the Cultural Revolution from 1966, and not seen somewhere that was about to implode?

This was truly a dark place. Libraries of commentary and analysis went into looking at aspects of this dismal, heartrending tale. Those who emerged to the outside world, as refugees, or asylum seekers, confirmed the worst. From journalists like Liu Binyan, to writers like Jun Chang, the harsh stories they conveyed built up a fearsome image. Influenced by some of these writings, it meant my own direct encounter with the country, living there from 1994 to 1996 in a remote provincial city, was often confusing. Knowing so much about the dark and terrifying past, how was it that anyone I was now amongst showed any happiness or optimism at all. And yet it seemed that people were no more nor less anxious, or visibly depressed than in my native UK.

That tone of earnestly seeing China as a place which deep down is unstable, dysfunctional, wounded by profound internal fractures which predestine it to one day fall apart, haunts much of what is written and thought about the country to this day. Weak China has given rise to an accompanying syndrome in the West – the conviction that the country is the forever underdog, the also-ran, the victim, which will always screw up in the end. This is a paradigm so many have invested in for such a long time that to contest or seek to reframe it means hitting against powerful vested interests. Weak China has also metastasized into other ideas, where its recent success is partially acknowledged, but dismissed as ultimately fraudulent and inauthentic. It is the sham adopter of fake capitalism, riddled with debt and made-up statistics, trying to lift itself out of its subordinate place by lies and secrecy. It is an unfair player for those in business who find that the competition from this new practitioner of capitalism is a little fiercer than they expected (witness the trade wars under Trump from 2017 to 2020 and the reasons driving them) and who seek to undermine what it is doing by calling it out as acting illegally or immorally and refusing to play by the rules everyone else follows. These days, too, the conviction amongst its fiercest detractors that China does not undertake social and political modernization because there is something wrong with it is still very great. It is not our ideas that are at fault here, the refrain goes, but the country that refuses to conform to their predictions. For the holders of the faith in a Weak China about to fall apart, even acknowledging a world where the country is, in many respects, strong proves a step too far. This is all, the riposte goes, from fake images conjured up by lying Communist leaders – not rooted in anything real or long lasting. This place is running on luck, trickery and dud statistics. Its comeuppance is imminent. It is only a matter of time.

If we set aside for the moment questions of how precisely one defines strength and power, and how China relates to these, and simply look at tone and language, then today, under Xi Jinping, the country sounds strong. The days of the country speaking in a low-key way, and acting with deep humility, are at an end. In his remarks to celebrate the hundredth anniversary of the foundation of the Communist Party in July 2021, Xi declared that those that attempted to bully the country would 'face broken heads and bloodshed'.[7] This phrase aroused worried comment and analysis. Once more, the more hawkish claimed, the world was seeing the true face of a country that harboured resentments and anger towards it. More considered voices however did point out that in the original Chinese the phrase used was a common one, and often deployed in situations referring to the well-established 'national humiliation by outsiders' storyline. Even so, the prominence and boldness of the statement was striking. This was a country speaking with a forcefulness that had not been seen before.

The tone of Xi's language is one thing. But signs of China's contemporary strength can be seen in actions. Internationally, the country is more proactive than ever before. China the weak was also either China the excluded and marginalized (as in the Mao years) or China the passive (as in the early years of reform) – a place that followed where others led and was obedient in fitting into the global system. Under Xi, however, it has articulated its own narratives, from the BRI to the notion of Common Prosperity, and a New Era. These are not domestic, or not solely so, but relate to, address and are meant to have impact on the wider world. Some of them contest or try to reshape that world and its own narratives. The BRI particularly has aroused a huge amount of speculation. It has resurrected the notion of an Indo-Pacific area in response by Washington and its allies. China's reach is shown not just in inspiring counter-narratives, but also in setting up bodies which convey multilateralism with Chinese characteristics. The Shanghai Cooperation Organisation is a longer established example. More recently there has been the Asia Infrastructure Investment Bank (AIIB) and forums associated with the BRI. A BRICS (Brazil, Russia, India,

China and South Africa) bank is now hosted in Shanghai. To supplement this, China has managed to insert itself in a number of United Nation (UN) bodies, supplying key leadership figures, and seeking increasing input. Chinese multilateralism is no longer something theoretical and imminent, but a real, and growing phenomenon. It carries the country's aspirations and messages out into international space. Even more strikingly, in outer space too China is very much present, planning landings of craft on Mars and running a space programme increasingly comparable to the US's NASA.

While we can acknowledge that China is strong today, we also have to be clear about how we evaluate and understand that strength. Perceptions of China's influence and reach in the outside world have been dramatically accentuated by how the West feels about its own loss of power and potency. This has created complex new dynamics, where the relative decline and deterioration economically, politically and socially of the US and Europe since the mid-2000s, because they have occurred at the same time as China's rise, are sometimes given a causal connection to each other. The West is becoming weaker at the expense of China being strong and being able to influence and undermine it. But the core moments of western deterioration and disunity – the 2008 Great Financial Crisis and its ravages of western capitalism, and the chaos of European and American politics culminating in highly unexpected and disruptive events like Brexit and Trump's election – came from complex causes, the most important of which (domestic inequality, frustration at political elites, poor management of banks) were either unconnected to China, or only indirectly linked. The West is more conflicted and confused now and its confidence is at low ebb, but these are from long-term issues within itself. China may figure as a convenient scapegoat for these ills, but if we want to subscribe to truthfulness, then we need to be crystal clear: since 2008, China has become stronger at the same time as the West has become weaker, but while these two trends are simultaneous and have some connections, they were and are not contingent on each other.

China as a Sea Power

Where does the abstract idea of Strong China become real? Where can we see it, experience it and feel it? Saying the phrase 'Strong China' is one thing, but for many outside working out what it really means is something else. The first issue, as mentioned above, is the most obvious

– that at least since the end of the eighteenth century, there has been no precedent for China being strong, so no one really knows what to make of this idea now it has cropped up. Lack of a precedent means that even were China not to be so politically different to the current dominant players in North America and Europe, its cultural differences are already enough to pose challenges to accurately assessing and working out what its real capacity and intentions are as it becomes the world's largest economy. On top of this is the thorny issue of the lack of clear-cut evidence about what China's power is and how it manifests itself, beyond stronger and clearer language and more muscular diplomacy. One of the great paradoxes is that in the era from 1949 to 1976 under Mao when it was much more marginalized as a geopolitical and economic player, the country was a far more fractious and bellicose actor and gave more tangible evidence of what kind of power it was. It fought the UN and the Americans in the Korean War from 1950 to 1953. It clashed with the Indians over the unresolved border between the two countries in 1962. In 1969, there were nasty and worrying skirmishes between the USSR and the PRC, which resulted in fatalities on each side. These occurred in the northeast border of the country. The final overt incidence of real military aggression was the invasion of Vietnam in 1979, at the start of the Deng era. The latter did not go well and brought to an end the era of physical aggressiveness for Beijing.

Since then, while China has grown wealthier and richer, and put a lot more capacity in its military, making it one of the world's most impressive and extensive, examples of behaviour that could be classified as bellicose not just in word but in deed have been confined to a few skirmishes in the South China Sea. While its air force often flies threatening training missions close to or into Taiwan air space (with sharp increases over 2021 and extremely aggressive actions after US Congress Speaker Nancy Pelosi's visit to the island in August 2022), and its civilian fishing or sea rescue fleet clash with other boats in the South and East China Sea, in terms of formal use of the People's Liberation Army (PLA), there has been precious little. A powerful China therefore, as of 2022, does not automatically mean a more interventionist or militarily active one. Beyond support for UN peacekeeping forces, and repatriation occasionally of its own citizens, particularly after the Arab Spring when Libya fell into civil war in 2010 and 36,000 Chinese were taken from there back to China, what is remarkable is how passive and inactive this newly powerful country is.

The more Machiavellian might accuse China of in fact waging psychological war. It is in the business of playing mind games, unsettling and unnerving the West by being mercurial and capricious in its behaviour. Its preferred field of operations are in cyberspace, rather than the real world, where strength is hard to calculate accurately. Here to be shadowy gives force and potency. These ways in which China power operates are striking. As the philosopher and sinologist François Jullien wrote, Chinese power 'haunts, but does not act'. He presents the reasons for why this may be so – in long established modes of thought where the key quality is not to try to mould and change events so that they deliver pre-planned outcomes, something more akin to a western way of behaving, but understanding the innate nature of things and then trying to read this and work with it. One way or another, this is a different method of manifesting potency and dominance, something more intuitive than assertive.[8]

Such large cultural descriptions are often contentious and subject to counterarguments and caveats. Even so, the non-use by China of its vast new military creates questions about whether the country is simply waiting for its time to strike, its current inactivity simply a temporary ruse to deceive and unsettle the outside world, or is indicative of patterns of behaviour which run far deeper. People are given to quoting the curt, often gnomic phrases from Sun-Tzu's 'Art of War' from the Warring States Period, two and a half millennium ago, about the premium placed in Chinese strategic thinking on subterfuge and deception. This is supplemented by more recent Maoist lines about the need to confuse and hide from the enemy. The Communist Party of China, like its patron in the early years, the Communist Party in the USSR, has never been fond of transparency and openness and tends to use this as a tool of diplomacy and to gain it influence.[9]

To add to the confusion, we now deal not just with a China that manifests its power through a massive but so far passive military into which it is pouring large amounts of funds and effort, but one that for the first time in modern history is starting to rank as a significant naval power. In at least the previous half a millennium, this issue has simply not been important for the outside world. Ming and Qing China, from the fifteenth to the nineteenth century, made sense as land powers. In the Qing in particular, land campaigns into inner Asia meant that the territory now covered by Xinjiang and Tibet were brought in complex but clear ways under central Qing control. Even what is currently Mongolia was within the borders of the Qing empire at their most expansive, in the nineteenth century. China's naval capacity throughout this time was minimal to non-existent. It was through overwhelming technological superiority in its navy that Britain was able to enforce its will from the First Opium War of 1839. China's navy was simply too ill managed, primitive, small and weak to offer any meaningful response. The only period in which China did figure as a naval entity was long before this, in the early fifteenth century. It was then that the celebrated eunuch admiral Zheng He undertook his voyages in vast ships that reached as far as the east coast of Africa and the edge of the South China Sea. That period, approximately two decades in length, ended as abruptly as it started, possibly for economic reasons (the costs of these campaigns nearly bankrupted the relatively young Ming state).

Today, China is undisputedly a major sea power. The decision was made in the 1980s by the leadership then to ensure that the country had the ability to defend its vast coastline, and to be able to reach deep into the waters around it. This was as much to secure its supply and export routes as it placed more emphasis on its economic development as it was about claiming maritime territory. Liu Huaqing, an admiral and member of the Politburo was the great architect of this. He was to live on to 2011, dying that year at the age of ninety-five. His vision has been amply realized. By 2021, China's navy, in vessel terms, is larger than that of the United States, with around 360 vessels compared to America's 300. Technologically, it still lags far behind. Aircraft carrier, crucial for projecting firepower and capability, is one such area. To China's current two, America has eleven. The latter's are far more advanced and better equipped. In terms of nuclear submarines, too, while China has a number of these, they are inferior to those of their key competitors like America or France. But the fact four decades ago they barely registered in any of these areas must give anyone foolhardy to be in the business of making predictions pause for thought. Across almost every benchmark, the one thing one can say with any confidence is that China has exceeded whatever expectations were set it in the past and developed more quickly than any expected. China as a naval power now is a reality unlike at any other time in modern history – or most of premodern for that matter. This too gives a new dimension to its power, and new challenges about how best to conceptualize and understand its intentions.

As a naval power, the country has ability to assert its historic and strategic claims in the maritime area around it as never before. It also means that it has the capacity to open naval bases beyond its shores. The first of these, Djibouti, on the east coast of Africa, was established to much commentary and speculation in 2015. Since then, despite many worried predictions, particularly focussed around the Pacific, Beijing has not followed up with a second. As a naval power, China has been able to up the ante in the South and East China Seas in particular, intensifying what were, at least till the 1980s, simmering issues that most people knew little about and treated as diplomatic spats rather than live military worries. Armed with a new fleet of ships, since the late 1980s China has been able to exert a fresh kind of influence in the space immediately around it. This has ranged from low-level clashes between nationalistic activists and fishing vessels, to constructing structures on usually submerged features to make them more akin to permanent islands.

Much could be said of the activities post-2010 in this space. Words like assertiveness, aggression and prosecution of Chinese imperial-style intentions have been bandied around to interpret China's actions. But if one strips away all the current (and often understandable) emotions because of the level of feeling between contesting parties from Vietnam to the Philippines, one is left dealing with an incontrovertible fact; the period of history in which Ming, Qing and modern China were land powers is over. The country that exists now as successor to these former dynastic entities is in this significant respect a wholly different kind of actor. Its ships can now reach European ports, not just as carriers of trade and goods, but as parts of a large, and expanding, navy (something even more remarkable when one remembers that in the whole of the nineteenth century only one Chinese vessel, the *Keying*, reached Europe, as an exhibition boat, in 1849). The Chinese navy has been hosted in Australia and appeared in the oceans around Africa. It gives true content to the notion of a global China. It makes Chinese power tangible and visible rather than something that is just speculated about and lies just beyond the edge of clear vision. In this respect, Strong China is not a chimera. It is real. The challenge is once more how to interpret this.

The Issue of Values

A China that not only sounds strong, but economically and geopolitically *is* strong, and one which is not only a land power but can project that power across water and into real and virtual space, mark an historically important change. The China that exists today has never existed in this form before. And while all countries to some extent undergo transformations through time, with China the scale of these, and the size of the country itself, magnify the impact. If, for instance, a medium European country like Greece were to appear literally from nowhere, and over a couple of decades, acquire a vast new navy and a sense of prowess, power and economic confidence utterly out of step with its former image, then that would be startling and destabilizing enough. But even in this scenario, the West would at least be able to manage things because of one simple fact – that the new emerging power (in this very hypothetical case, Greece) shared a set of religious, cultural and political values with those powers it was competing with, and was already a part of them. That might not allay tensions and a final clash. In many ways, as Germany and Britain proved in the first half of the twentieth century, it might make these in the end very catastrophic. But it would mean that at least from the start there was a little less confusion about what kind of problem one was looking at, what sort of challenges were emerging and what options were available to deal with this.

With China, we have no such starting point. Its history is one which differs greatly from that of Europe and North America. There have been plentiful connections over much at least of the last few centuries. But the distinctiveness of the intellectual and cultural history of inhabitants of the space now occupied by the People's Republic of China is undeniable. In terms of language, modes of governance, economic behaviour, and fundamental views about how the world operates and how society should be shaped, the Chinese tradition is a long, complex and sometimes (but not always) contrasting one to that which has created the Europe and North America of today. This sort of work of comparison is treacherous business. One should never oversimplify, nor should one overcomplicate. But in one very broad area the difference is clear. The Judaic Christian root of Western European belief systems is hugely unifying, even if the history of religion, with divisions between Catholic and Protestant, and then amongst different groups and belief communities within these, has been anything but. The Western European proclivity has been to maintain the conviction, at least until recent decades, that there is a final, truthful, unifying vision of the world, and of attitudes and beliefs that one could have about that world. To even state in one breath that one was sincerely at the same time a Catholic and also a Protestant, for much of the last five hundred years, would have been regarded either as incoherent, or as dangerous heresy. One had to take a stand – as Martin Luther famously did – and say what one's unified, coherent view of the world was, and whether it fell on one side of the divide or the other. Hybrid belief systems were unwelcome, a sign of confusion and lack of contact with reality. Truth with a capital 'T' was the aim not just in religious discourse, but across all the other disciplines that grew up as the Enlightenment and then the Scientific and Industrial revolution occurred. Over this time, one could argue, this was the great source of European strength intellectually. But in the twenty-first century, it is becoming their greatest vulnerability.

This is not the place to get into almost unfathomably complex arguments about what truth is, and whether it exists. Philosophers like Bernard Williams in any case have issued powerful, knowledgeable, and profound treatments on the subject.[10] What is germane to this discussion is the ways in which in intellectual traditions in the Chinese world, from at least the Tang dynasty from the seventh century onwards, hybridity was not an issue. Like the Roman Empire centuries before, the only rule was that there were no absolute gods. People increasingly practiced Buddhism, introduced into Han dynasty China from the second century onwards from its historic home in India. They subscribed to forms of ritual which revolved around Confucianism, in various iterations, increasingly from the eleventh century after a great revival in the Song under figures like Zhu Xi. Daoism remained a powerful influence, with its celebration and acceptance of contradictions, as did other forms of folk religion. East Asian resistance to some grand, unform vision of the meaning of reality was commented on by the historian F. W. Mote.[11] What have been called the three great teachings (Buddhism, Confucianism, Daoism) with their widespread acceptance, and their mutual accommodation of each other, means that very broadly, while Chinese dynastic history has many ethnic and political clashes (such as the catastrophic Taiping Rebellion in the mid-nineteenth century), it is hard to see easy parallels with events fired by religious convictions, such as the Crusades from the eleventh to the fourteenth century or the Thirty Years War from 1618 to 1648 in Europe, or the vicious struggles between Catholic and Protestant believers that occurred through much of the early modern era. This difference in behaviour historically shows that there is also something different about the underlying values of these two broad cultural entities, the West and historic imperial China. Western European values sought and fought, even if they frequently failed, to find unity. In the Chinese world where a notion of harmony in the abstract was privileged the focus was on accepting different kinds of views and convictions for different spaces and occasions. This did not preclude dramatic violence at times, but for purely political rather than religious reasons. A syncretic world view is the result – one that in the twenty-first century continues to puzzle and fascinate because of the ability of modern Chinese to place capitalism next to socialism, while seeming under Xi Jinping to be proud of Confucianism as well as having as many as 200 million Buddhists in various sects and about half that number of Christians.

This is why it is questionable whether China is asserting an absolute view of the world and promoting a competing set of values it wants others to adopt for themselves. That argument assumes that the only model of behaviour for China must be that of the West, with its default to unity and a uniform Truth as practised through most of the last half a millennium. For its critics, in order to align with this template China must not only have but be promoting a hard ideology which demands that those encountering it have to embrace. There is no other way to behave. If this is true, that is a significant threat and a major problem. The West and China will be doomed to clash, with each asserting the universal validity of their world view with no chance to compromise and tolerate each other. This would be a world where any alternative that appeared is a competitor just by being different, and in accordance with the law of survival of the fittest has to be eradicated before it eradicates. We arrive at the Clash of Civilisations thesis of Samuel Huntingdon. But what if Chinese values in the end have no such pretensions to universal scope and reach? What if they are implicitly related to China as a place, a culture and a world view, and have acceptance of this limitation embedded within them? If that were true, its critics would be seeking a fight with China that doesn't have to be fought.

It is for this reason that China's current officials and intellectuals like international relations expert Yan Xuetong are so insistent on stating, time and time again, a fact which is so obvious to them: that Chinese values are, well, very Chinese.[12] These values are framed in an excluding and exceptionalist way. While there are no barriers between those wanting to espouse universal concepts like 'socialism' or 'capitalism' if they wish, when you tag the phrase 'with Chinese characteristics' an immediate barrier comes up, marking off a place and community where these have validity and, at the same time, making clear a similarly vast area where they don't. The whole logic of Chinese nationalism is built on this insistence that to be Chinese is to be different from those who are not Chinese. As anyone knows who has ever had discussions with Chinese officials about resolving some of their demographic problems from ageing and declining birth rate by adopting a liberal migration regime, becoming Chinese for outsiders is either not an option, or one to which almost insurmountable barriers have been placed. This even leads to areas where, for instance, largely benign and supportive commentators on China's current global rise and its national mission like British writer Martin Jacques can at the same time be fiercely critical of Chinese attitudes towards other races, which are often intolerant and at times out and out prejudiced. The Chinese world view is not only a uniquely hybrid one, but on top of this a very excluding one. That makes it harder, not easier, to create a set of values the rest of the world can adopt and then be governed by. If China does plan to conquer the rest of humanity and remake it in its image, it has chosen a path and a means that are making it next to impossible to achieve this end goal. That implies that this is in fact not an aim China wants.

The main question posed in recent times is how a world pushes back against a China rolling towards it promoting its own values and seeking to undermine and replace those of the Enlightenment West. The better question is how China can be a global player when its world view is constructed in ways which are both immediately alienating because of their syncretism and complexity, and because of the way they insist on being uniquely and distinctively Chinese? A world where China plays an increasingly larger role is not likely to be one where its belief systems and world view swamp the minds of everyone else and where everyone then magically become practitioners of Sinified Marxism-Leninism, with important traces of Confucianism, Daoism and Buddhism. It is much more likely to be a world of long-term, structural divisions, where the issue is not so much that China is a power rising to global prominence with a competing coherent belief system the rest can adopt, but for precisely the opposite reason – that in fact it does not have an alternative, and its rise will make the world more complex, not simpler. No one, in the end, knows what a world run on Chinese values looks like. The greatest likelihood as of 2022 is that they are unlikely ever to find out.

Making Sense of Things: An Initial Conclusion

When we are discussing anything to do with the People's Republic of China in the contemporary context therefore, these three factors are good places to start. One could almost say they are necessary embarkation points. China as no longer a weak, marginal actor, but a strong one, with connections through supply chains, trade links, geopolitical reach and investment stretching to every corner of the planet. China is no longer a land power, expressing its main interests along its great western borders adjacent to India, Pakistan, Russia and South Asia, but a sea one with capacity to reach deep into the Indian and Pacific Ocean in ways that run completely against its habitual mode of behaviour for almost all of the last 500 years. While these two fundamental changes are happening, China is also a place with a cultural and intellectual tradition underpinned by a set of values that are structurally different to the Enlightenment West, ones which are hybrid, complicated and exclusive and excluding, and do not want to have universal pretensions.

The most striking aspect of this story we see emerge therefore is how lacking in clarity it is. This is a strong power, and one that speaks in an increasingly forceful way. And yet so far it has been less bellicose and willing to use its military beyond its borders than it was in the Maoist era when it was a much less impressive global actor. In many ways, the brunt of Chinese deployment of force and physical violence is borne by China's own citizens, within its borders. If the PLA acted externally the way it acts domestically, we would have a vast problem. But so far, it doesn't. On current evidence, China is more a self-harming nation, rather than a violent one to others. We have a comprehensive land and sea power now – only one that once more seems to act more through passivity than overt action, even over issues like Taiwan that directly relate to its interests and are regarded as belonging to its domestic space. And even with these two issues, around the manifestation of China's real physical power and capacity now, we have to take into account all the complexities that result from a full understanding of the final, far more vexing problem – that around values. Does China look like a proselytizing nation, something akin to the US, a 'house upon the hill', keen to spread its wonderful allure across the globe and have the rest of the world embrace its convictions for themselves? Or it is more accurate to see China as profoundly self-interested, a player who on the contrary cares little for what others chose to think about themselves, and often sounds baffled when it hears language about a China model being adopted by the world outside. With these three key factors firmly in mind, now we can start to think in much more detail about the matter that lies at their heart: what is the nature of Chinese power?

Chapter Two

THE ENIGMA OF CHINESE POWER

China is now powerful and manifests its power through being both a land and a sea power. It has a military installation in Djibouti, Eastern Africa. It has research stations along with other major powers in Antarctica and sits as an observer on the Arctic Council. Once upon a time, in the Maoist past, the country was not even a member of the UN. Its engagement with multilateralism was minimal. These days, it is hard to set up a single entity where China does not want to play a role. It is the largest contributor to UN peacekeeping forces. It is involved with the Association of Southeast Asian Nations (ASEAN) through ASEAN plus one, and ASEAN plus three. It joined the WTO in 2001, and is a 3 per cent stakeholder in the International Monetary Fund. It has strategic dialogues with dozens of countries, and comprehensive strategic dialogues with dozens more. With the US it runs eighty bilateral dialogues covering everything from fishing to intellectual property (IP) protection and human rights. With the European Union (EU) it has a similar kind of architecture of engagement, all of it captured by a bi-annual high-level summit. For the fifty plus countries in Africa that recognize Beijing over Taiwan, there is the Forum on China African Co-operation. Similar bodies apply to relations with Latin America, and the Middle East. China has nuclear weapons, and an active and expanding space programme. On top of all this, it owns more US debt than any other country in history. As Hillary Clinton while Secretary of State in the 2000s put it, how can the US really argue with its banker.[1]

It takes no great prescience or insight to put these threads together and conclude that one is looking at a powerful entity – or, at the very least, an entity that looks like it has power. It is as though one were let into some estate where there are fortifications, fences, the latest surveillance technology, and guards everywhere. Surely, this is the place where someone important with things to protect resides? When one looks at the clear signs of China's reach across the world, one has to draw the same conclusion.

But when one asks the simple question, what is the precise nature of Chinese power, things start to grow vaguer. Is this a nation into colonization and imperialism? Is it about to set up a new Pax Sinica to replace that of the US, which has prevailed till now? If so, it is going about things in a radically different way. China's public diplomatic language is sometimes shrill and defensive, and often full of unclear platitudes about wanting win-win and global peace. But there is precious little sign that it is, at least rhetorically, in the business of imposing its values on others. On the contrary, it is forever preaching the doctrine of non-interference, even if its actions are sometimes inconsistent with this (for instance, where it has direct interests in terms of investment or energy supplies abroad and has to get involved for reasons of self-interest). Excited media coverage of China the new Africa colonizer from the late 2000s had to then reckon with an approach that was problematic more through its cautiousness and deep reluctance to get sucked into local problems than for the opposite. China takes the same stance in the Middle East, or anywhere else for that matter, showing deep resistance to being regarded as a new US-style policeperson coming in to underwrite others' security and shore up stability. It does everything it can to either involve itself in issues multilaterally in concert with others or keep away. The only rule that one can make about Chinese global behaviour, now it has started to appear, is that it bases itself on doing everything the opposite way to the US.

That alone prompts endless speculation about the nature of Chinese intentions. Here is a country with a whole suite of new powers. Power is meaningful only if it acts on others. So, the argument goes, China must be up to something. But it is also a power that is astute enough to conceal and hide what it is doing. The twenty-four character phrase attributed to Deng Xiaoping after the 1989 Tiananmen Square uprising is often cited here. 'Bide your time, hide your strength, just build up your capacity' the mantra goes. With the unstated part of the phrase hanging int the air: 'until the time when you are strong enough to strike.'[2] In investigating a crime or trying to understand others and how they behave, one looks for motives. With China, one has plenty of evidence of deep resentments towards the West from a history of what it sees as victimization and suffering as the result of enforcement of others' will. Patriotic education campaigns since the 1990s have muddied the waters, creating a confusing nationalism where it is unclear if the party state is in charge of the story and the feelings that flow from it, or simply following in their wake. Lee Kuan Yew, the late statesman from Singapore, once tartly commented that the problem in Asia was that

Japan never remembered anything, and China never forgot. Chinese memory is a vast and powerful thing, an historic consciousness that has real impact on the present and shapes the future. This is about more than the five thousand years of continuous history so often claimed, and so often questioned by historians outside. It is about the conviction that to be Chinese is to be something that carries with it an almost permanent sense of identity, a bedrock going deep. The world outside might change, and the material circumstances of one's own country transform, but for Chinese its deep structure and underlying values remain semi-eternal on this account. No wonder Xi Jinping in the 2021 Plenum resolution on party history was spoken of as someone who stood up for both the Marxism-Leninism creed, with Chinese characteristics in place since 1949, but 'traditional Chinese culture'. This latter is indeed the core ground on which to stake out political longevity, with its claims to reach back thousands of years, and the assumption it will stretch for similar lengths of time into the future.

The sense of anger at the way the country was treated before amongst contemporary Chinese, often given forceful expression in social media, and the clear ways it has been stated so often both by elite leaders, and in more popular material, is a worrying phenomenon for the outside world. With this level of unhappiness about how the country was treated in the past, and with new capacity and ability today, surely the Chinese are seeking vengeance? Why would they be so sanguine and merciful when others doled out such cruel treatment to them? Japanese in particular because of the Sino-Japanese War from 1937 to 1945 arouse intense fury in online forums, with Chinese nationalists berating them for what is perceived as their lack of contrition. China's anger is manifested in populist works from the 1990s onwards, with bestsellers like 'China that Can Say No' appearing in 1998, or the more recent 'China is Not Happy' from 2009.

If China does have these motives of seeking retribution, it is unsurprising that analysts in the US and elsewhere often work within a framework where pessimistic and negative interpretation are given to almost all the country's behaviour. It has the kind of navy it does, they argue, and is involved in the kinds of projects it has supported through the BRI from 2015 because this is all driven by some blueprint constructed over the last few decades where getting even with the West is the real game. In that master plan, the aim was always to play along with the West when China needed technology and know-how, and of course capital, to build up its economic capacity, so that bit by bit it could start to enjoy advantages. China is after all, many say, a planning culture, one, we are forever being told, that likes to make long-term strategies.[3] This is the country that produced some of the oldest documents talking about the need to forever have plans and goals. With that mentality ascribed to their policymakers, it is easy to see how intentional and purposeful the accruing of so much financial capital and economic growth may look for doing something long term and big. But this fondness for attributing China with a culture so comfortable with articulating and then pursuing long-term plans is often contradicted by Chinese politicians themselves frequently acknowledging the precise opposite – how many important things have happened which were neither planned for foreseen, and how a strength of their system was to embrace this rather than negate it like other highly planned systems such as that of the USSR. This should prompt us to think a bit more deeply about what kind of strategic culture the country has rather than ascribing one simple characteristic to it. To give an example, domestically at least Deng Xiaoping himself famously accepted in the 1980s that Town and Village Enterprises, one of the most important promoters of growth during that era, were innovations that happened with little input from the central state.[4] Opper and Nee have written a whole, masterful book on how over the 1980s into the 1990s it was precisely the lack of planning and central control that inspired rapid growth in China, rather than the reverse.[5] If control is easier to exercise over domestic policy, and Chinese seem hesitant to assert strong controls for long-term planning even here, then that should give us pause for thought when claiming to see grand overarching goals in far less predictable, harder to control external affairs.

It is easy to see why intelligence agencies, think tanks and many others would invest so much in the narrative of China with a long-term, clear plan, and one that involves domination. For them, the professional default is always to assume the worst – after all, if there were no threats and no problems, their function would disappear. This relentless focus on negatives achieves two other things. It keeps them relevant and well-funded by their political masters, and it covers their backs on the few times when, in fact, the worst actually does happen. No one gets sacked easily for prudently planning for scenarios that show they are concerned and care about people and want to prevent disaster happening. At best they get mildly mocked for being worriers – until the kinds of scenarios they have been predicting come to pass. Even so, the intensity of the China Threat discourse over the last decade since 2010 has been startling. Faced with the kinds of complexities and ambiguities we noted in the first chapter, it seems that many people's minds have been made up – not least a large number of American and European politicians. For them China is not just a problem, but *the* problem. For example, Christopher Wray, head of the Federal Bureau of Investigations (FBI) in the US, has stated that 'The greatest long-term threat to our nation's information and IP, and to our economic vitality, is the counterintelligence and economic espionage threat from China.'[6] China in this sort of discourse is clearly in the business of power, and of exercising that power in more and more expansive ways as it gains military and economic capacity to do so. For holders of this view, the world is becoming a vast crime scene, with the signs of China's intentions stretched all the way across it.

But even for the most committed holders of this sort of opinion, there are nagging questions. Motive might be there, and threads of evidence. China has the reason, and the means to do more and want more. But so far, the real, crucial piece of evidence that might nail this whole 'threat' scenario and clear away all ambiguities for good has yet to surface. Militarily, the PLA is huge and well-funded, but as already noted has not been meaningfully active since 1979, and then not very effectively. China's skirmishes with India on the border in recent years have been brutal, but almost primitive in their reliance on knives and fists, not high-grade weaponry and kit. Even when the US chaotically evacuated Afghanistan in 2021 right on China's western border creating a huge vacuum, it was hard to see China being able to formally involve itself in the country, even though it had immense self-interested reasons for doing so (unlike for the US, China actually shares a land border with the Afghans). China is a power that looks, sounds, and feels, like it should be engaged in military disputes. It has a standing army of 1.3 million soldiers, with increasingly impressive levels of training, and more and more advanced technology. In the military parade held in September 2015 to mark the 70th anniversary of the Second World War in Asia, it was assessed that 84 per cent of the equipment moved through Beijing before Xi Jinping's approving eyes had never appeared in public before.[7] Each year sees more evidence of how in terms of technology, the country is catching up with its main competitors in ways which would have been surprising even a decade ago. Chiu Kuo-cheng, the Taiwanese Minister of Defence, gloomily predicted in 2021 that the Mainland had the ability to mount a credible amphibious attack on the island by 2025.[8] In the past, that was usually consigned to decades into the future. Regardless of how much longer the world will need to carry on waiting for the final, conclusive sign of China's hidden aggressive intent, however, as of the time of writing (January 2022) it is still waiting.

There is a different possibility – an alternative framework to see this issue in. That hinges on the question not so much of what China intends to do with its power, but what, in the end, its power actually is. If we take the position of thinking that power is a quality that is the same across all of those that exercise it, and has some almost transcendent, universal quality no matter who it is attributed to, then for sure, China will need to act in a particular way. A rigid definition of power will dictate how the holder of that power acts, just as a person will only be able to open a locked door if they have the right key for it, not if they have the right personality. If, however, we view power as fundamentally relational, something which is intrinsically culturally conditioned and context dependent, where these factors are a part of the definition and meaning of the term itself, then things start to look different. There is American power, with its melding of values and military might, and European power today, with its stress on cultural and enlightenment beliefs. And there is Chinese power – something founded on the kinds of hybrid, complex and different world views alluded to in the first chapter. These are loosely related to each other, but vary massively in their scope and function.

Once more, François Jullien's idea of how Chinese power haunts rather than acts / did not act is helpful to think about here. The era of cyber wars, and covert, often invisible, conflicts, where the virtual world is a key field of conflict, and the physical wars so popular in the past are becoming increasingly outmoded and defunct (a fact only likely to be reinforced by Russia's invasion of Ukraine in early 2022 which underlined how risky, ugly and inefficient real armed conflict is) has only served to illuminate this aspect of China's modus operandi. Technology far from being a threat has proved to be the greatest gift given to the one-party system in Beijing, creating new spaces for promoting its particular kind of power, one that does not involve operating in the light of physical day. This explains why Xi's government has embraced the new opportunities coming from this with enthusiasm. Without face recognition ability, and the artificial intelligence that propels mass surveillance and big data mining, the horrors of Xinjiang and the extensive internal controls in the last decade would not have been possible. While the intent to have such extensive and sophisticated control was there in the Maoist period, the capacity always fell far short. Then it was all down to human intelligence, with neighbour committees and internal snoopers filling out written reports, which had to be processed by other humans. In such a clumsy, laborious system, many fell through the net.[9] In Xi's China, tabs can be kept on people, and assessments made of their opinions by which to craft policy.

The simple fact is that if ever there was a technology made to suit China, then cyberspace, the internet and the web are it. As the great sociologist Fei Xiaotong noted in 1947, the country is a vastly networked society, one consisting of an almost impossibly dense framework centred on every Chinese individual.[10] In this highly elastic system, it is not surprising that when a new way of communicating comes which can somehow create unity across this atomized and fragmented landscape and harvest information about those active in it, but also provide new means to control expression, it gets embraced with passionate commitment. Nobel Prize Laureate, the late Liu Xiaobo, commented once that God had created the internet for China.[11] So much for the Clinton era predictions that this was the technology that would cut autocrats down to size. Far from it. It has given Chinese leaders a whole new lease of life. In view of this, they should be more grateful about this western invention, which was originally viewed by them with such apprehension. What a wonderful gift it has been! And one largely given for free.

Virtual space has certainly also given the country not only a new capacity to operate domestically, but a host of opportunities suitable to its kind of powers abroad. Here it has really taken on the guise of an effective but frustrating aggressor, forever suspected but never quite caught red handed at the scene of the crime. This is because in cyberspace, it being a virtual geography, there is no real scene for crimes to be committed. Instead, China has been blamed for mounting operations against websites and IT infrastructure abroad. Claims in the last decade that Chinese managed to get access to the confidential emails of western leaders like Germany's Angela Merkel, and the Westminster Whitehall network in the UK, along with massive attacks on the US and in Australia, culminated in the President Obama era in five named personnel being put on a FBI most wanted list in 2014. This was in the forlorn hope that in naming and shaming some of their people the Chinese would desist. Whether that worked or not, it was at least a recognition that the Chinese had been effective enough to provoke the US to take this unprecedented measure. They were drawing blood. More positively, however, Washington and Beijing attempted to establish an initial code of conduct in this new space, so that at least there was the possibility of some shared protocols and operational rules. But because virtual space is much like the great German theoretician of war Clausewitz's description of a perfect battlefield where events happen at uncontrollable velocity, and confusion reigns, it has proved hard to organize chaos. The internet in and of itself is a space uniquely suited to lack of clarity and invisibility, where people can act facelessly in the dark web, or via proxies that only the most expert can hope to get to the bottom of, and where governments have proved expert at issuing blank denials. When one sets this new situation alongside the confusing and ambiguous qualities of Chinese power or perceptions of that power discussed above, it is easy to see how this phenomenon intensifies the sense that the fact that it haunts *is* the way in which it acts. The two are intimately connected.

China in cyberspace for all its blurred confusion gives us unique insight into understanding what kind of actor the country is and what is the nature of its power. And once more we seen an opportunist, not the creator of a new paradigm it wants others to embrace and follow. We have to remember that the World Wide Web was a creation made in the outside world and bearing all its hallmark, identity and values of promoting free expression in the early days. Western politicians were keen to promote this wonderful new entity within China, insisting in 2008 that the web be open during the Olympics held in country that year. This was because there an assumption that the Chinese authorities could not tame this wonderful new western creation. It was the ultimate Trojan horse. Healthy democratic ideas would flow like pure, cleansing water into whoever used it. A standard, flat global space would be created, where liberalism and the force of universal western reason would be promoted by the internet's global democracy of ideas. Almost two decades later, in 2021, however, two fundamental parts of this story have proved utterly wrong. Despite predictions to the contrary, the Chinese government has shown huge ability in controlling the internet for its own ends and imposed its own values on this space. But on top of this, in the West itself, this wonderful creation has ended up becoming not an unalloyed good but something akin to a Frankenstein's beast, causing division and weakness. That in essence symbolizes the change that has happened on both sides.

For the first of these, the idea that China would not be able to create a duplicate internet and virtual world ruled by its own standards and fully under government control, even as it freely roamed where it wanted in the outside one, has been comprehensively disproved. It was the work of university official and technician Fang Binxin for the now disgraced Bo Xilai while leader in the vast city of Chongqing in the 2000s that created internet restrictions resulting ultimately in the Great Firewall of China. For this reason, Xi Jinping today can talk meaningfully about the sovereignty of the internet being as tangible, and defensible, as that of physical space. Since 2010, as western players from Google and Facebook to Twitter and finally LinkedIn have shifted out of the country no longer able to bear the rules and inhibitions placed on them, a group of indigenous equivalents – Sina Weibo and Douyin (the version of TikTok in China) – were cultivated. Obedient to the security parameters laid down by the party state, they have allowed Chinese to become as addicted to endless scrolling, internet controversies and mindless videos as anyone else – but all with content regarded as politically and culturally healthy, at least to the government. There is the World Wide Web, and the Chinese World Wide Web – the two running parallel to each other as though they were in parallel universes.

For the second, as this process of the Chinese internet metastasizing from the global one has happened, the internet in the outside world became a vicious battleground, aiding the rise of populists like Donald Trump, and exposing but also inflaming and creating divisions in society so deep that it often seemed like a new civil war had started. Even the most cautious who engaged with this brave new world could easily find their fingers badly burned by the abuse, vituperation, and hatred that spilled from hundreds of millions of Tweets and memes, many of them coming from artificial bot accounts set up precisely to aid this process. Chinese officials could look at this with a knowing prescience, aware that at least in their own territory they had tamed the beast. To add to fury, Chinese officials such as Zhao Lijian of the Ministry of Foreign Affairs and others made their own unique contribution to the ill-tempered external debates, while knowing the virtual world within China, as far as the government was concerned, was a haven of supportive peace and harmony. What was originally regarded as a sign of the West's superiority and stability has become a colossal monument to its division, weakness and self-doubts.

These virtual parallel worlds are new, but they illustrate longer established factors. Virtual China, and the virtual world with China in it, perfectly illustrate the ways Chinese power shadows that of the West, and operates around it, duplicating it in some respects, but in one fundamental area – asserting a final aimed for unity – simply not following the established rules. The Chinese cyberspace simply exists in its own fortified space. It can be visited, and its boundaries can be seen through acts of censorship and control. But it does not seek to usurp and overturn the rest of the global cyberworld around it. The world of Facebook, Instagram and SnapChat are fine for the rest. They just don't work for China. While China unintentionally subverts, irritates and complicates, it does not seek to monopolize, nor does it seek to destroy the alternatives that run beside it. In many ways, they suit its form of power, and their existence is in its interests in the disunity and ill feeling they create in the outside world.

Virtual China is a separate domain. But the perceptions and interpretations of its meaning cause real issues. This virtual domain contributes to the perception of a country whose power is ineffable, unsettling, hard to pin down – truly a place that haunts. Underpinning this is the sense that China has some strange influence – it is, in the words of at least one popular and terrifying account issued in 2020, operating like a 'hidden hand', reaching deep into the minds and worlds of the unknowing West, slowly moulding them to be compliant to the bidding of the all-powerful, almost demonic Chinese Communist Party (CCP). The world war raging in 2022 might not be a physical one. But psychologically, it is all too real. And for those in the US, Europe and elsewhere who see China as a proselytizer and malevolent disrupter come to bring us all down, then the very structure and nature of Chinese power with its elusiveness and intangible qualities as manifest in the virtual world is deliberately designed in order to undertake and succeed in that war through spreading confusion and disobedience to western norms. One would have to say, standing apart from this scenario and trying to view it objectively, that if (and one has to repeat here, if) Beijing is intentionally prosecuting a psychological war, it is so far winning handsomely.

Those convinced of its existence feel that the Hidden Hand of Beijing can be seen not just in the virtual world but in the real one – in the ways, for instance, in which this potent power has seeped into universities corrupting them through funding of key areas of research and the establishment of Confucius Institutes. It can be found in the cultivation via the Chinese United Front department which oversees foreign relations of elite political figures, and in the manipulation and enforcement of Chinese messages through diplomatic, media and other channels. As with Russia, while it forbids our companies working and operating in its space, China operates in our western world of social media. There it stands accused of running hundreds of thousands of fake accounts, a people's army waging a war that spreads disinformation and confusion. Sowing chaos in the West is the aim, these claims go. Ironically, being gripped by the 'hidden hand' syndrome means that this chaos comes early, as one sees almost everything China does as signs not of inexperience, or its own confusion, or even ineptness, but of some subtle, masterful strategic game. All too often via this route we come back to touching against unpleasant stereotypes of the past – the Fu Manchu syndrome from the fevered imagination of fantasist Anglo-

Irish writer Sax Rohmer in the 1920s and 1930s that spawned the vile yellow peril sinophobia of that era. This author went no further towards China than the coast of Britain. But in reflecting on this racist stereotype of the cruel, inscrutable oriental one can acknowledge the role that imagination has always played for Europeans in their long engagement with China. While that veered from idealization on the one hand (the mystical east with its wonderful resources of wisdom) and demonization on the other, these were always two sides of the same coin. Hidden hand today is part of that tradition, and while not claiming that all those that espouse this creed (and it is a creed, based more on faith than real evidence) are sinophobes, the idea they promote certainly supports the more lurid claims about oriental otherness for those that want to go along that route.

For the central claim is that Chinese power has a new assertiveness and tangibility which ranges across the economic, political, cultural and military spheres, evidence is far less clear cut. In each of these areas, the People's Republic that exists today is clearly a far more visible and active player than ever before. But the issue we need to examine here is at what point this goes from being understood as the inevitable side effects of its economic growth which simply give it a new prominence and capacity, or whether it is seen as evidence of a deeply well designed and highly deliberate process where the aim was always some ultimate dominance. Even were the latter wider and more worrying claim to be the case, here too we must distinguish between things that we can expect with a high degree of confidence, such as China attempting to promote, by open or covert means, its oft stated and clear interests over issues like Hong Kong, Taiwan, the South and East China Sea, and its internal human rights problems, and other, far broader issues where its interests are less overt and direct. On the former, there should be no surprises, as the Chinese government, far from being shy, has been persistently, almost obsessively vocal. This behaviour long predates the era of China's greater influence and engagement with the outside world. It would be a far more curious thing were China to have fallen silent on these matters it has expressed such clear interests in before once it acquired the wherewithal to do more about them. There is no hidden hand here. On the contrary, the hand is all too clearly out of the velvet glove and has been very visible for quite some time. But for China to enforce its views, for instance, on the need for democracies like America and those in Europe to adopt its political values and its systems, and to align with it – this is something it is hard to see happening, let alone find much evidence of now. China's behaviour preys on the weaknesses of others, as any opportunist would. But as for effectively, successfully promoting a positive vision of how everyone needs to govern themselves and conduct their domestic affairs, China barely registers. The hidden hand in this context is more likely non-existent.

A final point before we move to details. On all of the ways in which China seeks to utilize its power today to get traction abroad, it is following along paths already well-trod by others. If we look at the Confucius Institutes and the claims about their promotion of propaganda originated in China, and hosting of events that overtly promote the Chinese government's line on issues from Tibet to Xinjiang, we see the same kinds of attempts to influence the public opinion of others that, after all, Americans and Europeans tried to wage in China from the 1980s when the country opened up and came much more accessible to the outside world. I have personal experience of this. In the mid-1990s while working for the British charity Voluntary Service Overseas in Hohhot, Inner Mongolia, in the northern part of China, I remember well that in a city of a million inhabitants, of the dozen or so foreigners who were based there long term (meaning periods of over one year), all of whom were employed as 'foreign experts' teaching English at universities or colleges, apart from myself and a couple of other examples, the majority remaining were closely affiliated with religious institutions. Their mission was clear enough. However benign, they had come under using the cover of aid work to proselytize and save souls. This was explicitly forbidden by Chinese laws at the time.

Attempting to influence China for its own good and saving the place by well-meaning outsiders is an interesting, and long running project. It particularly figures in China's relations with Europe. From the era of the Jesuit (and at time the competing Franciscan) missionaries in the sixteenth century onwards, the Catholic and (and some time after) the Protestant churches had invested personnel, and huge effort, in reaching out to the vast ocean of human souls awaiting salvation in Ming and then Qing China. The results historically were complex, but in the area where the intention had been most specific and clearly articulated – converting Chinese – underwhelming to the point of verging on catastrophic failure. While emperors like Kangxi and Qianlong in the high Qing of the seventeenth and eighteenth century enjoyed educational and cultural exchanges with eminent Christians from Europe, some of whom even took up important positions in their courts, the number of Chinese brought over to practicing the new creed were tiny. The Chinese authorities regarded Christianity as a threat, and at times closed the door on the activities of proselytizers. They had many reasons for doing this, not least their dislike of a religion that demanded absolute fidelity and wanted to eliminate all other belief systems. That did not sit well with the syncretic and pluralistic nature of Chinese belief systems and threatened their desire for harmony.

Communism from 1949 did, under Mao at least, demand uniform loyalty. One could claim that in the whole of Chinese histories through the imperial into the modern era, the brief decade of the Cultural Revolution was the only one that saw anything like a uniform, singular spiritual faith imposed on Chinese people. The intensity and ecstasy of adherents of Maoism from 1966, the claims they made about how seeing Mao in the flesh changed their lives, about how Mao was able to cure diseases, and bring about miraculous changes, had parallels with religious literature from the European mystical tradition. Mao's presence in people's intimate lives, and the levels of adoration given to him, were hard to differentiate from the kind of adoration given to a divine figure. But the Cultural Revolution was the exception, not the norm – a period, today, regarded by scholars inside and outside China, and by people who experienced it and afterwards remain bewildered about why they behaved as they did, as one that is strange and needs explanation. China has returned to the default of broad pluralism since then. Official adherence to Marxism-Leninism with Chinese characteristics while the rest of society commits to other kinds of faith means that the country has returned to a multiple, almost impossibly complex, set of belief systems, interlocking, interconnecting, and often running aside each other, and seldom, if ever, forced to clash to the point where one takes absolute precedence over another. In the political realm, Marxism rules. In matters of inner life and social practice, Buddhism, Christianity, Daoism, Islam all have space. This might not be the space that outsiders would like to see. The non-recognition of the Catholic Church is one long standing bugbear. The other is the crushing under Xi Jinping of more forceful forms of Wahhabi Islam. But to say that the Chinese government forbids religious practice and faith per se is simply not true.

Once more, too, there is evidence that experience, some of it negative, has shaped the current posture in Beijing. The Chinese government was liberal in allowing missionaries into the country under the guise of teachers and experts in the early reform era from the 1980s. But even despite there being clear restrictions on how one could conduct one's religious practices in the country as a foreigner, liberties were often taken. One adherent, sent to China by an American Protestant organization, told me that they could not actively proselytize, and had to ensure no Chinese nationals were involved in their weekly Sunday worship, held at one of their houses. Even so, the box of bibles translated into Chinese they kept in the room which they handed out whenever they got the chance, and the way that they could weave discussion of Christian belief and its role in western society into their English lessons, meant there was plenty of chance to use other, more subtle approaches. Perhaps it was the work from this that lifted the number of Christians in the country to an estimated 100 million by the 2010s.

That proclivity to seek to influence and subtly change people's fundamental ideas so common amongst Enlightenment Europeans is the kind of behaviour that is easily able to see others try to mirror and copy. If we were trying so hard and so persistently to influence and change them, the mentality goes, then this is what they must be doing to us. The assumption is always in the end that they must, whoever they are, be like us, and therefore act like us. If one accepts this description, it is easy to see why today's Europeans and Americans with some awareness of their modern history might be on edge, ready for China to turn into an unwelcome duplicate of their behaviour when they were on the rise. But as David Graeber and David Wengrow in their new history of humanity point out, this kind of behaviour in terms of scale, length and intensity, was very specific to westerners.[12] Their aggressive sallying into the outside world at times using the most brutal methods to promote and enforce a specific belief systems at the costs of all others it encountered over such a sustained and long period was unusual. There is a reason why the sun never set on the British Empire – and that was because no one before had tried to spread themselves so proactively and aggressively across the rest of the world before. The only similar example at least in China's long history had been the Mongolian conquests from the thirteenth to the fourteenth century. But one could argue that was hardly a typical imperial regime, and it fell apart after only a matter of decades. The Japanese in the Second World War had huge territorial ambitions too. But that also was an aberration, a form of behaviour that had simply not been seen in the centuries of Japanese history before. And again, it collapsed after less than a decade.

Whatever the motives for the sustained, global expansion by western powers from the seventeenth century, we all now know too much about the colossal human and cultural cost of this on indigenous peoples in places from South and North America to Africa to regard it in any straightforward way today. And while modern westerners should not be immediately held responsible for the sins of their forebears, divisive and passionate contemporary debates show how far from consensus people are about the best way to interpret this long era. For some (historians like Niall Fergusson) empire is still seen positively. For others, it was a catastrophe. Observing this, those living today in countries with experience of colonization such as China find it hard to take the moralizing lectures accusing them of pursuing similar kinds of behaviour by the countries that were historically the most enthusiastic and extensive practitioners in the not too distant past. Nor do they see solid evidence that those old western habits of interference and meddling have fully stopped. Witness the endless operations in the Middle East since the 1990s by Americans, and Europeans. This assumption that China will be and act like the West in its pomp because that is the only option open to it must account for some of the almost paranoid levels of fear of Chinese hidden influence that have occurred since the turn of the millennium. This has been growing progressively shriller as time has gone on. But whether it accurately reflects China's real intentions is a completely different matter.

It is also important to remind those most invested in this particular narrative of China the emerging dominator and hegemon that, if the People's Republic is indeed simply duplicating western behaviour, then in the long term it is using a strategy the West itself has shown will end in failure. It only needs to look at the concerted efforts of western soft culture and influence campaigns on it since the 1980s to see this. Despite the vast resources, and the attractive values that were promoted through literature, films, language learning, and other means promising happiness and freedom (however far reality fell from this), with the much greater economic advantages the West had at the time, the American and European efforts to win hearts and minds of Chinese people has culminated in the curt rejection of Xi Jinping. It has, to be blunt, failed. This is a place where despite this colossal charm offensive, the political elite have overtly, and repeatedly, said no to what they call western universalist models. Nor should we kid ourselves with the simple explanation that this is because the Chinese government stubbornly continues to subscribe to the ideology of Marxism-Leninism, ironically one of the most successful non-Chinese, semi-western imports into the country, and will not let its people free to experience better things. Amazingly, the Communist Party in China and the West have to bow down to one thing neither has been able to change. The great wall facing down our zealous, proselytizing campaigns in the last four decades has ended up being something far more epic, and profound standing behind this façade – the vast terrain of 'traditional Chinese culture' and the edifice of Chinese identity built on that. Even the mighty Communist Party now increasingly stands beside this after concerted efforts in the Maoist era to bring it down, seeking authenticity and legitimacy from what it once rejected and despised. This is not something created by Chinese politicians, but a thing with a far more complex reality and far deeper and wider hold on people who regard themselves as Chinese. The simple fact is that it is not the Communist Party that has said no to making itself a copy of the West, but Chinese people, meaning those daydreams in the recent past of western soft power melting the hearts of the grateful locals and letting them run towards mass conversion to western values was a doomed quest from the start.

If the West has the courage to see the massive soft power campaign it waged, consciously or otherwise, in China from the 1980s onwards as something that can be evaluated as a failure today, it can use this experience to inform its own current frenetic fear of China's claimed nefarious influence in the West more analytically and critically. Once the abhorrent but ever lingering issue of sinophobia has been stripped away, a more proportionate view appears: that is that it is not surprising China might be using the same methods on the West that the West used on it. It does so however with significant disadvantages. It is dealing with an audience for one thing who are either ill-informed about its own cultural and political ideals, or, until recently, indifferent and uninterested in them. It is doing so with a complex message, one which is very hard to make accessible and attractive for people from a non-Chinese background. While capitalism in its heyday could use its clear impact in improving material standards of living as its greatest advert, for socialism with Chinese characteristics the incentives to follow are far harder to grasp. People in Europe and America do not want a Chinese style of living, and do not idealize life in China in terms of standards and comfort the way that Chinese did towards the West in the 1980s and 1990s. At best, we can say there is increasing parity here. In many ways too, right or wrong, those that do think about China or have an awareness of the place in Europe or America are unlikely, even if they regard China positively, or even neutrally, to want to embrace its political or social values. They would see them as different, not as something that might be of utility or relevance to them. That too was not the case at times in the 1980s and 1990s for Chinese the other way, when some did feel western liberal values had a chance of being embraced in their country.

These are very significant impediments and differences. They are ones which the Chinese government probably knows as well as anyone. This is why it has scaled down its outright support for soft power promotion in the last decade after an initial period of enthusiasm. The question is therefore not whether China has effectively managed to influence and confuse the outside world and undertake campaigns to brainwash and control it. It is more about how it has managed to even get to the place where a perception like the 'hidden hand' scare story and others of its ilk can take hold. Why, in the end, did the West become so convinced that Chinese power is so potent, threatening and invasive? It's not China's assertiveness and ambitions that should interest here. It is the complete collapse of the West's confidence in itself which has been so dramatic.

Confucius Institutes and the Infiltration of Foreign Universities

In their various hard-hitting, and well researched reports, Human Rights Watch have repeatedly focussed on Confucius Institutes. Established via the Hanban (the abbreviation for the Office of Chinese Council International) under the Ministry of Education in Beijing in 2004, as of 2019 there were 530 across the world, with an aim of opening 1,000. It has to be said that Confucius Institutes are curious entities. Unlike the Goethe Institute of Germany or the Alliance Francaise from France, they are almost all located within established non-Chinese universities. Some of these are very eminent institutions. The School of Oriental and African Studies in London, for instance, and the University of Chicago all had such Institutes. The former still exists at the time of writing (late 2021) while the latter was closed down in 2020. This means that from the start, they exist in a far more complex environment that the stand-alone, more autonomous representative entities from other countries. The British Council, too, tends to operate either independent of the other arms of the British state, or, in China, as the cultural arm of the embassy due to regulations there. Even so, in terms of office, badging, governance and identity, there is a lot of independence.

Nestling in universities, it is easy to see why, however bright the idea operating in this way in the past may have been, they were doomed to experience a vexatious fate. Human Rights Watch in a document issued in 2019 put this unequivocally. They are, it said. 'fundamentally incompatible with a robust commitment to academic freedom. Confucius Institutes (CI) are extensions of the Chinese government that censor certain topics and perspectives in course materials on political grounds, and use hiring practices that take political loyalty into consideration.'[13] Despite this, it is clear that the *perception* of what the

Confucius Institutes do races ahead of what any significant body of evidence showing that they actually do. Across the very different environments in which they are active, through different countries and in different local terrains, and according to the specifics of the institution they happen to be embedded in, Confucius Institutes are a mixed bunch. My own experience since being aware of them from the mid-2000s onwards bears this out. Even back then, there was plenty of speculation about what these things were up to. Their closed doors and the ways in which they seemed to operate as an extension of the Chinese state right at the heart of liberal institutions, gave force to the worse possible interpretation. But the overwhelming impression I started to get was just how *odd* they were.

Confucius Institutes don't, for a start, have a common narrative they tell. They each testify to a very different story. For a lot of that time, this depends on the leadership each one has, and the opportunities offered to them wherever they are located. Chinese power as it flows through these is more akin to a somewhat reactive, opportunistic force adapting itself to the environment it flows into. If countries or particular universities want to allow large scale events celebrating the noble achievements of the Communist Party's great leaders, where an audience might even turn up (even if only to devour the food after the formal event), then there are plenty of Confucius Institute directors who would be glad to step in. But most of the time, Confucius Institutes are involved in language learning, very broad cultural education, and doing what they said they would be doing – addressing the vast knowledge and linguistic deficit of the outside world. If some of that looks like it might be presenting China in a positive light, then one has to ask the simple question – with a global audience that clearly has limited knowledge of China, and a country that is fast becoming more prominent, what is better – the provision of some knowledge about the place, or none at all? If education systems in the outside world provided more material on Chinese culture and language, Confucius Institutes would have a far smaller audience. Their limited success in the past decade or so has been almost wholly on the back of having no competition in supplying this very basic education.

What is clear is that in a few cases, for entities run by an organization meant to promote China's image abroad and increase what is sometimes called its soft power, they have been excellent at achieving the exact opposite. China's worst enemies could not have done more damage to the nation's image than the remarkable attempts made in 2014 at a convening of the European Association of Chinese Studies (EACS) in

Portugal. As one of the co-sponsors, zealous officials from Hanban and the local Confucius Institute were accused by conference attendees of taking the printed booklet for the meeting, some of them in the hands of attendees, and ripping out a page acknowledging support from the Taiwanese Chiang Ching-kuo Foundation.[14] This was made even more inflammatory because of the presence of Madame Xu Lin, the global head of Hanban who was due to speak. Her hasty departure after protests were lodged with local authorities was an inglorious and humiliating exit, rather than the victory lap of someone who had made a good point well.

Why the Chinese government does not want to funnel all its work through far more transparently marked Chinese cultural centres like the one that exists in the centre of Sydney is an interesting question. One has to acknowledge too that Confucius Institutes in Africa, Latin America or the Middle East are very different beasts to those in North America, Australia and Europe where the political hang-ups are different. As lightning rods for complaints and suspicions, and sources of seething discontent by some universities where large numbers of staff disagree with Confucius Institutes being present, it is hard to imagine a more clunky and counterproductive model. Despite that, hard evidence of Confucius Institutes really effecting deep change in the mindsets of those around them, wherever they are located, is hard to find. And there are examples of some hosting riskier, more diverse events, ones which were often critical of the Chinese government. This too is wholly dependent on who is in charge of them. In my experience, the main issue with many Confucius Institutes is not their activism, but that they do precisely nothing, and frustrate their hosts by taking up space and sometimes funding while simply stagnating. That, more than any other reason, is probably why there were cases of some closing from 2019.

The Chinese government was unwise a decade and a half ago to invest so much optimism into Confucius Institutes. It was a marriage made in Hell from the start for the simple fact that anything that placed foreign universities in direct relationship with the Chinese state in this way was going to become very complex, and without very clear terms of reference and mutual understanding stood a good risk of being often very messy. Leaving aside the rest of the world, one need only look at the situation in the UK to bear this out. Of the major universities there, for places like Oxford and Cambridge their internal governance and sheer byzantine opacity competes well even with the Communist Party itself. Unsurprisingly, Confucius Institutes made no inroads here. At the

London School of Economics, and Nottingham, and other places, their fate was tied to the complexities of these very different hosts. In the UK, no two universities are wholly alike. Their leadership too changes remarkably quickly. Today's vice chancellor with a keen interest in China and desire to do more work there is often replaced by one with a completely contrary view. In the heyday of university engagement with education in the PRC, Nottingham and Liverpool opened different kinds of campus or learning centres in country. They therefore could link their Confucius Institutes to larger strategic plans. Some like Manchester University, could in parallel have large numbers of Chinese students, a Confucius Institute and a centre for the study of China with completely parallel objectives and different governance, funding and staff. In other places, like Lancaster, Confucius Institutes gave an extra capacity for language and cultural learning that was unlikely to have funding were the Hanban not at hand. The one thing one can say, about this single example of one country in Europe, was that the Confucius Institutes may have been derived from a common model, and come associated with a common mother institution in Beijing, but they had to fit into radically different, of often fast changing, contexts.

On top of this was the very inconvenient truth that of all western institutions, universities were going to be the least easy for the Chinese government to deal with. Beyond their huge diversity, there is also the one underpinning feature they share – a commitment to Enlightenment ideas of pedagogy which, in the words of dissident Liu Xiaobo, privileged analysis and self-criticism. The British government, were it asked, could tell the Chinese government exactly how easy its own universities were to organize. Academics are infamously hostile to management of any kind – thus the remarkable decentralized model of Oxbridge where the Vice Chancellor is no more than the servant of college heads where, in some cases (Trinity in Cambridge for instance) the incumbent might be a far more powerful and higher profile figure. Enforcing consensus and gaining friends in this kind of environment is either exhausting, or impossible, even for those that spend their life working from within. The question is therefore why China decided to try to forge partnerships with a vastly complicated set of institutions where the only commonality was their fierce resistance to being told what to do by anyone outside. Surely, they were naïve and did not know what they were getting themselves involved in.

There are other ways in which universities have been put in a far more complex relationship with China than through hosting of Confucius Institutes. For separate reasons, and largely through their own agency and compliance, in the case of the UK, Australia, Canada, New Zealand and the US (the Five Eyes, though in this particular case more akin to the Five Takers) enormous and ever rising numbers of Chinese students have come to do undergraduate, or post-graduate degrees. From a slow trickle at the end of the 1990s, there are now 140,00 Chinese students in Britain alone, with about the same number in Australia, and double in the US. The University of Sydney is a case in point – with 6,000 students from the PRC in 2012, this has now climbed to something closer to 25,000. These contribute well over a quarter of all university revenue. This means that, through active and willing collaboration, the great bastions of free speech and dispassionate enquiry are now largely bankrolled by citizens from a totalitarian country consistently accused of imprisoning anyone who dissents from the government line. It is not, therefore, Confucius Institutes that should be watched fiercely as the great source of influence here, but the vast, high fee-paying cohort of students. The Confucius Institutes are a mere tiny side show compared to this, even if the worst fears of their behaviour are assumed to be true.

Even in this narrative, however, reality when viewed dispassionately turns out to be less amenable to those committed to the pure China Threat creed. Around 2014, while at the University of Sydney, reports in some Australian papers started declaring that the Chinese government was running spy rings amongst its students in country. This was a bold claim. As someone actually based there day to day and dealing with this issue, it seemed I had not seen the compelling evidence the journalist working on this story had found. Nor, for that matter, had they ever bothered to get in touch to get my views. Our own research showed that Chinese students coming to study with us, if they had been working as deep cover agents, were at the same time dealing with isolation, immense pressure because of financial reasons (far from being from wealthy families, they were often funded by a network of friends and relatives, which meant failure was far more than an academic issue, and had long-term impact on the rest of their lives), and a good amount of well-documented prejudice locally. While most Australians were friendly and accommodating, there were a minority that felt it permissible to berate and discriminate on Asian-looking students that crossed their path.

In this context, the real, living, breathing Chinese students I got to know in Sydney were hard working, usually very low profile, and focussed on doing everything they could to get through courses taught in a second language. They were often homesick. The newspaper stories probably worsened that by creating a strong sense that they were far from welcome by some quarters in their new adopted, temporary home. Nor did many reports in the media look much at the story of the high number of suicides by Chinese studying overseas. It was easier and more dramatic to talk about spying.

Of the 6,000 students at Sydney University at this time, maybe a tiny handful had been tasked with sensitive work and might be categorized as spies. I am no expert on intelligence work, but I would hazard a guess that by its nature, not a lot of people can engage with it. This is for the simple reason that as an area of high risk, anyone running a spy ring would want to keep things small and tight. And it would probably have been easy enough to work out where the main areas for covert work might be – those with a high component for Intellectual Property that could be stolen, or working in computing, engineering, places like that. I can't imagine there being a great appetite for the Chinese government to receive top secret strap line reports on the musings of the members of the school of social science, or the literature department. Nor in Business Studies or Accounting, where the vast bulk of Chinese overseas students were based.

The 'Chinese students as a vast cohort of spies' is one of the more pernicious myths promoted by certain media outlets.[15] These reports were, and are, particularly corrosive because, of course, no one would ever overtly state they felt all Chinese students were indeed spies, but in making claims about a limited number that casts a shadow over everyone else. Paranoia ensues. In the worst cases, as one saw in 2020, there are crude, racist attacks.[16] Intelligent, evidence based, well contextualized reports on areas of real risk, with a proper analysis of what might be done to mitigate this – that is highly necessary. But that would be something anyone would do only when they understand the specific areas they need to protect, and why they need to do this. It would also need to apply for anyone, whether they are from China or Timbuktu.

What does the case of Confucius Institutes and Chinese actions in western universities support then? Are they clear evidence of a comprehensive, well focussed, destructive and (most crucially of all) effective contemporary Chinese power campaign? Or on the contrary signs of opportunistic behaviour by an entity with new capacity but one that clearly has severe limitations both on its mode of operations and what these yield for it? The best we can say when we review the evidence is that, yes, we do see China trying to influence, and use power, but over a specific and well identified set of issues. We do not see a masterful campaign, by an adept, well concealed 'hidden hand' which stretches across global issues, but one more akin to trembling, grabbing and upsetting things as it tries to promote its interests. In this area, therefore, the very best verdict we can give so far is unproven.

A final word on this. The greatest problem for Confucius Institutes, or for any Chinese campaign for influence, at least in Europe and North America, is the lack of an attractive alternative set of ideas to put before western audiences. Confucius Institutes are not effective disseminators of Chinese soft power for the government above and beyond the reasons given already because they do not have that fundamental thing that would make them so – a seductive, compelling belief system that can win hearts and minds. Marxism-Leninism with Chinese characteristics is not a world view that is either easy to understand at first acquaintance, or attractive when it is understood. That is not to say it doesn't work for China, its host country. But it is unlikely to work for anywhere which is not China. The clue, as ever, is in the name. And to reinforce this point, some in the West should pause their agonizing and self-doubt for a second and observe that still, today, universities in America, Europe and Australia are the ones that attract Chinese students, rather than western students suddenly flocking to be immersed in the attractions of China. For the moment, this shows that, for many young Chinese at least, the West continues to have potency and attractiveness. If only the promoters of the hysterical China Threat meme in the West would sound like they held this view too.

China is Buying Us Up

Since the Global Financial Crisis of 2008, news of China becoming one of the world's fastest growing outward investors has seldom left the headlines. In 2008, the *Financial Times* reported that the China Investment Corporation, a sovereign wealth fund set up around the time of the crisis, and the State Administration for Foreign Exchange (SAFE), the government body in charge of the trillions of foreign revenue the country has accrued through its manufacturing, were buying up shares in companies as wide ranging as Tesco and British Petroleum. In 2004, Lenova (formerly Legend), a computer company from China bought the IBM Think Pad brand in the US. American congressional concern stopped a similar purchase of the small energy company Unocal a year later. Chinese overseas investment is a relatively new phenomenon, not figuring in any volume till the late 1990s. Since then, it has been watched hawkishly and almost obsessively. China is buying up the world, the narrative goes. This, rather than the ideological worries brought by Confucius Institutes, gives tangibility to Chinese power – exposing a country with a vast economy willing to use this to enforce its will. There is even a term for this – Chinese economic statecraft. Unlike ideological power, which is much harder to discern and track evidence for, with investment one can assemble data and speak empirically.

In terms of trends, things are clear. As a bigger economy, China has accrued more capital to use abroad. On the surface, the country's motives are not mysterious. Researchers at Leeds University, amongst other places, have tracked the drivers of Chinese overseas investment for over a decade and a half.[17] Supporting sales markets for exports, gaining security of supply for raw materials and energy, acquiring managerial and IP know-how – these are some of the main elements. Where things get more confusing is around the idea that because of the stronger role of the state, and of State Owned Enterprises (SOEs), for Chinese Overseas Direct Investment (ODI), that must mean that there is a master plan for all the acquisitions run by the central government. After all, in 2002, the 'Going Out' strategy was announced to great fanfare at a Communist Party congress held that year, supporting fifty national champions to enable them to become world class through targeted mergers and acquisitions.

When the BRI started to appear around 2013 (though then in the guise of the New Silk Road, before it was renamed a couple of years later) one of the responses was to see this as a further intensification of the Chinese government engaging in economic statecraft.[18] There was a blueprint, it was clear, an agreed plan whereby China would use ODI to promote its interests and enforce compliance from others. Debt trap diplomacy became the new guise for this, with claims that China was providing unrealistic aid and finance packages. When the recipient could no longer service these, it led to them either handing everything back to the Chinese state to manage or showing obedience in some other way for kinder treatment. Chinese investment was accused of being largely in the interests of China, of involving deals whereby Chinese labour and Chinese companies were set up to be the net beneficiaries. Technology and IP were sucked into China by this route.

Here was the hidden hand coming stuffed with Chinese currency and gifts too good to be true. There was, as one image conveyed it, a great wall of Chinese RMB currency being assembled, trapping those who were naïve enough to engage, allowing levels of interference and involvement that seemed to go contrary to the hypocritical stance of the Beijing government that said it overtly stood against such exploitative behaviour.

Some countries offered various kinds of horror stories. These differed in scale and gravity. In Latin America, from early on, mines and extractive industry projects China put money into often became environmental degradation black spots. Unions and local laws were not respected. In Poland, initial interest in Chinese assistance in building roads turned sour when the very attractive sums originally talked about failed to add up. Cases like this showed that Chinese ODI certainly aroused one quality in the outside world – and that was naked greed. China kindly offered to supply the African Union headquarters with telecoms equipment in the 2000s, only for the new inhabitants to find out their building was bugged (the US couldn't complain about this kind of behaviour, because they had played the same kind of favour on the presidential plane supplied to then Chinese president Jiang Zemin in the early 2000s). And a partly Chinese investment in a golf club in the UK, at Wentworth, offered a text book of malpractice, with fees being raised through the roof, and the local community alienated to such an extent they protested against the new owner, billionaire Yang Bin, and took their complaints to the British government and the Chinese embassy in London.[19] Chinese investment aroused such ire in Australia that after a number of major attempts to buy stakes in the state grid, and in a huge parcel of land in the norther part of the country by Chinese associated entities, a new official board scrutinizing foreign investment, largely originating from the PRC, was set up. Similar bodies have now been established in Europe. America has long had one of its own.

In some cases, as this short list of examples shows, Chinese investment poses problems. The question is more about what specific problems it might pose that make it generically different from any other ODI. After all, there are plenty of examples, going back decades, of foreign investors misunderstanding and misbehaving in places they chose to invest in, whatever the origins of the money. Chinese entities have no monopoly here. The main argument from critics was that Chinese ODI, whatever badge it came with, was more obedient to the diktats of the central state in Beijing, and therefore much more of a political tool.

This claim is a sweeping one and depends once again on that illusive issue of what Chinese intentions might be and how coherent they are. If we look at the evidence from the period after 2008, then it is hard to see straightforward patterns. This lack of coherence argues directly against Chinese ODI being an intentional, vast, concerted push for influence.

That China is active as an investor abroad is not mysterious. The anomaly is more that as the world's second largest economy it is not doing more. Netherlands, Japan, South Korea, Germany, the US and the UK were for much of this time far larger outward investors, even when their economies became smaller than China's.[20] Despite all the excited commentary in 2008, in the ensuing years China became more cautious, never quite embarking on the huge buying spree of cheap, foreign assets that was expected of it.

Its path as a foreign investor too has been a rocky one, with some sobering commercial failures. In the decade after the Great Financial Crisis, far from constructing a grand takeover strategy, China has learned some hard lessons. So have those who have engaged with it. The Belt and Road offers a topical case study. Accused of being the epitome of predatory capitalism, it is assigned responsibility for buying political allegiance in places as far flung as Tanzania, Sri Lanka and Greece. That it has been clothed in high sounding, friendly rhetoric from the Chinese side since the time Xi Jinping announced it first in 2013 has alerted more critical and sensitive observers to suspect something nefarious going on under the surface. It all sounds too good to be true. The media has piled into this with abandon, covering lurid tales of China's state sending out feelers deep into the Asian region and further afield. In Sri Lanka, the Hambantota Port Development Project aroused intense interest around 2018. According to the *New York Times*, writing that year, 'Every time Sri Lanka's president, Mahinda Rajapaksa, turned to his Chinese allies for loans and assistance with an ambitious port project, the answer was yes.' But the story didn't end up well. 'Over years of construction and renegotiation with China Harbor Engineering Company, one of Beijing's largest state-owned enterprises, the Hambantota Port Development Project distinguished itself mostly by failing, as predicted. With tens of thousands of ships passing by along one of the world's busiest shipping lanes, the port drew only thirty-four ships in 2012. And then the port became China's.'[21] The author continues: 'The case is one of the most vivid examples of China's ambitious use of loans and aid to gain influence around the world – and of its willingness to play hardball to collect.'

A similar tale is given of the Piraeus port in Greece, where the Chinese state shipping company COSCO has been buying shares since 2008. 'The Chinese-lettered banner hanging over the entrance is one of the few signs that Beijing now controls Europe's fourth-biggest container port,' a *Financial Times* report stated in October 2021. 'Yet this month the Piraeus Port Authority handed a further 16 per cent of its shares to

COSCO, cementing its control by the Chinese state-backed shipping group, which bought 51 per cent of the Greek port in August 2016.[22] Such investment sees Beijing cementing control of EU infrastructure, the report continues. It also ensured that at least in 2017 the Greek government was willing to veto criticism of China's human rights record in an EU resolution for the UN.[23]

In Tanzania, too, the Chinese were associated from 2013 with Bagamoya port plans. This was set to be the largest deep-water port in Africa. 'In addition to building what would be the largest port in Africa,' one account said, 'China Merchants agreed to construct railways and a special economic zone with the goal of making Tanzania a regional trade and transport centre. If completed as planned, the Bagamoyo port would be considerably larger than the Kenyan port of Mombasa, the largest African port on the Indian Ocean and a key economic driver for East and Central Africa.'[24]

Robert Erskine Childers in his famous 1903 espionage classic, 'The Riddle of the Sands,' describes Caruthers, a British Foreign Office official divining sinister intentional activity by the Germans in the Frisian Islands off the coast of Mainland Europe. What looked like innocent ship movements and construction for purely commercial purposes at first inspection was ultimately exposed as a masterful, well concealed plan by the government to conquer and control. The same could be said of much of the narrative of Chinese behaviour overseas. Every part of the BRI is closely inspected, with a political motive sought for even the most commercial activity. The Chinese words are telling one story, those doing this watching say, but we, the critical observers, see something absolutely different. The most common default is the simplest one: to always assume the worst. This is the guiding principle of much media and commentary. From the String of Pearls notion beloved of American analysts in the 2000s where it was claimed China by stealth was gaining interests in ports around its region to aid its naval ambitions, to the behaviour of China in the South China Sea with its island building and in the BRI today, the conviction remains the same: that there is a highly deliberative, strategic, long-term plan. The riddle here is not in the sands, but written across the BRI, and in the seaways and investment projects with any link to Beijing. The only frustration with this line of approach is that the moment of irrefutable revelation of the grand final ambitions lurking behind China's actions is forever in the process of being exposed. It has not become clear yet. For the sceptics, as each year goes by, the question intensifies: was there ever such a single, clear aim from the word go? How much longer do we have to wait till we see

Beijing's hand fully exposed? What if, in the end, it really was all mainly commercial?

This issue of how to best interpret China's behaviour matters because of that vast question referred to before. If China is indeed a power driven by the desire to remake, reorder and completely reform the world in its own image, a sort of US model, then something like the BRI offers crucial indicators of its long-term intent. If however it is an opportunistic, exceptional, more limited power, driven by self-interest, then the BRI becomes a different kind of vehicle, and a different kind of problem. As with the Confucius Institutes in the ideological realm, what the case of Greece, Tanzania and Sri Lanka show is that whatever plans and strategies China might have, they have experienced fierce headwinds, raising major questions over the way they have been executed. That sits more with an inexperienced, exposed and often incomplete power, one with ability in some areas (capital, technical ability to build infrastructure) but ongoing challenges in others (the political, ideological and cultural). The common point about the three examples given above is that, as of late 2021, none are going that well. If these are symbols of Chinese strength and success, then they show the world needs to worry more about how limited that is, rather than how potent and overwhelming.

In the case of Sri Lanka, the handing of the port to the Chinese saddled them with a hard project, along with a changing government, and increasingly hostile and sceptical attitudes towards China. Were Beijing of an imperial mindset, it would be up for the raft of responsibilities and commitment to run not just the port but the whole island. But clearly it isn't, as is shown from what has transpired since 2018 where the absolute opposite of the preferred modus operandi attributed to it has occurred. It has had to commit even more money, expose itself to even more risk, and become sucked into complex local politics. Exactly the same could be said of the port planned in Tanzania. Negotiations with the government have ended up going down a blind alley. After 2008, and significant criticism about China's involvement in the continent, with accusations it was a new kind of colonizer, China adopted a far more cautious approach. Despite a decade or more of extra experience and time to reflect, the obstructions its plans have met in Tanzania are illustrative of the comment an African analyst made to me around 2006 when this story first started to arouse interest. 'Africans will use China the way they have used all others who have come to work with them. The principle will be the same, despite the friendly rhetoric on the surface.' In Greece, too, the attitude by Beijing that Europeans are an impossible, complicated, fickle partner has been proved right. With the change of government in 2018 in Athens, attitudes towards China became far more negative. Criticisms escalated. And while Chinese shipowner COSCO's involvement in the Piraeus port has increased, it has received precious little praise for the jobs creation and support in an economy that has been afflicted with unemployment, weak growth, and vast government debt for almost a decade now.

The complexity of China's exposure in different environments is well spelled out by Eyck Freymann in a 2020 book on the BRI. There, the conclusion after detailed examination of each of these three, and other examples, is that the sheer scope of the geography covered by the BRI, along with the hesitancy of the Chinese government to be more explicit in setting out aims for fear of being accused of being an imperialist or colonizer create immediate problems. Finally, there is the manner in which it is trying to operate in vastly different areas, on very different kinds of projects, for very different aims, meaning that the elegant simplicity of labelling the whole operation a huge geopolitical power grab to control territory, supply lines and space is easily undermined.[25]

None of this is to say that China does not have motives. Its economy is now deeply integrated into the rest of the world. It needs supplies from the outside in terms of raw materials and energy. It also needs markets for its goods. Efforts to create more autonomy with the Dual Circulation idea announced by Xi Jinping in 2020, where domestic consumption, local creation of technology and internal markets would be the focus of development as the outside world became more difficult to deal with have not as yet fundamentally changed this situation. It is hard to see the return of a world where China lived behind its own boundaries and barriers. Chinese investment has a major role to play in this interaction globally. But the quandary it poses is as tricky for China as for everyone else. As an integrated and important economic actor, it has to seek new opportunities and sources of growth. But that very act of seeking is seen all too often in a political rather than a commercial or economic prism abroad. The assumption of most when they hear China saying that what it is doing is not politically motivated is that the opposite must be the case.

China as a Hard Power

In the late 2000s, in the twilight of the Hu Jintao era, there was an increase of incidents of clashes between lifeboats and fishing vessels in the South and East China Sea area. In one of the most infamous, in September 2010, Zhan Qixiong, captain of a Chinese fishing vessel, was detained by Japanese coastguard vessels after encountering them near the disputed Senkaku/Diaoyutai islands. These are currently under Japanese control, but bitterly disputed by both the government in Beijing and Taiwan. Two weeks after being taken in, Zhan was released.[26] By that time his case had become a prominent one amongst the nationalists in China. Demands for his liberation became shrill and menacing. Furious patriotic Chinese online unleashed a barrage of insults against a country they felt had been constantly undermining and insulting them in the last century. In Japan and the US, however, the worry was more about Beijing's new assertiveness and pushiness. Claims about the country being more vocal and taking a much more prominent stance on issues that matter to it, therefore, predates the Xi era. The proactive foreign policy stance attributed to him has its roots well within the period before he became the main leader.

What China might look like as a power with real hard military capacity is a tricky question to answer. We know what Japan looked like under a nationalistic, militarized government which had a strong economy in the Asian region, because that it precisely what we saw up to 1945. Japan as number one in Asia resulted in tragic, appalling outcomes. But for Chinese nationalism, while the history stretches back a long way, the trail of evidence is, once again, more ambiguous. As was argued in the first chapter, the world does not know what a strong China looks like because, until now, at least in modern history, such a place has never existed. Now we confront a country that in terms of its unofficial, and sometimes its official rhetoric, sounds like it means business and has the physical wherewithal to enforce its own will if it so choses. The question is what sense to make of this. What does China being a serious military power actually mean in the twenty-first century?

If these is a place where one would see this Chinese hard military power in action then the area immediately around it is the most likely. In terms of land borders, beyond the settling of these through disputes, and sometimes skirmishes in the Maoist era up to today, it is hard to see China wanting to deploy its troops over the vast and inhospitable Tibetan Plateau in order to attack India or Bhutan. It has live and ongoing interests in areas along the border with both of these – but not beyond them. China harbours no larger ambitions too with Russia or Mongolia, despite persistent fears in both countries of an imminent Chinese landgrab for the vast empty spaces of Siberia, and the resources that are there. As anthropologists Caroline Humphrey and Frank Bille explain, in a fascinating book from 2021 on the Sino-Russian border, the numbers of Chinese attempting to settle long term in Siberia has declined in recent years rather than gone up. Why go to a place which is undeveloped and harsh when there are so many more opportunities back in China?[27]

China as a land power is a well-established narrative, with clear precedents and modes of behaviour. What expansiveness Chinese dynasties showed were either in the Yuan Dynasty, over eight centuries ago, as part of the vast Mongolian conquests into today's Central Asia, Middle East and Europe – a truly exceptional era that has never been duplicated – or in the Qing when Tibet and Xinjiang, and Mongolia, were brought into the sphere of central control from the mid-seventeenth to the early eighteenth century. These were territories that from a strategic and historic perspective already had deep links with previous dynasties. They were also geographically right next to it. The idea of duplicating this sort of behaviour for areas further afield never happened. It is hard to see much strategic rationale supporting it ever happening. Historically at least, from the era of the Yuan, empire building with Chinese characteristics was very much a local affair.

China's maritime area however offers a more promising target by which to expose new aspects of Chinese power. With its huge new navy, and the need to protect supply chain and logistic links for goods and energy, Xi's country has the means and the motive to be a greater presence in the waters around it. It also makes strategic sense. Having the US Seventh Fleet, now joined by aircraft carriers from Australia, France and Britain, parading up and down next to its southern coastal border is both an irritant for China, an affront to its sensitivities about sovereignty, and an impediment to its own freedom of movement and action. In the end, it is another tangible sign for Beijing that China simply does not have, even in its own neighbourhood, the kind of space the world's second largest economy feels it deserves. This is probably why Xi when meeting Obama in 2013 declared that the Pacific was big enough for both powers – with the underlying message that this was as long as they both kept to their separate ends of the vast pond.

If we see the South China Sea as a platform on which Chinese contemporary intentions are played, and as a place where its hard power is tangibly visible, then it is clearly a location of immense geopolitical significance. Chinese hard power in the Atlantic, or the Artic Ocean, or along the west coast of Africa, or the east coast of Latin America, is an elusive, to non-existent, thing. At best, one can fixate on the meaning of the Djibouti naval base set up between 2015 and 2017, and recurring reports that China is about to add another like this somewhere in the Pacific. Within the South China Sea, however, there is far more real activity. Since 2014, Chinese have been accused of building new structures on rock formations there to make them classifiable as islands, constructing runways for aircraft, enhancing their naval capacity and presence, and escalating their rhetoric. Contesting claimants from the Philippines to Malaysia have all engaged in different kinds of pushback. These tensions are real, not imagined. There is no place to hide for China in this game, and no ambiguity about what it is doing.

If we have tracked down the reality of Chinese hard power in the South China Sea, this is a huge thing. But once more complexity emerges. Henry Kissinger in a book about China written in 2011 expended a lot of time on explaining his conception of the differences between Chinese and western strategic culture. For him, the metaphor of Chinese chequers (the game 'Go') versus international chess helped illuminate this.[28] In the former, the objective is to identity spaces that one can hedge in and control; in the latter it is about clear lines of strategic flexibility where pieces can move across the board, sometimes to the whole length, taking others and achieving dominance by eliminating their opponents and blocking in the single piece of the King. Looking at the physical terrain of the South China Sea there is an eerie appropriateness to these two conceptualizations. China has been busy increasing the spaces it can claim it controls. The submerged islands made into ones that have a permanent existence above the waves and the fortified rock formations have all allowed China to exercise dominance over more discrete territory dotted across the region's waters. This has provided an alternative physical reality to suit its claims. For the US and its allies, the priority is to maintain freedom of navigation, preserving lateral lines of access and movement across the sea, ensuring that the attempts to block and inhibit this are thwarted. Nevertheless, between these lines, China has constructed a whole parallel territory which has slowly accumulated in the period after 2010. This gives it pockets of influence which while not continuous, reach down to the coast of Indonesia 2,000 kilometres from its southern land coast.

The attractiveness of the Kissinger framework is that it has at least some explanatory power. It seems to show that Chinese behaviour is different from the West, because its ways of thinking are different, and that one territory can have two very different kinds of strategic games played on it. Françoise Jullien gives a deeper and more sophisticated description of these contrasting approaches. For him, Chinese contemporary strategy is rooted in long and well-documented historic traditions of thought and philosophical outlook. This strategic culture concentrates on, to use Jullien's terms, releasing the 'imminence of things', and working with their already extant nature to optimize and develop them rather than bring about radical change. It does not strive after pre-decided objectives which bring about a complete alteration of reality and demand total change. It simply looks at fulfilling actuality and bringing to bear things which are already there, in a situation, but have not yet been made manifest. 'The "European" way of "model-making", Jullien argues, 'involves a means-end relationship. Once an end is ideally conceived, we set about finding the means whereby that end can be made to enter the realm of fact.'[29] In China, however, 'we find a way of thinking . . . [that] does not need to envisage behaviour from a means-end point of view. In these circumstances, one's behaviour does not result from an *application* (with a theory conceived in advance being imposed upon reality in such a way as to be eventually imprinted on it). Rather, it is determined by an *exploitation* (the best way to profit from the potential implied in the given situation).'

For China's basic claims in the South China Sea, its behaviour is also different to other competing parties because it is framed by history and by the belief that this gives the contemporary PRC far greater legitimacy. This mindset faces two problems. The first is that others involved do not accept this history. They are far keener to look to modern international law as having greater authority. Even if one does accept the importance of history, there is the constant problem of how dramatically notions of China have changed in the timeframe we are looking at. The Ming, Qing and now modern China cover the six centuries that are most recent, and most important for current Chinese claims. Over that time, there were multiple, very different Chinas rather than anything uniform and singular. The territory of the Ming were not those of the Qing. Over its two and a half centuries in power, the Qing changed radically as it acquired more space through land conquests. China today has been constructed through these pasts in ways too complex to go into here. The main point is to simply note this complexity and acknowledge that it exists. That alone explains why China brings an internal understanding to the whole space of the South China Sea and how it should be interpreted and understood that is different to others. It means that the place China starts from differs from everyone else. Until all those involved work towards a more common, shared framework and starting point, then it is hard to see how, diplomatically at least, the issues in this area are soluble.

Is China gaining its own way in the South China Sea? Before we get too excited by the Kissinger and Jullien visions of a place pursuing deep and sophisticated strategy, and slowly gaining what it wants, one has to dwell on more prosaic realities. One would have thought in territory so close to home, and with a vast military and new naval capacity, China today would have the capacity and the levers to enjoy hegemony over this region. Nor is it dealing with partners who are wholly uncomprehending or alien to it, but have all sorts of incentives to seek to work with it (mainly economic) and many problems confronting them if they chose to pick fights. All those involved have much more of a common cultural and philosophical basis between them than China has for instance with Europe or the US, which should at least aid communication. Despite these advantages, things are not going China's way. All of the involved powers resolutely do not accept the framework that China wishes to use. They resist, subvert and defy it. It seems the stronger China is seen to be, the worst the situation in the South China Sea becomes for it, with powers like the Philippines and Vietnam pushing back even more (with the former going to the International Court of Arbitration in the Hague in 2015 and winning a significant victory against Chinese claims), and the US, France and even the UK sending their navies to parade the region from 2020. The South China Sea can be seen as many things, but one of the most striking but least commented on is as a theatre not of Chinese success, but of failure, where it is not the scope of its power that is on display, but its frustrations and limitations. If it really is playing Go rather than chess here, it seems to have forgotten that this is a game than can literally go on forever, with no easy checkmate. So too might the Chinese South China Sea claims.

China as a Technological Predator

Previously the fear was that a China deep in technological deficit was forever stealing IP secrets to make up for its vulnerabilities. In recent years, the worry has changed slightly. Inspired by the West's superiority in know-how and innovation, and seeing this as a clear problem, Beijing has invested eye watering amounts in research and development. Now it has at least some indigenous technology which is either equal to or in some cases superior to that of the outside world. Some of the highest profile examples of Chinese technology successes are now used not as something to celebrate as a part of the world wide fund of capacity and understanding but to provide further evidence for why Chinese power per se, wherever it is seen, and whatever shape or form it takes, is a problem and carries some underlying narrative that is subversive and threatening to the outside world. In short, just as the Chinese state politicizes and weaponizes educational collaboration, cyberspace and investment, so it does the same to technology. There is technology, and then there is the Chinese variant – and the latter is very much not what the West likes because it comes with concealed intentions and hidden meaning, and it is all part and parcel of this grand, terrifying thing called Chinese Power.

Huawei is a cause célèbre in this area, and one that we can look at for more illumination on this question of China's technology strategy and whether it has links to a larger geopolitical ambition. Few companies have become such lightning rods for suspicion of nefarious actions and claims of state involvement. Huawei can argue, probably truthfully, that it is a Chinese non-state company in name. But it is certainly one that has to comply with security legislation in country where that means whatever the Beijing government asks. On paper it is private. In spirit, it very much belongs to an environment where the state and the party that sits behind is all powerful in certain areas. This is even clearer in view of the legislation that the Xi administration passed in 2017, the National Intelligence Law. This stipulates in its seventh article that 'all organizations and citizens shall support, assist, and cooperate with national intelligence efforts in accordance with law, and shall protect national intelligence work secrets they are aware of.'[30] Such a regulation is extremely broad, meaning that if the government deems issues of importance to security, then anything and everything can be demanded. And being the kind of company Huawei is, with the kind of role it plays, it is no wonder that its state role is so intensely scrutinized.

Huawei is not a straightforward story though. It poses a particular quandary for the outside world. On the one hand, its provision of services is broad and provided by very few others. This includes American companies, none of which quite match Huawei in their comprehensiveness. Huawei's technology is good. To add to the headache, it is also cheap. This is why it has become so favoured in Africa and across Latin America. It was also why for some years it was used widely in British Telecom in the UK. But fears that it is a company working to a different set of imperatives than other multinationals took root early on. In 2009, the *Sunday Times* in the UK reported concerns about Huawei equipment potentially being used for a hostile cyber-attack.[31] Australia blocked Huawei from tendering for its national broadband network three years later and from involvement in 5G in

2018. Since then, the doors in America and Europe have progressively closed, with the UK committing in 2020 to ensuring all Huawei equipment would be out of 5G networks by 2028.

But what precisely is the risk that Huawei poses? As one analyst speaking on the subject at a conference on this issue I attended in Europe in 2019 stated, for evidence that China was indeed a security threat then all one needed was to find one piece of coding or any evidence there was a backdoor in Huawei's equipment linking it to the Chinese state. From that moment, its global operations would be dead. At one point, this evidence seemed to be found. Bloomberg reported that Vodafone when using Huawei equipment in 2011 and 2012 had found such a backdoor. But more technologically literate commentators pointed out that these were technical glitches that any complex new systems suffered from, rather than something intentionally designed and targeted.[32] Another IT specialist I spoke to at the time wearily commentated that because there were millions of lines of code in Huawei's systems it was next to impossible to say whether there were security issues or not. We just had to accept the risk knowing we could never dispel the doubt. That is the Huawei quandary.

With this much uncertainty, it is better for everyone, Chinese and non-Chinese, that Huawei does not operate in certain markets. The suspicion about it is impossible to dispel. In any case it has proved in its success in other markets that it can prosper without conquering the US or Europe. This case doesn't clarify the nature of Chinese power in this area, but simply illustrates how its ambiguity and lack of clarity are the problem, rather than the opposite. The sole certainty is that technology, particularly in sensitive sectors such as telecoms, have presented China with a wonderful field of opportunity. Huawei is the best exemplar of what a two track world looks like. Look at Huawei's sales networks and customer base, and there you have it.

And for the larger point, on the nature of Chinese power, once more the state's activity here is evidence of how predictably China is a self-interested opportunist and not a confident new paradigm creator. It acts according to its nature, even when different modes of behaviour might serve its interests far better. A more effective commercial strategy would have been to have done everything to make clear that Huawei was truly free of state involvement. That would have meant setting up a parallel foreign structure totally unconnected to China, and demonstrably free from not just real Chinese state interference but even the suspicion this interference existed (one could argue that this is what has been attempted with TikTok). In the end, Huawei proved that the state in

Beijing just couldn't countenance this happening. Despite the significant initial impediments from lack of access to major North American and European markets, and vast amounts of effort by Huawei to reassure and lobby its potential partners in Washington and London (spending multiple millions on this each year up to 2020), dispelling suspicion about its true intentions and how far they are tied to the Chinese state has proved impossible. The evidence and signs of the Chinese state being deeply controlling are everywhere – but they are a huge disadvantage to it, rather than a benefit. Far from taking François Jullien's 'working with the nature of things', deeply ironically, the one entity in the whole of China that does the exact reverse and imposes end objectives and ordering strictures is the most important – its ruling party state.

Here, at least going from the evidence offered by Huawei as an important case study, one can say that the West is prudent to take a worse case view of Chinese ambiguity and lack of transparency in technology. For all the attractiveness of a company like Huawei, and others similar to it, the default has to remain that because there is so much uncertainty and doubt, it is best to err on the side of caution. It is a geopolitical failure on both sides that the Chinese are unable to convincingly show that they would not exploit technology cooperation for their own security aims, and that the West has come to such a firm, decided position that where the PRC is concerned, to assume the worst is the safest option. If there is a monument to the cognitive dissonance of our era, this is it. Had the Chinese state a real, viable, effective strategy towards the opportunity its new technology and the companies spearheading this (Alibaba is another example) presented, it would have been less ham fisted and tried a little bit more to not be so controlling. But with almost constant interference in its main non-state, hi-tech companies from 2018 onwards (witness the disappearance for a few months of Jack Ma over 2021 into 2022) it has given the outside world plenty of opportunity to find evidence to back up their already nervous hunches and make them cast-iron certainties. Huawei, far from being a symbol of the success and Chinese state use of technology opportunities, is an example of their limitations.

Neither Guilty nor Innocent: An Unclear Nation seen Unclearly

Those from the Enlightenment tradition must be comfortable with a sceptical view of life. The mantra was, and remains, to question everything. As the motto of the Royal Society in Britain goes, 'Nullius in verba' – 'take no one's word for it.' This is why in the Xi era the relative lack of circumspection and self-questioning about the nature of China's power, its intentions, its nature, with so much assertion of clarity and certainty about these questions is so puzzling. Were this a country that behaved like Nazi Germany (and some people insist that the Communist Party in China is little better than the rulers of Germany from 1933 to 1945) aggressively annexing countries on its borders, and breaking international treaties that forbad it to rearm, then we would have very clear actions to interpret and offer as evidence. But most discussions are about what China currently *threatens* to do because the evidence we have is ambiguous. So far, China displays its vast new military, but as yet there have been no tanks rolling across the Chinese border into India or Myanmar. It refrains from deploying. It sets up Confucius Institutes, which then undertake activities that intensify rather than alleviate criticism and suspicions about the country's motives. In cyberspace, China agitates, snoops and disrupts – along with everyone else. China is a problem, for sure. But is it *the* problem, justifying the words of figures like former American Vice President Mike Pence labelling it the greatest threat facing the US and therefore the rest of us?

In the face of this, the conclusion about the nature of Chinese power and the issues it poses has to be a very tentative and mixed one. We can certainly see opportunism about gaining economic advantage, and assertiveness about a specific menu of issues that matter to Beijing. The effectiveness of the means by which it tries to achieve its aims has been variable. China offers evidence of being self-centred, and willing to use power when it can. The issue is the strength of conclusions that can be drawn from this. With at least the ideological and the economic instruments, as they are illustrated through Confucius Institutes or the Belt and Road projects and debt associated with them, these must be seen as at best unclear, and at worst more tending to prove the limitations of Chinese power rather than its potency. Things in the cyber and virtual world, by their nature, are far harder to be categorical about. But even there, one has to say that China operates in a way that many others do, taking opportunities coming its way.

For those that make stronger and firmer claims from what they see, the evidence base is flimsier. Can we really see categorical proof that justifies the levels of outright paranoia promoted by the 'hidden hand' and the 'silent invasion' thesis? Like in the McCarthy era, the conviction underpinning this approach is that Chinese power is like a highly infectious mental virus, seeping into the minds of those exposed to it, changing them in ways that mean they no longer act with any freewill. Its potency is in its invisibility and opacity. If one wants to hold to this view, then it is a matter of faith, not reason, that such a thing exists, because it can never be seen or pinned down.

Clearly, I don't subscribe to such a view. I don't believe in a mysterious, ineffable, insidious kind of Chinese power that operates on us all like invisible anaesthetic, largely because I don't believe in this kind of power period. In my experience, that's not how influence and power operate. When Chinese, or non-Chinese, start talking like sorcerers and mediums, then I revert to the rationalist default. As a rationalist who likes conceptual clarity, and a strong sense of what counts as empirical evidence to support arguments and conclusions, I come back to the question that started this chapter: What is Chinese power? Clearly it exists, because claims about it figures in the minds of so many today. But what is it? This chapter has argued that whatever it might be, it is not straightforward. That could either be because of remarkable skills of manipulation and subterfuge by the Chinese party state, or the far more prosaic reason that Chinese power is simply by its nature just as it seems – conflicted, divided, confusing and uneven, moulded as much by the environment it is deployed in as moulding. We know American power much more clearly. We can see it in the 600-plus military installations across the planet, and in the huge budgets each year spent on defence. We know it through the vast reach of the American dollar in the international economy, and the central role of American finance and investment in the rest of the world. We can see it spelled out in the various alliances, treaties and pacts that the US is a party too. American power is visible because it does not need to hide, as the number one economic and military player. Chinese power offers us none of these clear pieces of evidence. Is that because it in fact has similarly potent instruments it can deploy in the dark that counter all of these listed above, or because, as number two, it has to work within a context where it must be perpetually sensitive to provoking the competitive attention of its superior? The question here is which is the more realistic interpretation. Like Groucho Marx said, 'Who are you going to believe – me, or your own eyes.' We cannot see the infrastructure of rising, overwhelming secret Chinese power, which either means that it is deviously concealed – or, the far more radical conclusion, that it simply is not there.

Chapter Three

CHINA AND THE QUESTION OF VALUES

If there is one area where China and the Enlightenment West (here meaning North America and Europe) are on collision course, it is in what is broadly called the realm of values. This is a story with a long tail. From the earliest era of Sino-European engagement, there was deep interest in the question of what Chinese believed by Europeans. To this day, that haunts much of the discussion about China's relations with the outside world. There are plenty who have concluded that Chinese believe nothing. They feel that the conflict between their practice of capitalism in their own economy, and yet their adherence to socialism is an indication of complete incoherence and an underlying nihilism where they simply have no holistic belief system.

This western notion of the souls of Chinese being almost empty of compelling convictions and a coherent faith have made them greatly desired by missionaries of one sort or another for hundreds of years. The struggle continues to this day. In recent decades it has shifted from religion to promoting the great political causes of democracy and western liberalism – what we can very broadly call Enlightenment values. On both sides of this battle, of course, there are vast areas of haziness and confusion. No clear answer to what Chinese values are has ever really been accepted in the West. And Enlightenment values remain hard to pin down. Perhaps one of the boldest attempts was by François Jullien who simply admitted that the West since the time of the ancient Greek philosophers in the fifth century BC, was the home of universalism – of the belief that certain forms of knowledge had a claim to complete acceptance because they were *a priori* and in themselves true.[1] Since then, types of knowledge, and how they might be arranged not in a hierarchy of truthfulness, but more along a spectrum where one moves from one framework to another to find meaning and sense, with no framework pre-eminent, have been deeply discussed. The Kantian philosophical revolution, where the most fundamental categories of space and time were related to subjective observation and understanding, was only one of many stepping-stones along the pathway of redefining and re-understanding, and in some places jettisoning, this notion of the Universal.

There are many reasons for why the Chinese view of the world came to be regarded so negatively in the West. The parlous condition of the country for much of the late nineteenth and twentieth century was one. The remarkable success of western industrial and economic development over the nineteenth century was another. But in the end, the simple fact that Europeans and Americans were able to enforce their will on the Qing, and then Republican China, manifested the great asymmetry of power. This more than anything else nurtured this sense of disdain towards a China seen as weak because it was archaic, backward, confused, and had an almost fairy tale like view of the world. John Barrow, already mentioned, a young participant in the Macartney Mission, in his subsequent work was a hugely influential proponent of the idea of a decaying, ancient, premodern China that would never succeed in the modern world.[2] And while Chinese philosophy and history did come to be better understood in Europe, the fact that sinology ended up being such a forbidding, highly exclusive and specialist area was symptomatic of the great marginalization of China.[3] It was a place that deserved pity, rather than admiration. Chinese needed to modernize their world view, for most Europeans, which in some quarters equated with simply abandoning their own chaotic, incoherent belief systems and adopting those of the outside world. Western modernity was not just a way of behaving, but one built on values that somehow read the world right. It had colonized not only the physical world, but the notion of Truth. Without ceding to these values, China would always lag far behind.

Chinese traditional values are talked of by contemporary political leaders in the People's Republic in ways which raise the hackles of many external observers. For them, it seems abject hypocrisy to say in one breath one is a Communist, and yet also a Confucian. Those of more historic bent remember the Maoist past when feudal traditional cultural was the great enemy. These days, however, tradition has certainly made a great comeback. This is all fresh testimony to the amazing proclivity of Chinese thinking towards to move towards hybridity. Such hybridity is the most unsettling issue, because it is becoming clearer that whatever Chinese believe, these are plural values, not singular ones. Hybridity is therefore the great intellectual crime of the Chinese view of the world for universalist westerners. But it is also, in the era of post-modernity, something that looks more and more like an immense advantage in engaging with a world that does not easily fit into uniform, universalist discourse.

Europe as a Values Superpower

The place where the clash of values between China and the West might be best illustrated is not so much the US, where the history of engagement is more time limited because of the relative brevity of American national existence in its current guise, but with Europe, with a history of interaction going back 700 years or more. The intensity of this dialogue over values has been increased by the insistence, at least in the last two decades, by the EU that its interactions with others must be underpinned by a set of principles and a mode of interaction which, at least on the European side, are understood as central to the relationship. This has given its links with China a fractious, and ill-tempered tone. As one Chinese academic said to me when we discussed this in Beijing as early as 2009, the moralizing and grandstanding of the Europeans was something that triggered Chinese far more than America berating them about their manifold human rights failures. With America, one had to politely listen to them venting off because of their vast military in the background to enforce their point of view when discussion reached stalemate. With Europe, at least in this individual's view, all there was were words, words, words.

For any Chinese with a sense of modern history, one can forgive the slightly puzzled look when they see Europe come to them in the guise of a saviour with shining values which they wish to see the rest of the world not just admire but validate and adopt. This is, they learned at school, the continent that from the seventeenth century engaged in a global trade in slavery, the terrible consequences of which are still evident today. It is a continent that may well have been the home of Shakespeare, Beethoven and Einstein, but also gave the world the polar opposites of these creators of high cultural masterpieces – Hitler, colonization, and the concept and practice of Total War. If any continent can claim to be a dark one for Chinese, Europe can. And yet, in the twenty-first century, the EU's proposed constitution and its key political documents gleam with liberal, democratic values, and a noble proclamation for embracing diversity and pluralism. It is truly, as its more enthusiastic promoters like former British and European diplomat Robert Cooper insist, a post-modern power, operating in new ways, and with an expansiveness that eschews the messy business of being about nation states and their limited, parochial aims and ambitions.[4]

The sceptical view of Europe and the EU is reinforced by the historiography of modern China. In the narrative of national humiliation promoted in patriotic education campaigns from the 1990s some of the key actors in this grim tale are from this continent – France, Germany, and in particular Britain. With its bullying, its desire to smash open a new and potentially vast market, and its deep sense of cultural superiority along with a mercenariness and focus on the bottom line in terms of trade returns that verged on the psychopathic, the latter attracts particular depths of antagonism and feeling that linger till this day, in the language of China's emotional diplomacy and their wider collective consciousness.

This is all compounded by another issue – the confusion Europe's identity poses. What, after all, is Europe – and what in particular is the European Union? As far as Chinese can see at least from external behaviour, it is a collective of countries that all say they work as one, and are from one common family and root, and yet seem to belong to a dysfunctional, fractious home that delights in airing its differences in public. A European diplomat in the early 2000s on a visit they were making to Beijing made the point succinctly at a talk I attended while working as a British diplomat serving there. How can the Chinese government make sense, he said, of a place that on the one hand talks the soothing language of unity, and stresses the need for all to work together, and yet on the other endlessly scraps in front of their interlocutor when things move from abstractions down to tangibles like receiving investment or gaining trade for separate countries. This was partially ameliorated as the EU evolved from 2000 to 2009, when the Lisbon Treaty was signed creating a strong sense of European collective action in foreign policy. But China remains deeply sceptical of such displays of unity and is not averse to using what is sees as underlying divisions to further its own ends. It has been all too successful in achieving this, as multiple examples of causing member states in the EU to fail to agree on human rights strictures against China over the years testify to.[5] To exacerbate this, Europe lacks hard power, the one thing that China might be able to respect more. There is no European army, or coherent European security strategy. It differs from country to country. For Poland, Russia is more of a priority than for France, where worries are often about containing Germany ambition in the EU. The UK sticks close to the US no matter what the issue, particularly now it has exited the Union. France however seems to delight in antagonizing Washington – witness the huge differences in attitude on the 2003 Second Gulf War. Despite intense study and inspection, Europe and the EU have evaded China's best efforts to merit being treated as a unitary entity. Xi Jinping's label deployed during the first ever visit by a Chinese head of state to the capital of the Union, Brussels, in 2014 captured this amorphousness by calling it a civilization partner.[6] There he was reduced to the same vague language as those Europeans in the past who talked similarly about China with its complex histories and shifting identity as a civilizational state.[7]

Europe, with this highly problematic history, its complexity, its lack of any clear geopolitical or cultural identity, but with its immense confidence verging almost on the hubristic, was able in one of the key documents issued in 2006, an EU Commission paper dealing with Chinese policy, to set out a clear set of ways in which China (and one has to say these words slowly to appreciate properly their full rich irony and import) might improve itself. Like a stern teacher dealing with a talented but recalcitrant pupil, the EU opined that its function was to assist China in building a better rule of law, becoming a better defender of its own people's rights, becoming a cleaner, more responsible, more diverse, tolerant partner. 'A stable, growing China is in Europe's interest,' the document stated. 'Europe has a critical interest in China's transition to a stable, prosperous and open economy. It recognizes that the openness of the EU market to Chinese exports will be a key factor in China's further development . . . To build and maintain political support in Europe for this policy and the adjustment it requires, the benefits of openness and change must be fully realized. This means China must show that it is committed to embracing globalisation as a two way street. China should use its growing influence to champion open markets and fair competition.'[8]

This condescension was not just a European habit of mind. Britain in 2009 publicly issued one of its first (and only) bilateral strategies towards a country in a document of similar zeal: 'The UK and China: A Framework for Engagement.'[9] Again, areas were set out from assisting China in its legal reform, to helping it develop its civil society, to improving its finance sector and supporting political reform and improvements in governance. One wonders at this point what the view in Brussels or Westminster might have been had the Chinese displayed reciprocal altruism and issued their own policy paper proposing assisting these respective partners in improving their own governance issues, from the democracy deficit the EU often stood accused of to the continuation of a hereditary monarchy with vague and unstated powers in Britain, an unwritten constitution and a wholly unelected second chamber. No doubt the views of politicians in these places would have been somewhat less than indulgent when they detected that a major counterpart, far from seeing them as an equal and a peer, regarded them as still inferior. To add to the problems, this was happening at a time when China's economy was already exceeding in growth and gross size all of the major states in Europe.

Altruism usually starts from a position of superiority and power. This is not to denigrate it. Charity by definition is seldom something experienced between equals. But most times, there has to be a desire on the part of the entity given to that they are in the business of taking. The Chinese government could have said words along the lines of Emperor Qianlong to Lord Macartney: 'I set no value on objects strange or ingenious, and have no use for your country's manufactures.' Just as two centuries before western largesse from London presaged objectives and aims which were tougher and more self-centred, something proved a few decades later when the Opium Wars started and the British gloves really came off. At the second time of Europeans coming bearing huge gifts in the twenty-first century, China's hesitancy is understandable. Who precisely stood to gain from adopting the raft of bright ideas about how to run their own affairs, and how to view the world, that was emanating from a party outside their borders, they may have asked themselves?

The Marxist-Leninists in Beijing adhere to a view of history which is rigidly deterministic and teleological. China, in the world view of its current leaders, has to rise because that is the inevitable and ineluctable law of historic development. Things ever move forward and happen by necessity. Just work out the laws guiding this and you can see how the future goes. But the European mindset towards China around 2006 was infected by its own variety of determinism. China would *have* to politically reform, it would *have* to change, it would *have* to adopt the sorts of social structures and governance and rule of law that the developed world had. These were the Europeans own version of inevitable historical progress. The most crucial part of this was that one day, China would need to make the transition to a more democratic, pluralistic political system. Assisting that particular outcome was spelled out in the 2009 UK document. On page six, under the headline 'Promoting sustainable development, modernization and internal reform in China', it talked about 'influencing China's evolving domestic policies and helping China manage the risks of its rapid development'. But just as the British government would have regarded statements emanating from the Chinese Ministry of Foreign Affairs saying they wanted to influence Britain's evolving domestic policies and help them manage the risks of Brexit as an insult to their own autonomy and sovereignty, Beijing's response to the diplomatic charity being expressed by London was to maintain a telling silence.

Changing Tack

In an admission that this approach was ineffective, by the time of the second major document by the EU about policy towards China issued in June 2016, the tone and content had changed completely. This was partly due to the humiliation that the 2008 Great Financial Crisis had delivered to America and Europe. It was also derived from the complex impact of the Arab Spring uprisings, where mission creep saw NATO intervention in Libya in 2010 transform into something far more ambitious and ominous for China – the attempt to establish democratic systems by the West and bring about regime change. In a pincer movement, the financial crisis removed much of the admiration and respect that China had towards Europe in an area it was still regarded as competent in, while the political machinations of the US and others around the Arab Spring deepened distrust. Both of these phenomena created a more unstable world. The financial failure and economic turbulence it saw over 2008 and 2009 made Beijing acknowledge that westerners were not even particularly good at their one great specialism – capitalism. The Arab Spring only made them even more convinced that whatever the failures and crises particular states might experience when they went their own way, adopting remedies or assistance from US and Europe stood a good chance of making things worse. The turbulence in Egypt and Syria after the initial rebellions confirmed this view for them.

These were the main factors that made the EU's maintenance of a high minded, high sounding altruistic tone, where its greatest ambition was to help and aid China to be a better place simply unsustainable. How could a continent that had sent officials to China in 2009 and 2010 to beg for funds and financial aid to bail out its own currencies and protect countries like Greece in its region that were economically standing on the precipice continue to pretend they were speaking from a position of strength? From 2008 to 2010 Europe learned a lesson China had long since worked out: the key criterion for success was simply to survive. That meant spending less time thinking about what to do for others, and more of its deciding what to do for yourself.

All of this is made clear in the updated strategy issued from the European Commission in 2016. Published on the same rainy, oppressive day in which the UK held its referendum to exit the EU, the paper received little attention when it came out because of the shock of the British events. And yet its structure, content and tone, because they were so different to the predecessor document, were noteworthy. The clue started right from the title, with the somewhat prosaic 'Elements for a new EU Strategy' rather than the grander designation from 2006. With its bullet points at each stage, its seven areas of different engagement clearly set out, and an action plan for forward steps at the end, the tone is businesslike. It is also assertive about the need for the EU to keep its own interests at the forefront. As the preamble says: 'The EU needs its own strategy, one which puts its own interests at the forefront in the new relationship; which promotes universal values; which recognizes the need for and helps to define an increased role for China in the international system; and is based on a positive agenda of partnership coupled with the constructive management of differences.'[10]

This is a posture that points in all directions – to be self-interested, and yet to subscribe to the promotion of universal values which happily work not just for you but everyone else, while at the same time granting space to China and its interest, and on top of that managing differences. The last element in particular sounds like a pre-emptive admission of defeat. If the values espoused are meaningfully universal, the assumption would be that at some point everyone has to adopt them or pay the consequences. But in this EU statement there is a tacit admission that this neat unfolding of the Enlightenment vision was experiencing fierce headwinds in the case of China, and that a different tactic had to be taken. All that is left of previous hopes however is a faint residue.

Between 2006 and 2016, the Great Financial Crisis had resulted in almost three years or turbulence in Europe, where the Commission had ended up as a perpetual crisis management entity. Italy, Greece and others had come close to economic implosion; bailouts were agreed on the back of high levels of intervention, much of these emanating from the central bank in Germany. Old spectres of European divisions leading to nasty diplomatic fights and arguments started to appear. By 2015, the ongoing military action in Syria had resulted in a wave of immigrants which, in the case of Germany, reached almost a million. Chancellor Merkel's humane response in accommodating such numbers of new arrivals was brave, but divisive, and gave political grist to the far right, who experienced a wave of support in elections across the continent in the following two years. Over the same time, a series of vicious terrorist attacks in Europe intensified the anxiety, feeding a narrative that politicians had lost control. The June 2016 Brexit referendum was a shock – a moment when a whole constellation of issues came to the head, from immigration to austerity policies, and anger at elites and inequality, where in the eyes of its critics the EU figured as the ultimate globalist cabal. How could the great home of Enlightenment values, Old Europe (as it was once disparagingly called by the late Donald Rumsfeld, Secretary of Defence in the US under Bush the younger) maintain its high sounding, moralizing tone when it itself was in such poor shape? The dismissive attitude newly elected US President Donald Trump also displayed towards Europe deepened this. Chinese could observe for the first time since the Second World War the main official in the US castigating Europeans for their poor record in preserving their own defence because of low spending and threatening to walk away from NATO unless more contribution was made.

In the early part of the Cold War, commentators talked of how the US 'lost' China. That may well have been hyperbole. It was hard to see how Mao and his fellow Communists might have easily worked with America after 1949 in view of their ideological and strategic differences. But by 2016, in a far more profound way, one could say that through the way it behaved, and how it seemed forever beset by crises and issues, Europeans, and to some extent Americans, had 'lost' China. Since 2008 they had shown they were poor at the one thing that truly mattered – practicing what they preached and showing that their values were universal because they were universally useful. Uncertain, unstable and frequently dependent on China to carry on being stable while they fell into their own instability, there were times when Europe was closer to implosion than the long predicted crack up of the People's Republic, particular after the events of June 2016.

Humility is not easy for Europeans. But from 2016, whatever strategic documents issued from Brussels, they were circumscribed by a new awareness that things weren't what they used to be. In 2019, before the pandemic, the division of 'competitor, collaborator and adversary' was deployed. In 'EU-China: A Strategic Outlook', the Commission stated that 'China is, simultaneously, in different policy areas, a cooperation partner with whom the EU has closely aligned objectives, a negotiating partner with whom the EU needs to find a balance of interests, an economic competitor in the pursuit of technological leadership, and a systemic rival promoting alternative models of governance.'[11] A similar trilateral structure was deployed by the US and the UK in key documents they issued over the following two years.

How had China changed its strategic outlook in the period since 2006 towards the EU? Had it also gone along a path where initial ambitions were superseded by a more complex understanding which had brought about a fundamental reappraisal and a scaling down of their posture? To some extent, Chinese attitudes did go through a mild transformation towards Europeans, for the reasons outlined above. It thought less highly of them as capitalists, and loss what little respect it had once had for their political models. But as far as formal statements of position go, the various government White Papers over this period from the Chinese State Council (the equivalent of the Cabinet), never deploy the language of wanting to help Europe change and reform, and from the start are relentlessly self-interested in their focus. Mutual benefit is the one constant. China was always engaging with Europeans over this period for specific things – markets, technology and investment. The main difference was any sense that China had a need to promote 'universal values' with Chinese characteristics into the Eurosphere. Unburdened with this missionary purpose and with narrower focus and greater clarity, China's approach to the EU was more consistent than the Europeans were towards it. The one more overt change was the sharper tone of Chinese statements about their core interests as time went on back at the Europeans. In 2018, the most recent such paper, China's core interests occur early in its statement:

> Honoring (sic) the commitment to respecting China's sovereignty and territorial integrity, upholding the one China principle with concrete actions, and respecting China's core interests and major concerns bear on the long-term stability and growth of China-EU relations. The EU should explicitly oppose "Taiwan independence" in any form, support China's peaceful reunification, and handle Taiwan-related issues with prudence. Exchanges between the EU and Taiwan should be strictly limited to nonofficial and people-to-people activities, and there should be no official contact or exchanges in any form. The EU should refrain from signing with Taiwan any agreement with sovereign implications or official in nature. No institutions of an official nature should be established. The EU should not endorse Taiwan's membership in any international organization where statehood is required, not sell Taiwan any weapons or any equipment, materials or technologies that can be used for military purposes, and not carry out military exchanges or cooperation in any form.[12]

Similarly assertive language was deployed on Hong Kong, human rights and other issues germane to China's interests. This were signs of a greater sense of strength towards a partner once seemingly so far ahead of it.

This consistency on the part of China as far as it regards its own values and its own standpoint, is important. It meant that by 2020, despite immense efforts and commitment by the EU, China had not grown closer to it as Brussels had originally hoped back in the mid-2000s.

Pragmatic recognition of this meant it was Europeans who needed to change their position, and compromise, not the Chinese. Europe was undertaking a diplomatic tactical retreat. In the early phase of their relationship, there had been misunderstanding by Europeans both of China's own beliefs, and the commitment it was willing to give to these. At the start of this process, the Europeans did not believe that Chinese world views and mindsets were sustainable. At some point they would need to change to come closer to European views. As of 2022 this has not happened. We are therefore back to the initial question, but with a difference. EU–China relations prove that there are things that Chinese believe, and which matter for them. The question is what those things actually are and how outsiders can understand and work with these.

What Do Chinese Believe?

The standard place to start in answering this question would be the party state doctrine espoused by leaders like Xi Jinping and his predecessors. The striking thing today is that these statements of belief are homogenized and consistently expressed. China is in the primary stage of socialism. It subscribes to a view of material dialectical historical development. This is adopted to the unique conditions of Chinese society. While the indigenization of Marxism-Leninism is understood and accepted by analysts and commentators, what is less accepted is that in a certain, very specific and unique way, Chinese contemporary leaders do probably believe in the socialist view of the world. The depth and quality of this belief certainly changes a lot from individual to individual. But in the public, social and political realm, socialism in China is an important faith, at least amongst the elite. This is not dissimilar to the ways in which, for instance, in other examples of a faith community there are huge disparities in kinds of belief and their intensity and articulation. In the Catholic church, the average active churchgoer might have a clearer idea of what Catholic belief means than someone who simply puts that they are a member of the church on a census form but is entirely inactive and passive in terms of practicing their faith. As one works upwards from this, the extent for instance of a priest's knowledge of what they believe is going to be probably less worked through than that of a high-ranking church theologian. They all say they share the same belief. But there are big differences in how explicitly and knowledgably that faith is expressed and understood.

Marxism-Leninism is not so dissimilar in China to the belief system of the Catholic church in some of the outside world. To say one believes in this creed means vastly different things according to who says it. For many people it means nothing more than to say they belong to certain institutions and undertake specific practices in their daily life. It is important to note two things here. First, while this belief system plays an important role in some areas of Chinese life, it fades away to the point of being background noise for many other areas of society and for different groups. For businesspeople, people working in the countryside, people working in cultural and technological fields, those working in finance and banks, socialism with Chinese characteristics mostly serves as a part of their environment, one they accept to various degrees because they have to to get by, but are largely able to operate around, rather than engage deeply with. The second is that socialism on these lines, beyond the era of high Maoism from 1966 when it really was a national faith, claims exclusivity only in certain key political spaces. In many other areas of life and activity, it recedes to irrelevance, and other sets of beliefs and ideas which are equally non-exclusive kick in. The Chinese inner world is a remarkable place, and one that is ill understood. But as sociologist Fei Xiaotong and others have expertly described over the last century, it is a deeply layered, networked, and complex one. That complexity is seldom appreciated when focussing exclusively on the repressive state and its total annexation of all ways of thinking and world views in China. The fact is that most Chinese have a light and flexible relationship with ideologies, and that includes socialism with Chinese characteristics.

The question should therefore be not so much what Chinese believe, but how. Ideology even for the inner group of the Communist Party is instrumental. It has utility, a pragmatic function, in giving the veneer of unity and coherence in an environment pervaded by what Fei Xiaotong called 'elasticity' – complex social interconnections that come down to the individual, creating a unique and dynamic world around them.[13] This is one of the great paradoxes that his work outlined – that for a society which is often accused of being so collective in its spirit, in many ways the average Chinese lives in a self-centred way building a dense network of relationships from family to friends focussed on those around them to enable them to function well. This atomized structure of society partly explains the spectre of deep disunity and chaos that haunts the Chinese collective unconsciousness. Social fracturing and divisions are a real risk because of this atomization where the larger sense of society can quickly break down into clans, families, smaller and smaller networks, each focussed on its own interests with no wider aims. It is for this reason that Sun Yat-sen talked of China being like a handful of sand. The disunity that comes from this is an immense bogeyman, one that occasionally raises its head. The chaos of the early twentieth century, and then the breakout of semi-civil war in the Cultural Revolution, give at least some explanation of why great effort is put into having a common belief system on the surface. That it is on the surface and goes no deeper is important to note. The rhetoric is the thing that matters. As long as this is given the status and prestige necessary, then beyond it many other things can be thought. This is not the same thing as saying that Chinese people believe nothing. On the contrary, they believe many things. That hybridity and multiplicity is the core characteristic.

Europeans through the lengthy period of their acquaintance with China have had issues with this hybridity and syncretism almost from the start. One of the greatest intermediaries between the two civilizations is Matteo Ricci. An Italian Jesuit who was sent first to Macau, then under the long era of Portuguese management, before going to work in Ming China proper in 1576, Ricci's life and experiences as a missionary stand as an immense symbol of the kinds of deep contradictions and internal compromises that any profound engagement from one cultural and religious background to another cause. Ricci's early years in China were ones in which he immersed himself in the language of his new home. The late Jonathon Spence describes in painful detail the kind of journey he had had to take to reach his new home the other side of the world. The likelihood of surviving even this initial period, on vessels with primitive living conditions, subject to the vagaries of the weather, and with health conditions where infectious diseases were rife, meant as many as a third of any ship's passengers never made it to their destination.[14] Nor did Ricci ever have an endpoint of his great venture to look forward to. Letters home took up to three years. Responses meant that people may have long since died by the time he got their letters. Many letters went missing. Ricci was only to hear, indirectly, and incompletely, about his father, and those few of his communications that survive read like 'dead letters sent' (to use the poignant phrase of poet Gerard Manley Hopkins), where it is clear that both sides of the conversation were never quite sure if the other would ever hear what they had to say.

Ricci's evolving response to his environment is testified to in those of his personal writings that have survived, and in the works that he produced during his long years in China. One of the earliest was a selection of paragraphs and statements on friendship, where he was able to find a happy medium between the world view of his new home, and that from where he had come. Confucianism proved a seductive creed, one that Ricci grew to increasingly admire to the point where he even adopted the robes of Confucian scholars common at the time. With Buddhists however, he took an increasingly critical stance, appalled by their lack, in his eyes, of morals and their laxity. It is true that the Buddhist monks of the time were infamous for being recruited from poorer, less educated families, and that Buddhist practice in Ming China had become corrupted by popular superstition. Even so, this division in Ricci's mind between an admiration for one side of the Chinese belief system and repulsion towards the other would be a familiar pattern from others in the centuries to come. It sees its expression today in those who loudly declare that they hate China's Communism, but love its culture.

Ricci's most important later work, 'The True Meaning of the Lord of Heaven', was originally written in Chinese. It is an extraordinary document because of the level of Chinese proficiency it shows Ricci had attained. Ricci was truly one of a few groundbreakers. He had come to a culture very little understood and known. The main missionary activity starting from the foundation of the Society of Jesus in the mid-sixteenth century was only a few decades prior to his own arrival. Saint Francis Xavier had embarked on his mission from India and then Japan to convert the Chinese in 1552. It was on this final great mission that he died, on Taishan. He is buried on Shangchuan island, now in today's Guangdong province. After his mission, a few others had come to China to spread their beliefs. But they were literally embarking on a 'terra incognita', a world which was unknown. To learn Chinese, Ricci had needed to write his own textbooks and be his own teacher. In view of how difficult Mandarin Chinese is regarded in the twenty-first century for foreign learners, with infinitely more aid and exposure, it is daunting to think how Ricci must have felt as he made his slow progress. His final mastery was complete. In the process, in some respects his mind had almost become Chinese.

'The True Meaning of the Lord of Heaven' is the archetypal dialogue between a western scholar and a Chinese one. It is a work which is important not for any of its intellectual content, but for the context in which it was written. Throughout, the western scholar is able to express the superiority of the Christian creed, bringing down on the head of the other partner in the discussion a torrent of disproof and disapproval for their own statements on their belief system. Large sections of the work are simply statements made by the Chinese scholar which are set up to then allow their elegant and complete demolition. Throughout the work, other parts of the text allocated to the Chinese scholar consists often of nothing more than peons of praise for the new doctrine just articulated by Ricci. After one such exposition, on the unity and omnipotence of the Christian deity, the Chinese says 'what a rich doctrine! It explains what man is unable to explain and tells exhaustively what man is unable to tell exhaustively.'[15] The next day of the dialogue, the Chinese scholar continues that 'your profound doctrine satisfies the ear and intoxicates the mind'.[16] Later in the work, when discussing the question of spirit, the scholar states: 'After taking my leave of you yesterday I went over what you had taught me and, sure enough, discovered truth in it.'[17] Sure enough, for the rest of the book, the scholar continues to cede to his interlocutor's world view. In life, too, Ricci had engaged in discussions with Buddhist practitioners. It is not recorded if they were as similarly one sided and offered him the kind of complete victory that the 'True Meaning of the Lord of Heaven' does his imaginary debaters.

Intellectual annexation is what Ricci's work represents. The design of the arguments, their content, their structure, like a Platonic dialogue, provide a home territory for Ricci to display mastery and achieve dominance. The Chinese scholar's statements are hollow, shallow and full of illogicality. Is this really what Ricci thought of the Chinese around him and their world views? It is hard to know now what might have gone through his mind, in the years in which he was based in Beijing up to his death in 1610. But whatever ideas he had they must have been complex. Subsequent missionaries in the years that followed were often accused of going native by their headquarters at the Vatican in Rome. In the nineteenth century, the Abbe Huc undertook a long journey across what is today's Inner Mongolia and into Tibet. When that account was published in the West, in French and then English, it attracted claims that he had also compromised his real belief system by being too sympathetic to the Chinese world view. A book he had written about Chinese religion in the 1860s was regarded as displaying almost heretical levels of empathy for Confucianism, and even Buddhism. Simon Leys, the great sinologist of the late twentieth and early twenty-first century wrote towards the end of his life that engagement with any culture different to one's own in any depth involves changes and revisions to one's own world view, a process of transformation and evaluation.[18] Ricci, unlike Xavier, was never canonized, but were he to be, he would best be made the patron saint of the conflicted, those caught between cultures and values. His life personified the attempt to intellectually assert universalist views while embracing and having lived experience of radical relativism and diversity, where the Jesuit priest ended up dressed on Confucian scholar garb. In 'The True Meaning of the Lord of Heaven', he is shown trying to convince himself what his actual life disproved – that far from being universal, western values existed in a world where there was much other competition, and that their greatest problem was not that they could be attractive and worth living by, but their dogmatic assertion that no others could do the same.

Over four centuries later, the superiority of western values is still taken as a given implicitly, and, as the earlier EU documents about engagement with China looked at above, often explicitly. Groups like Chinese officials who set their faces against this are seen as not just dissenting and disagreeing but posing a threat. With a group like this too, things get particularly complex. The assumption is that they have to believe in something which is an alternative universalism, having the same ambitiousness and all-embracing quality as the western idea of its values. This immediately sets up a conflict. There can't be two different sets of universalist values. Logically, this is an either/or scenario, with one necessarily needing to be right and the other false. That implies a dichotomy, and a values clash. But with their constant stress on everything in their belief system having 'Chinese characteristics' haven't the Chinese side made clear they're not presenting ideas everyone else has to adopt as their own, and that therefore this dichotomy is not relevant? Even more damaging, this conviction that Chinese believe in something, that it is singular, neat and tidy means that the most striking aspect of their world view is ignored – and that is its intrinsic complexity.

Belief systems, faiths and values in contemporary China are multifaceted and multilayered. Understanding how best to understand this has resisted many attempts at categorization and straightforward analysis. In the Maoist era, with limited links with the outside world, it is unsurprising that Chinese struck non-Chinese as fanatically all believing one thing. But now, with so many Chinese students, tourists and businesspeople travelling all over the world, and with huge connections on social media, the resistance to rethinking this conviction Chinese subscribe to one set of values and one world view is more the problem of the observer than those being observed. Plenty of excellent English language material has even spelled this complexity out in recent years in very compelling and accessible ways. 'The Path' by journalist Christine Gross-Loh and philosopher Michael Puett about contemporary Confucianism and its use in modern China, or Roel Sterckx's broader work on Chinese thought and its varied historic roots are good examples. Both have laid out the immense richness of the country's intellectual heritage.[19] This past is part of China today. This all makes clear something that should have been apparent long ago: there is no such thing as 'Chinese Thought' in the singular. There are instead multiplicities of thinking. Lack of familiarity, and a conviction that the Chinese intellectual tradition has to be like the West's, all pointing to the aspiration one day to uncover the singular, universal 'Truth' have delayed the appreciation of this till very late in the day. So too has the fundamental disruptiveness of China's position. Just by being what it is, how it is, it poses immense questions, before even acting.

Chapter Four

WHAT DOES THE WORLD WANT FROM CHINA?

In thirty years of dealing with China in different ways, while I remember often being asked what China wants from the world (for which see the next chapter), I've seldom heard its twin – what does the world want from China. For the Enlightenment West in particular, the argument in this chapter is not just that there was a fundamental mistake in misunderstanding the complexity of China's belief systems and the challenges these posed for western universalism, but also of the aspirations, desires and plans directed towards China. China was not the only complex one. For a proper diagnostic of the torturous and incoherent policy posture adopted towards China today by Europeans and Americans, one has to look at what the West wants of it, and how contradictory that is. If we can introduce at least a little more coherency and self-awareness here, than some of the pain the world has experienced in the last few years might be alleviated.

First, some clarification is in order. The Enlightenment West clearly wants some things from China, but it also has other things it doesn't want. The positives and the negatives tussle with each other. They are intertwined. The challenges start where we reach a point where the wants and the don't wants come into conflict with each other. China stretches this to the limits, because, in essence, it offers the ultimate quandary – potential material inducements because of its economic size and the growing role of its new, higher consuming and newly wealthy middle class, but with a country that does not share Enlightenment values, and in many places behaves in ways that are regarded as inimical to those values. There can be few other cases where such a stark dilemma poses itself. There are, of course, many smaller cases that offer this sort of problem – countries like Saudi Arabia where the desire for energy and arms sales has to be set against the issues of human rights abuses there. Or Russia, where it's supply of natural gas and oil to Europe comes alongside its disruptive and aggressive actions like the Salisbury poisonings of 2018 or the appalling war in Ukraine in 2022. The West has to do business all the time with partners it doesn't see eye to eye with. But in terms of sheer scale of the challenge, China is in a class of its own. The Enlightenment West's self-interest in terms of economic growth, environmental protection and public health involves them working more and more closely with a partner who they also feel is competing with and threatening them. This is a remarkable bind to be caught in, like a knot that only gets tighter the more one tries to unpick it.

Listing the positive and negative wants from China is easy. The Enlightenment West votes with its feet on the kind of things it wants from China. It wants, clearly, to source vast amounts of manufactured goods. Even over the COVID-19 era the trade flows between the US and China have maintained high levels (USD600 billion-plus predicted for 2021, similar to previous years despite the trade wars and the imposition of tariffs).[1] With the EU the figures rose to around EURO600 billion, a third of it in Europe's favour. These too showed no major change apart from a slight growth of current trends over the last decade.[2] For the UK, China rose from the 26th largest export market and 15th largest importer in 2000 to the 6th and 4th respectively by 2020, with £30 billion in exports and £49 billion in imports, 4.4 and 6.8 per cent of the UK's totals respectively.[3] By 2018, China was the largest trading partner of 128 out of 190 countries, an almost total reversal of the situation in 2000.[4] Simply because of iron ore exports and meat, Australian trade with China flourished in 2021, despite the worst political relations in living memory, achieving a record surplus in Australia's favour by August.[5]

As a trade partner, China's integral role in supply chains became even more glaring as the COVID-19 crisis developed over 2020. Personal Protection Equipment (PPE) was largely sourced from China. Of these, face masks for use by the public were particularly symbolic, with China sending what it called aid to countries like Italy when their levels of infections started racing up. From the mid-2000s, China enjoyed a major role in the manufacture of microwaves, fridges, other white goods and electrical appliances. Since 2010, China has been the world's largest exporter, with USD2.641 trillion of exports, making up a sixth of global trade, by 2019.[6] This was almost 50 per cent more than the US, which constituted 8 per cent of global export volumes. If we stand by the principle of people voting with their feet, or at least with their wallets, then the need for China has certainly been clear over the last decade or so. It has also been growing.

The debate about whether in the end this has ended up as a good deal for the trading partners, or China, has raged amongst economists since the phenomenon of China's trading increases started. One of the key issues during the rise of Donald Trump in 2015 into 2016 was the 'terrible deal' (to use his word) America had with its great competitor, resulting in loss of American jobs, and economic growth as more manufacturing shifted to the People's Republic. Those that supported globalization stated that the gains were by consumers in developed markets able to buy cheaper goods from China through outlets like Walmart. Walmart, the world's largest retailer, as of 2019 reportedly still sourced over a quarter of its products from Chinese suppliers.[7] The globalizers stated that this kept down costs for customers, meaning they had money to spend elsewhere. Critics of this view countered that this was not much use when the jobs they should have had to earn money to buy such things had been destroyed by trade with China in the first place!

Nor is this solely about sourcing things cheaply to take out of China, but also trying to seek large amounts of profit within by getting access to the Chinese market to be able to sell to the 1.4 billion eager consumers there. Glimpses of what some had called as far back as the early 2000s the western version of 'the China Dream' were frequent. Indeed, in the Victorian era manufacturers in the north of Britain had drooled over the vision of every one of China's then 400 million people buying a single British manufactured cotton garment as a quick way to make them immensely rich. Carl Crow, an American businessman based in what was then Republican China in the pre-World War Two period wrote his own famous account of this, along with some initial debunking.[8] As economic reforms started in China from the late 1970s, something akin to a China consumer along western lines that one could sell products to appeared. Some companies managed early on to see to this brand-new cohort. Coca Cola and Kentucky Fried Chicken were early operators in the PRC, the former opening one of the earliest joint ventures allowed after 1979 between American and Chinese business in Tianjin. Both are still making good profits in China. Others appeared afterwards in automotive (Toyota and Volkswagen) and avionics (Bae Systems). Airbus and Boeing continue to fight over the huge opportunities that China offers with its new discovery of mass air travel – at least before the pandemic.

Selling goods into China runs alongside the dream of selling services. This too has become more appealing as the Chinese have urbanized, and more work in the services sector. Middle-class China under Xi Jinping is a dazzling prospect. It is a country where per capita levels of wealth are reaching USD13,000 per year, where there is a preference for foreign brands, and a bias towards foreign providers of services because of higher respect and trust – at least for the time being. This was why the dismissive comments made by J P Morgan bank head Jamie Dimon in November 2021 about his organization probably outlasting the Communist Party of China were unwise. As a recognition of just how important the China market was, J P Morgan had just signed a major deal there. Goldman Sachs, HSBC and Standard Chartered had also been in on the action. A more sophisticated China in terms of economic structure is also a more potentially lucrative one for those seeking to sell services into it.

A common complaint in the past by those looking to make their way in China was that after some help in the early stages of it reforms, it would start to repay on the investment as it became more like their own economies. In the early days, it focussed on using its main advantages – plentiful and cheap labour – and a world keen to shift their more polluting, less profitable and technologically less advanced production out of their own environment and into China. At the start, China would be exporting more as it became, in the words of the much admired premier of the 1990s Zhu Rongji, the 'factory of the world'. But even this early on, in the era around the time the country joined the World Trade Organisation, the hope was that the trade surpluses China amassed with Europe and America in particular would be a temporary phenomenon, and that they would ease down and level out. One day the situation would become one more conducive to the developed West. The entry of an upgraded Chinese economy into the services sector was usually taken as the moment when western companies would see this happen and the big rebalance would occur.

So far, this hasn't come to pass. But the hope it still might has not entirely dissipated. What is loosely called the Chinese middle class exist more tangibly now than ever before. Any visitor can see representatives of them, and sense their economic potential, when they look at the vast and gleaming new cities spread across the country, and at the new cars, new shopping malls, and new housing estates. To access this demographic would truly be a dream come true. Shanghai is a case in point – the future of Chinese consumerism existing in the here and now, with shops and restaurants heaving with people (again, before the pandemic) and signs almost everywhere of conspicuous consumption, from the clothes people wear to what they eat, to how they travel. Being able to sell goods and services to these people would be to make inroads into the world's most important single economic group, one bursting with potential. To be a stakeholder in their future is a massive advantage. As Apple experienced in the 2010s, if Chinese indeed become addicted to one's products, the roads can become paved with gold.

The hunger towards conquering the Chinese market for the riches it will bring is a deep one. If we forget the more remote history and look simply at the period since China entered WTO, then the amount of time and effort invested by major partners from the US to UK, Germany, Canada and others into making money there has been considerable. Countless trade delegations, endless ministerial- and government-level meetings, hours upon hours of Chamber of Commerce events from countries across the world, and then signing of agreements, Memorandums of Understanding and contracts, along with actual investments, factories, study and research tours – all of this has been focussed on a hope for a future where material gains can be made. There is nothing wrong with this. It is the work of trade through history. But we must remember here just how massive a part of the narrative between China and the outside world in recent times this has played. It testifies, and continues to testify, to the single, irrefutable fact that the West wanted something for its own gain in dealing with China. It was not engaging through pure altruism and good heartedness. It wanted to sell goods, buy goods cheaply, invest, and provide services to the Chinese for the single, overwhelming and overriding aim of making money.

In the furious battle over values and beliefs, one that has only intensified since the early 2010s, this point about how strong the role of material self-interest is and has always been for the West in its engagement with China often gets obscured. One can argue that transactions in investment and trade, to be successfully undertaken, need to be underpinned by a set of convictions and protocols expressing the values which all sides involved share. They don't just happen in some transactional vacuum. The question is what sort of values these might be. There has, for instance, to be common understanding of reciprocity, due process, fairness, the meaning of promises and obligations in contracts, responsibilities, and common safety and product quality standards. In joining entities like the WTO, China up to a point accepted this. It has subscribed to the need for a common playing field, a space where there must be rules for trade and business to be possible between very different partners. It has operated like a team in a game of football. No game would be possible without everyone participating having a common understanding of how it should be conducted and abiding by certain shared procedures. But problems start when we are forced to acknowledge that there are more complex issues which go beyond the simple physical playing of the game: what sort of things, for instance, a game symbolizes (courage, fitness, national prowess, endurance, etc.) and how those engaged in it, and watching, generate significance and meaning from it. There may be one activity happening. But the way this is seen and experienced differs radically depending on who is the spectator. A game in the end is a symbol – but precisely of what depends on many different things.

In the same way, the rules of trading and economics may be global and standardized, but China's understanding of their meaning is utilitarian. They have value because they are aimed at delivering specific tangible benefits to it, rather than because they indicate some deeper, moral aspect of reality. This is where it is a truly disruptive new participant. It dissents from the ideology of capitalism, and the notion that capitalist-style trading and investing with others carries an added political or ideological dimension meaning that to do it well, you must also adopt a certain world view that is necessitated by this based on notions of freedom and the power and dignity of the individual. The shocking heresy that China has performed in being an effective economic actor since 2000 shows it is perfectly possible to engage well with the rules and norms of the global game of business while not subscribing to the values that are meant to underly this. This is a bit like playing in the World Cup Soccer competition but only caring about the financial reward of final victory if you are the winner, and not the honour and pride that should come from this. China in this way performs a double violation when it competes in the global economic system, because it upsets the other players not just through the keenness of its competitiveness, but it also because it sows doubts about one of their most fundamental convictions – that to be a good player one must have not just a great technique but the right set of beliefs, ultimate aims and attitudes. China has showed in the end a game is just that – a game. All you need to be to win is not a good believer, but just a good player.

The world clearly wants practical things like goods, investment, money and markets, from China. The statistics make that abundantly clear. In the late twentieth and early twenty-first century, as the quotes from the documents issued by the EU from 2006 show, there were also other expectations. These were along the lines of hoping China would become what was called a good global citizen, a positive member of the international community, an observer of the rules-based system, and a stable partner but one which embraced pluralism. From the 1980s, International Non-Government organizations like the Ford Foundation, Save the Children Fund, and the World Wildlife Fund, operated in China, with offices, personnel and projects. Aid agencies like the UK Department for International Development (DFID), folded into the

Foreign, Commonwealth and Development Office in 2021, and voluntary organizations like Peace Corps from the US, or Britain's Voluntary Services Overseas all were active, running projects to help with the country's development. In internal, and at times public, documents, outside governments and their politicians said that their aim through this was partly to help China become a more predictable and reliable member of the international community. They often spoke as though membership of this community was a gift that was in their power to give. They spoke like they were members of an exclusive club and had veto power over China's application for membership. But was this power to decide whether or not China could join real? China itself was becoming so significant as a global player as the 2000s wore on that the greater risk was not being engaged with it rather than the other way around. Increasingly it was clear that for an international system or stage to really be what it said it was, China had to be present. Otherwise, it was simply a limited clique.

Through this material engagement, we revert to an issue raised in the last chapter – the way that this support for WTO entry was seen as a means to see not just economic but political change. One has to only look at the language used by successive American presidents to appreciate this. Speaking just before the time of China's entry to the WTO around 2000, President Bill Clinton declared that 'The WTO agreement will move China in the right direction. It will advance the goals America has worked for in China for the past three decades.' These were, he went on to spell out, to see China 'play by global rules' observing the freedoms and liberties of Americans in the free West.[9] Speaking two years later in 2002, George W. Bush, Clinton's successor, told students at Tsinghua university in Beijing during a visit there that 'China is already having secret ballot and competitive elections at the local level. Nearly 20 years ago, a great Chinese leader, Deng Xiaoping, said this – I want you to hear his words. He said that China would eventually expand democratic elections all the way to the national level. I look forward to that day.' He went on to say that he looked forward to 'a stronger, more confident China – a China that can astonish and enrich the world, a China that your generation will help create. This is one of the most exciting times in the history of your country, a time when even the grandest hopes seem within your reach.'[10] Obama, after him, continued the same theme. Speaking in a press conference with Xi Jinping in 2015, he affirmed 'America's unwavering support for the human rights and fundamental freedoms of all people, including freedom of assembly and expression, freedom of the press and freedom of religion. And I expressed in candid terms our strong view that preventing journalists, lawyers, NGOs and civil society groups from operating freely, or closing churches and denying ethnic minorities equal treatment are all problematic, in our view, and actually prevent China and its people from realizing its full potential.'[11] Ironically, with his transactional view of the world, President Trump spoke very little in this vein, although his deputy Mike Pence articulated the main views of his administration towards the People's Republic: 'America had hoped that economic liberalization would bring China into a greater partnership with us and with the world,' he intoned, like a disappointed headmaster talking of a recalcitrant student. 'Instead, China has chosen economic aggression, which has in turn emboldened its growing military. Nor, as we had hoped, has Beijing moved toward greater freedom for its own people. For a time, Beijing inched toward greater liberty and respect for human rights. But in recent years, China has taken a sharp U-turn toward control and oppression of its own people.'[12]

This is an impressive record over two decades, and across four very different presidents, of a common aim. It is also an equally impressive record of its consistent thwarting. Reverting to the metaphor of the game, we have to acknowledge that the reason this thwarting has happened is not due to any failure of conviction on the US's part, or others of a similar mindset like the EU. They were sincere in their belief that to play the game of trade and investment you had to have other things beyond technical skills and strength. You needed to have an attitude and an ethos. In this latter assumption (and it clearly was only an assumption) they have so far been proved wrong. If the West does want China to change its behaviour and its values, economic engagement was clearly not the right tactic. As of 2022 it has failed, creating panic and disarray.

What the West Doesn't Want

Investment, trade on terms the Enlightenment West feels acceptable, and buying into a common global growth narrative where the Chinese domestic market and Chinese consumers from the middle class are key players are all positive things that are wanted from China. Then there are things that are not wanted. These divide into those already alluded to before of China becoming an assertive, aggressive military actor, or involving itself in issues outside its borders that complicate and thwart the plans of the Enlightenment West, or contesting and attempting to rewrite the global rules that currently run the world's business in ways that suit China and no one else.

For the first of these the Enlightenment West, along with much of the Asia Pacific region, clearly doesn't want a China with a massive military. China having more ships than the US, and with power projection deep into its region and beyond, arouses deep suspicion and fear about what its intentions are. This 'smoking gun' image of China brandishing a weapon it claims it has no ambition to use is unsettling. Observers believe that the investments it has put into creating new jets, new kinds of military equipment, and new ways of doing things through professionalizing its armed forces must portend something large, and unpleasant. A China that is out to dominate, conquer and suppress once it has the capacity to do so is profoundly undesirable.

To prevent, or impede, the building up of this capacity, the US and its allies have imposed arms embargoes on China. This limits the kinds of technology that can be sold to Beijing, or the sorts of dual use IP that it can have. The arms embargoes themselves were put in place after the 1989 uprising. The EU attempted to lift its own in the early 2000s as a friendly gesture towards Beijing. Washington however was not happy. The Bush White House was unimpressed by the argument that alternative legislation within the EU meant that it would not be able to export sensitive goods and technology to China, with or without a specific embargo legislating against this. North Korea, for instance, is the subject of no specific regulations, but no one would trade in armaments or military goods with it because they would be breaking general non-proliferation laws in place at a national level.

China took recourse to three things in order to gain what it felt it needed in this area to overcome these restrictions. The first was to undertake espionage. There is nothing surprising about this. Everyone wants good technology, and some try to get it by fair means or foul. With no formal alliance system and living in a space prone to radical insecurity, it is not surprising that China placed such a premium on acquiring good kit and know-how via this route. There are stringent countermeasures in place to try to prevent theft of IT or IP happening, but inevitably, many cases slipped through. The second was to get technology from powers more favourable to it, such as Russia. In the early 2000s, Russia was the provider of a large amount of military equipment. It did this because of the parlous nature of its own economy at that time meaning it had to pursue any revenue-raising opportunities, but also on the assumption (which in the end proved correct) that a militarized China was more of a problem for Moscow's common foes, the US and Europe, than for it itself. In the long term, this might prove to have been a huge miscalculation. But Russian planes, an aircraft carrier, and other systems figured in the earlier period of Chinese militarization. The third action China undertook to mitigate the impact of western sanctions was to place immense amounts of investment and effort into creating its own indigenous capability to produce proprietorial technology. Chinese-returned students with the right qualifications from abroad, and the immense effort in making Chinese universities better at research formed the two prongs of this strategy.

As of 2022, while these three actions remain a work in progress, they have already had an impact. China has achieved a track record of serving up unpleasant surprises in giving the world tangible evidence of the progress it has been making. In 2007, it carried out the first test of an anti-satellite missile. This, one report stated, marked 'a new sphere of technical and military competition' with the US.[13] In 2011 during a visit to Beijing by the US Secretary of Defence, Robert Gates, a new J10 stealth fighter was tested. When Gates asked the then Chinese president Hu Jintao about this he seemed surprised.[14] Almost a decade later, in August 2021, the US reported that China had launched a nuclear-capable hypersonic missile which had circled the globe before coming down close to its target. According to one report, 'the test showed that China had made astounding progress on hypersonic weapons and was far more advanced than US officials realized.'[15] As with economic predictions, China is perpetually ahead.

China's self-justification when its military technology and capacity building hunger is brought up is firstly that any country has the right to protect and secure itself, and secondly, that it does not accept why in terms of technology development and security the US and others should have one law and insist another applies to everyone else. The literature on the US as an exceptionalist power is long and detailed.[16] In the specific case of the 2007 anti-satellite event, for instance, a few months later in early 2008 the US Navy fired a missile to destroy a satellite of its own above the Pacific. Around the same time, it rejected a proposal by China and Russia for a treaty to ban weapons in space and for their use against spacecraft on the grounds that it was keener on confidence building measures. The official *People's Daily* in Beijing stated that 'The United States, the world's top space power, has often accused other countries of vigorously developing military space technology. But faced with the Chinese-Russian proposal to restrict space armaments, it runs in fear from what it claimed to love.'[17] Similarly, in the South and East China Sea, while China is a signatory of the

United Nations Convention on the Law of the Sea (UNCLOS), the US is not. With its troops hosted in Okinawa, Japan, and with over 30,000 still in South Korea, and a smaller detachment in Guam along with military installations throughout the Pacific the US is a different kind of presence in China's backyard than China in its. This asymmetry of expectations towards itself and others by the US is probably what inspired Xi Jinping to start talking of the Pacific as a common shared area. In this context, it states that its development of military capacity and its attempts to have a greater role in the region are simply catch up rather than any attempt to take over. But whatever they might be, the amount of anxiety and interest focussed on them certainly shows that for the US and its allies, they are regarded as undesirable.

Derived from this, the outside world does not want a China that is building new installations in the South China Sea and making ownership claims over territory that spread down to the coast of Indonesia. It does not want a China whose behaviour is assertive and pushy in the ways seen in the Nauru islands during a meeting of the Pacific Islands Forum in September 2018, when the envoy from Beijing stormed out because he felt his country had been slighted. The Enlightenment West does not want China to be spreading what it calls debt diplomacy and buying up strategic assets like ports or railways which it can then use to promote expansionist aims. It doesn't want a China that has a range of high-powered missiles aimed across the Taiwan Strait with the clear intention of pressurizing the island, creating the possibility of a catastrophic conflagration in the region. It certainly doesn't want a monumental clash between the US and China which ends with military action that might decimate the region, and much of the rest of the world, and plunge the globe into economic and geopolitical chaos.

Oddly enough, though, nor does that outside world want a China that falls into instability and fragments. This might sound odd. A China that became weaker appears to be the answer to the dreams of most of the more strenuous hawks in Europe and America. But any consideration of the kinds of cost this sort of implosion would involve should sober them up. A Chinese version of what happened after the USSR collapsed in 1991 would be a massive tragedy. It would be far more extensive and damaging than what happened in that case. In view of the horrible consequences for human development and prosperity for Russians in the decade after 1991, this is quite a claim. But if one remembers the impact of rising male mortality rates due to alcoholism and poverty, and the general decline of living standards to around 150 million people, and then appreciates that we are talking about the possibility of a similar thing happening to ten times that amount in China, this makes clear why. The collapse of the Chinese government would carry the strong possibility of fragmentation of the country along the lines experienced when the Qing Dynasty fell after the Xinhai revolution in 1911. Bearing in mind the importance of China to global supply chains, the integral role it plays in the global economy, the immensity of its population, and the fact that it is a major nuclear power, one occupying a huge, complex and intrinsically dangerous locality with sources of instability all around, ranging from North Korea to the India and Pakistan relationship, contemplating a China failure as a nation state would make most sane people baulk. It would lead to massive economic issues, immense migration challenges, and potentially prompt regional implosion. A strong China is at least manageable because it carries some degree of predictability. A failed, fragmented China would remove one of the most crucial pillars to global stability. In this context, the Communist Party for all its issues and challenges to the outside world, is at a minimum providing some level of stability. The world may not be happy with a China strong in this way and with improving military capacity. But it will want a failed China even less.

And then there is the converse of this. The ultimate 'what if'. A friend originally from China alerted me to this some years back. 'You guys are so funny,' she said once when we were talking about China's political system and political reform. 'I mean, don't you realize the only thing holding the country back today from becoming a total capitalist rollercoaster is the Communist Party. It's a weight on their growth not a help. If you got rid of that, you would be facing 100 million Jack Mas!' It was a fanciful and provocative point. But we weren't the first to muse on the idea that in many ways if there was such a thing as natural entrepreneurs, then China had a high supply of them. Businesspeople in China have to succeed against massive odds. As economist Yasheng Huang pointed out almost two decades ago, they have limited access to capital, they have to face off against state-owned enterprises with all the advantages they enjoy, and they need to be constantly aware of the hard, clammy hand of authority coming and messing about with their business.[18] There is no predictability in the legal system, or at least hasn't been until recently, On top of this they have to demonstrate political loyalty and be adept at reading the changing shifts and movements of the political winds. If the aforementioned were not enough as a final challenge they have to deal with an environment of savage competitiveness with their fellow entrepreneurs. It is a miracle people succeed in this environment. And yet Jack Ma, China's recently most famous and successful billionaire before he hit political troubles in 2021 and briefly disappeared from public view after criticizing state banks, is not alone. Hurun, a company run by a British analyst of Chinese business, produces lists each year of the most successful Chinese entrepreneurs. Those listed are just the tip of the iceberg. There are many more.[19]

My friend in their comments was speculating on what would happen if some, or all, of the formidable list of barriers and impediments ranged against entrepreneurs given above was removed. China might become a landscape where dynamic, successful entrepreneurs were everywhere, unconstrained in their ability to do business. What objections would the West have if China, reformed, politically aligned to their preferences, playing to the rules that they kept insisting had to be observed, ended up being not only very good and capable of this, but domineering and successful? There would be no space in this scenario to complain about the role of the Chinese state, unfair advantages, and immoral actions and attitudes. China would be playing the game, in the right spirit and the right way, and winning.

If the concept of a strong China has caused disruption in the mindsets of the outside world, where the narrative in modern times was more often about how to manage Chinese failure and instability, rather than its success and dominance, then a China that is working and winning, not on its own terms but ours, would be a mixed blessing. Would the world where this happens, however improbable it might be today, be one where anxiety and worry about China vanishes? Would it be one of harmony and stability? Would a China that dominates legitimately, speaks the same language of global order, abides by the same norms, and through sheer success and economic clout is able to dominate and command the situation – would that be the kind of world the West would be happy to live with? Even under this benign scenario, it is hard to see the US or Europe being happy surrendering their dominant geopolitical position. For an America that is so assertive of its place as the number one power, which is often so unsettled and unnerved by the prospect of this slipping from it, there are clearly underlying anxieties and vulnerabilities that even the overtaking of it by a democratic China would not allay. The issue is about being pushed into second place as much as it is about who does that pushing.

In fact, what would be the best scenario for Washington is a continuation of the status quo, one where the American and European dominance politically and economically continues, but where China, as a secondary player, with a reformed political system, and a supportive economy, occupies a subordinate, useful place. This would be one largely defined by the current dominant partners. It would be a role crafted and granted to China, akin to a vassal state relationship, a model ironically that Chinese dynasties were once accused of creating for others in the imperial period. China has good reason to be suspicious of offers like this for it to slip into such a convenient subsidiary role. First there is the problem of trust. The very structure of western power feigns altruism but practices the opposite. We have to remember that China never forgets. It knows how the Enlightenment West's current dominance was won over the last three centuries as much by weaponry, war and violence as it was by ideas and knowledge. Only when comfortably in the dominant position did the West start being a little more merciful in its behaviour. But as the Middle East and the record of constant intervention there proves, even in the twenty-first century, for the West, rather than Communist China, power grows first from the barrel of a hi-tech gun or a precision drone – even if it then gets fortified by ideas afterwards.

The Enlightenment West wants a China that works for it within that power structure and culture where its own dominance is assured. It wants a China that neither fails, implodes and creates colossal problems for the region and the rest of the world, nor a place that reforms and succeeds so much that it is able to legitimately dominate, creating new centres of power and usurping the West. It wants a China that reforms, but only so much that it does moderately well rather than excels. It wants a country that become like the West but does not duplicate it so well it overtakes it. It wants a humble subordinate, something a little similar to Japan, that obeys the global rules, does well economically, but forever stands beside the West and remains beholden to it. The West's China Dream, and the Chinese one, are absolutely different, because for the West the dominance of its power is in the end the ultimate monopoly. Even were it not the way it is, there would still be an issue with a rising China. That problem is not therefore primarily China's politics. That simply adds to the grief. The issue is the West's fear and sense of its own decline as it sees its period of dominance slip from its hand, and does everything to try to prevent this happening to whoever comes to compete with it.

What Everyone Wants

Finally, we can draw the perspective out and look at far broader issues. The outside world, and the Enlightenment West, have a deep interest in managing, and hoping to solve, key issues. Of these, combatting climate change, dealing with pandemics, managing the challenges of artificial intelligence, and dealing with nuclear proliferation are amongst the most critical. China is not a bystander in these, but a hugely important stakeholder. Its interests and those of the rest of the world align as never before here.

The world certainly wants cooperation and help with China in these issues. They are insoluble without China's participation. A global climate change agreement would be senseless without Chinese participation. The expectations in this area are specific and highly articulated. They have been hammered out in international meetings and agreements from the 1990s onwards. Over this time, China's position has become far clearer and closer with that of the US and Europe. The world must have China's cooperation on this matter. It needs China to significantly reduce its reliance on fossil fuels. It needs Chinese people to produce far less per capita emissions than their equivalents in European or American countries. It needs these same people to use clean energy cars, and to eat and live in ways which can quickly become carbon neutral. Even as China is developing and lifting people to the sort of wealth and prosperity levels of the developed world, it needs to do this in ways which are more constrained in terms of fossil fuel usage. For most of their periods of rapid wealth creation and industrialization, the environmental costs of what the West were doing were poorly understood, and there was little urgency in trying to combat them. China does not have this luxury as it follows the same pathway.

China's partnership in preventing and managing pandemics is also crucial. Events from 2020 onwards made that abundantly clear. The dark hints by some that China had created the COVID-19 virus deliberately are hard to shift because they rely on a conspiratorial view of the world, one where faith rather than evidence is the main factor. But in view of the huge impact of the virus on Chinese society and the economy, one would have to say that were this really unleashed on the world as some demonic scheme, it is one that China has borne, and is likely to continue to bear, a very high cost for. The more neutral idea that China created the virus due to experiments gone awry at a biological laboratory might have more rational basis to it. Even so, in view of what happened during the Avian flu in Hong Kong, and breakouts of SARS in 2003, the most likely scenario is that the whole thing was a terrible accident, one that happened in wet markets rather than laboratory petri dishes. If we exclude these ideas that China is in the business of a perverse form of biological warfare through assisting in the spread of pandemics, then one can assume that the world and the Chinese are fully committed to put in place measures ensuring future virus outbreaks either do not happen or can be dealt with much more efficiently as soon as they appear.

COVID-19 has seen deepening differences and arguments between China and the rest of the world. But on another level there is greater acceptance of common ground and the need for more extensive cooperation. The foundation of this is self-interest for everyone. At some points in 2020 there were hints that scientists internationally were working together to find a vaccine. In the end, vaccines were found, but separately and in different places. The main thing to note here is the awareness of the need for common research frameworks. COVID-19 has made both the argument for closer cooperation on public health more urgent and showed in some areas how it can happen better.

Combatting nuclear proliferation is another core area for working together. Here, the common ground is more uneven. China, unlike the US, does not believe humanity could emerge from a nuclear war with anything left of current civilization. It sees the costs of deployment of nuclear options in a more anxious way than the US. Despite reports by the US Pentagon in 2021 of China planning to increase its stockpile of nuclear weapons to around a 1,000 by 2030,[20] even if that were true, it would still mean its arsenal was relatively small. By June 2021, according to one international report, of the world's 13,082 nuclear weapons, Russia had almost half of these (6,257), and the US most of the remainder (5,500). China stood third, with 350, a little ahead of France (300), the UK (225) and Pakistan and India with 150 each.[21] China's stance on nuclear weapons is reactive and defensive. It holds a no first use posture. It has good reason to be cautious. Unlike the US, it is bordered by four other nuclear powers (India, Russia, Pakistan and North Korea). A country with the kind of longstanding anxieties over stability in the region and domestically, occupying such a complex terrain, is unlikely to be adventurous as far as use of nuclear weapons goes. That China tried, in the end with no success, to prevent North Korea getting nuclear capacity, and was unhappy in the late 1990s when Pakistan and India entered the small group of nations with nuclear weapons proves this. While it guards its membership of this club jealously and knows that possession of nuclear weapons is the ultimate guarantee of security from attack by others (the US has never attacked a nuclear power), it is also as keen as the rest of its fellow members to ensure that others do not join.

Artificial intelligence (AI) has already been discussed. Suffice to say here that if problems do arise from deployment of AI, it is unlikely that these will be ones unique to one country or region, but that they will be intrinsically global in nature. China's use of AI and face recognition domestically is a serious issue – but a domestic one before it becomes international. This is symptomatic of Chinese behaviour often being tougher and more of a threat to itself than to the outside world. There are also fierce arguments over whether in fact AI could ever have the sort of capacity feared of it. These lay beyond this book's subject. Although therefore the dialogue between China and the outside world on how to develop, and then use, AI is undeveloped at the moment, the kinds of threats and problems going forward are common ones, and the sorts of mitigation of them therefore global.

Climate change, pandemics, nuclear proliferation and artificial intelligence are four clear areas where the challenges are intrinsically global, and where any management or these will also, necessarily, be global too. For the first three, there are already venues and modes for discussion and shaping cooperation with some levels of specificity. In climate change, these are the most developed, with various already extant international conventions and UN sponsored meetings directing things. In others, the situation is less mature and the framework primitive, but at least something is in place. For AI, there is far less convergence. This is more due to the lack of consensus about the kind of threat this issue poses, rather than some deep chasm that exists between China and the rest of the world. There is one striking commonality linking these four areas however, and that is that no one, whether it be China or anyone else, has much choice in working collectively. If they want to face the threats these issues raise (and it is clear for their own self-interest and security they must), they have to cooperate. Partial responses are not possible. The burden of work might be spread unevenly (carbon emissions per capita will always be different between different countries, for historic and economic reasons) but there can't be a scenario where one or two partners alone magically solve the issue. For nuclear proliferation, if one of the current nine accepted members of the nuclear club do decide to deploy, then everyone gets brought down. Cooperation is not the preference here. It is the only option. The world in this space needs things from China that China also wants from it. China does not figure as a super-sized rogue state, holding everyone else to ransom. There is, thankfully, a clear, shared balance of interest. Everyone is locked in. China may well be a difficult partner in these negotiations, and a self-interested one. But thankfully for the rest of the world, it is a rational one.

Who Are the Complex Ones?

What does the world want from China? It's clear from the discussion so far, that the answer to this is not a straightforward one. One of the issues we can be more certain about is that while no one can deny the complexity of the object the People's Republic – we also have to acknowledge the complexity of others involved in this relationship. These too sometimes cause challenges.

For tangible things like trade, investment, manufacturing, the world has voted with its feet for what it wants. The complaints by figures like Donald Trump are not so much about the interaction per se, but about how uneven this is and where the real benefits have accrued. The developed world has willingly bought great mountains of goods like Barbie dolls, almost all of them manufactured in China, to fuel the vast trade surpluses China enjoys. But as economists have shown, the profits that Chinese companies and the workers get from each doll they produced is tiny. In 1996, according to one analysis, of the retail value of USD$7.99 for one doll, only 35 cents of this went to the person making the toy in China.[22] In the whole debate about the trade surpluses China has with the US and others that became a major political preoccupation since 2017, consensus remains elusive over where exactly benefits ultimately lie. China's keenness to move beyond manufacturing to higher value areas of the economy like services is some clue to just how much of a priority solely accruing vast amounts of foreign reserves through exporting more than it imports is for its government.

Once one moves beyond the world of straightforward transactions like these that can, to some point, be measured and tabulated, then the question of the outside world's wants and desires towards China becomes much less clear. An honest and comprehensive account would need to acknowledge some level of contradictoriness. The Enlightenment West as one important group seems to be conflicted between wanting a China that becomes politically and in terms of values more like it, but not one that going along this route could ever succeed to the point where it might be dominant over it. And while it has multiple issues with a China succeeding, unreformed or even reformed, it also has the same intensity of issues with a China that fails. It wants a country that is stable, predictable, and fits in. It doesn't want a country that is destabilizing, fractious, or argumentative, either as a failing or a succeeding entity. This is a unique space that has been allocated to China. There is a huge question over whether there is any way, structurally speaking, that a country with the history, identity, hybrid values and cultural difference might even be able to occupy such a place. There is a good possibility that the whole structure of western demands towards China is incoherent, intrinsically contradictory, and doomed to perpetual disappointment. It's not the complexity of China that is the issue here, but the complexity of the desires and wants projected on it, something we all need to be clear about.

All of this is compounded by the fact that there are also issues of massive importance which the outside world not only wants from China, but needs – combatting climate change, pandemic management, restraining nuclear proliferation and ensuring there is never a nuclear war, and managing the significant and pressing threats from artificial intelligence. In addressing these problems, a failing, unstable, fragmented China becomes the worst of all worlds. It makes cooperation either significantly more difficult or impossible. A strong, stable China on any terms, whether that be under Communism or whatever other forms of governance that might emerge, is better than the opposite in this context.

From this whole discussion we can understand that one of the reasons why the question of what the outside world and particularly the Enlightenment West wants from China is seldom explicitly asked is because it is so hard to offer a succinct answer to. In the past, language like the US in the mid-2000s when it talked, via figures like Robert Zoellick, then a US government official, of the desire to see China being a 'stakeholder' sufficed. But one of the many issues with this sort of formulation is that there are different kinds of stakeholder. The sort Zoellick referred to here was clearly one that is compliant with what the US government at that time wanted. Back then the EU wanted a slightly different stakeholder, one that it could work with to bring about benign internal reform. Others wanted a partner they could go to make money from. All the time, China itself wanted to participate in global issues, but on terms that were not wholly aligned with these various variations of stakeholder. Lack of clarity about this concept has persisted. Today, China is a stakeholder per se because it is such a major part of the global economy and so has to play a role whether it likes it or not. The real problem remains what sort of role. Zoellick would have been more accurate and more honest, to say that China needed to be 'the right kind of stakeholder'. That would also have helped to make clear, even this early, how unlikely it was that this was something China would be able to do, and how the issue was as much about the aspirations from the outside world towards it as it was about China per se.

Chapter Five

WHAT DOES CHINA WANT
FROM THE WORLD?

Listening to Chinese diplomatic rhetoric over the last three decades, an observer would be tempted to think that the country being spoken about has only ever wanted to be friends in a world where everyone is equal, there is multipolarity and harmony, and the rules of engagement are all about non-interference, mutual respect, win-win outcomes, and peaceful co-existence. The static quality of this language is striking. As one observer speaking in a conference in Prague commented to me around 2018, seen even from their own relatively small European country, Chinese diplomacy was unique because it was (in their words) one model imposed everywhere, no matter who the People's Republic were dealing with and where that happened to be. China's posture towards the Czech Republic (population in 2021, 10.7 million) is the same as its posture towards India (currently at 1.3 billion people) at least on paper, following the Five Principles of Peaceful Co-Existence in place since 1955 (non-interference, non-aggression, respect for sovereignty, equality and mutual co-existence). In terms even of the mechanics of diplomacy, China's willingness to grant audiences at the highest level to small African or Latin American countries, and to make a fuss of the leaders of these places when they come to Beijing, has been observed on many occasions.[1] Leaders who are fobbed off with either low-level meetings or barely any recognition in Washington or European capitals, can luxuriate in the streets being closed off as their car cavalcade bowls through downtown Beijing on its way to their meeting with President Xi.

China certainly behaves like it wants friends. And yet it also avoids gaining over-burdensome responsibilities that might come through signing formal alliances and bilateral treaties. The only one it currently has, created in 1961 and renewed for another two decades in 2021, is with the Democratic People's Republic of Korea (DPRK). This is the exception that proves the rule. Like Marx – though in this case Groucho rather than Karl – it subscribes to the philosophy that a friend in need is a nuisance! Soothing rhetoric about closeness, and the grand language used by the Ministry of Foreign Affairs of strategic and then comprehensive strategic partnerships, is fine. But these are furthered through documents of limited legal or political standing like Memorandum of Understandings containing high levels of abstraction, and a general lack of binding commitments and specific targets.

There are two attitudes one might take to answering the question of what China wants from the outside world. Neither are particularly helped by the kind of very unclear and ambiguous language contained in its formal diplomatic utterances and statement of general posture outlined above. One is to see it as being in the business of incremental domination and control. It wants, in the end, to be number one, with a world of vassal states around it, returning to the caricature of its position of premodern history where it was able to sit in dynastic regal splendour at the centre of the world.[2] That is an aggressive and disruptive aim. On the other, one might see China's role as framed by a sense of its own exclusivity, a high level of self-interest, and a desire to have space in the world, but not all of that space. China's words largely don't help in coming down on one side or the other of this argument. So this chapter will try to work out across a number of different areas, not just from what China says but from how in recent years it acts, which of these two descriptions is the more accurate. As with the previous chapter on what the world wants from China, it will look at the tangible, then the geopolitical, then address the question of what China wants in positive and negative terms (i.e. not just what it wants, but what it doesn't want from the outside world) and then its long-term aims.

Getting Rich Together

China clearly wants a world where it can make money. This seems an obvious point, but the most obvious things often gets overlooked. If there is one theme that runs through its interaction with others it is the priority placed on material gain. Unlike the Enlightenment West, China is unapologetic, unvarnished and unconflicted about this. Making money, at least since the Deng era, has been a good thing. The approach China has adopted through the language of its key leaders over this era has been to stress mutual benefit, doing that via the mode of business and trade. That has proved disarming. A communist country speaking the language of profit and mutual enrichment is unexpected. This was not a tactic that the USSR used. But China's has been consistent in words and action on this point. Speaking in 2017 as the first Chinese head of state to attend the Davos meeting of the World Economic Forum, the ultimate venue for members of the globalizing elite, Xi stated:

> We should commit ourselves to growing an open global economy to share opportunities and interests through opening-up and achieve win-win outcomes. One should not just retreat to the harbour when encountering a storm, for this will never get us to the other shore of the ocean. We must redouble efforts to develop global connectivity to enable all countries to achieve inter-connected growth and share prosperity. We must remain committed to developing global free trade and investment, promote trade and investment liberalization and facilitation through opening-up and say no to protectionism. Pursuing protectionism is like locking oneself in a dark room. While wind and rain may be kept outside, that dark room will also block light and air. No one will emerge as a winner in a trade war.[3]

That this statement was made at the same time as the world was digesting the looming presidency of Donald Trump and the strong signals of a protectionist and much more American focussed ethos emanating from the White House made its commitment to free global trade even more striking.

Early predictions that the broadly transactional nature of Chinese diplomacy would fit well with the similar mindset of Trump proved over-optimistic. China's desire for the world to happily make money with each other and leave other more complex issues aside is clearly a vast oversimplification. What needs to be recognized here is that it is in the business of doing business, and that the explanation for this is not complex. Firstly, trade and investment with the outside world on terms that suit China ideally have brought it, in the past, capital, technology, and know-how – things it identified after a period of reflection and research in the early part of the Deng reforms as ones it needed in order to develop and grow richer and stronger. That trilogy of capital, technology and know-how have always been present since 1978, but have evolved, rebalanced and changed in priority and intensity. In the beginning desire for capital was as strong as for technology and know-how. But by the era of Xi, while remaining happy to carry on taking generous gifts of cash that might come its way, the need not just for any technology and know-how, but for very specific forms of these had come to the fore. China in 2022 needs less hi-tech products from the West than it once did. But it would certainly want to be able to do a better job at creating semi-conductors and large bodied aircraft, two examples (there are plenty of others) where its reliance on the outside world remains a profound irritant to it.

China's investment overseas has also been driven by specific strategic objectives. Getting hold of good brands for instance, to support its overseas expansion plans when its own versions are either unknown or regarded negatively because of where they come from. Technology acquisition by buying certain companies has already been mentioned, though here the record has often been patchy. China wants to have decent overseas markets for its goods. The reduction of these during the impoverishment of American and European consumers, its main export markets up to then, in the 2008 Great Financial Crisis pushed Beijing to try to diversify. Trade figures a decade later show this was of limited success. Overseas investments are also an expression of China's desire for a reliable aftersales support network for its own manufacturing and exporting companies. For investments into China too, as stated previously, it clearly wanted competition and sources of pressure for its own companies from international ones, something that happened in the era after entry to the WTO. In the early 2000s, human capital was important, with a dearth of well qualified managerial level corporation people in China and a need to have this kind of highly skilled work imported. As more highly educated Chinese have returned from studying abroad since then, many of them with several years' experience of working in the outside world, this issue has eased somewhat.

China's engagement with the world is assisted by the fact that from the late 1970s, it had a clear awareness of the large set of challenges developmentally and economically that it faced and what the outside might have that could address these. This has not changed. Under Xi Jinping, the list has only increased in complexity. The country needs to deal with massive environmental, demographic and inequality issues. It still has a highly imperfect health care sector (only 6 per cent of GDP is spent on health, compared to almost three times that in the USA). Its pensions sector is also far below what it needs to be in a country which is already experiencing rapid ageing. Despite the seemingly limitless powers attributed to the Beijing government, even trying to raise the retirement age for women on state companies from the current fifty-five to a more viable sixty or sixty-five is still a task too much. Nor does this constant sense of internal vulnerability and need, present even in the confident era of Xi, derive solely from the country's sense of the huge challenges it still needs to face to develop fully. It also needs the outside world to provide a level of stability and predictability while if focusses on facing these. In the economic area that means investment environments where in terms of financial returns, and in protecting China's assets abroad, there are strong institutions and strong laws. China is accused of being a disruptive and assertive force. And yet, from the 1980s, its stance has been to look for predictability and be reliant on that in its chief markets and investment partners overseas. It did not enjoy the disruption of 2008. Nor did it look on Trump's rise and the bumpy progress since then with much enthusiasm. As Jiang Zemin said in 2002, the two decades till 2020 offered a period of consolidation and the opportunity for China to continue to build its capacity and enjoy a time of what Jiang called 'strategic opportunity'. [4] This was a period when the US was expected to be preoccupied by issues in the Middle East, with the war on terror that it had just launched there and in Central Asia. It was a time of gifts for China, one when it would be able to work to strengthen and enrich itself, without drawing attention to this. The leadership style of Hu Jintao proved to be an immense decoy over this period, almost soporifically calm and unremarkable on the surface at least, lulling the world into the false idea that China was silent not just because it could not speak, but because it had nothing to say.

This is not to claim that China wanted the series of unforced errors, mistakes and problems that afflicted the West over this period, from the financial crisis to the wars in the Middle East, and the terrorist issues in Europe. These were highly unwelcome distractions from its main mission, to continue to strengthen itself and answer its own problems. The great irony is that despite the conviction of so many in the outside world about its disruptive behaviour, one of China's greatest desires was for partners that did not rock the boat and cause turbulence. There are good arguments to support the idea that the more abrasive and assertive Xi posture since the mid-2010s is as much to compensate for this disappearance of predictability from key players like the US and Europe, and the need to fill the vacuum this has created rather than to proactively prove China is now newly strong. This mode of behaviour has been forced upon it by necessity, thrusting it into an unexpected situation before it was quite ready and making it overcompensate for the more important, demanding role expected of it. These days, for self-interest if for no other reason, China is frequently the more stable one – one of the true ironies of contemporary geopolitics.

Unwilling Wants

China may be strong now, but beyond know-how and technology it has some far more basic requirements from the outside world. Of these, provision of energy, food and raw materials are the most obvious. In China's ideal world, it would be able to revert to the 'zili gengsheng', the spirit of self-reliance that was one of the slogans of the Maoist era. In those days, China really did try to practice autarky, simply residing economically behind its borders, making a few modest transactions via Hong Kong (the convenience of which was one of the reasons Beijing never acted on the occasional impulse to invade and take possession of the city before formal retrocession in 1997). But the whole ethos of Reform and Opening up after 1978 was to buck this trend, and to engage once more with the wider world, though this time with a stronger sense of what China wanted, and a clear resistance to falling into asymmetrical agreements and arrangements that served to exploit it.

China in the era of fast industrialization after 1980 has not been able to avoid becoming what *Financial Times* journalist James Kynge called in the 2000s a 'hungry nation'. Its appetite for iron and other kinds of ore grew vast. They remain so. It gobbled up resources to such an extent that at some points it was the user of most of the world's concrete and steel. Despite vast resources of coal, and some of oil, its need for energy exploded. Using the Million Tonnes of Oil Equivalent (MTOE) as unit of measure, between 1980 and 2015, China's usage rose from under 500 MTOEs to around 7,000. [5] By 2020, China consumed almost a quarter of all global energy.[6] After 2011, It used more coal than the rest of the world combined.[7] Oil constitutes about a fifth of China's energy needs, and half of this is imported, predominantly from Saudi Arabia and Iran. Despite immense efforts to build nuclear power plants (the country had forty-seven of these operational by 2019[8]) and rising numbers of renewable sources, the reliance on coal (70 per cent of China's energy) and oil has not notably shifted in the last two decades. That this oil needs to be sourced beyond China's borders poses a longstanding strategic threat, both because of the instability of the region where much of it comes from, and the ways in which in terms of supply routes via sea, China is reliant on territory still dominated by the US Navy. The narrow Malacca Strait has been a much commented on phenomenon, a tight passage where much of China's sea-borne oil is transported, and which, if necessity called for it, the US and its allies could easily control.

Australia is a good example of highly unwelcome supply dependence. In 2020, despite the increasingly unfriendly and fractious relations, already noted before, China imported USD70 billion of ore from Australia, three times as much as the second largest source, Brazil, and almost half as much as the rest of the world combined.[9] By August 2021, in one month alone, this had hit a record USD20 billion.[10] China expressed its reluctance to continue being in a relationship where for once the Australians had the upper hand, by seeking alternative sources in Africa. Geology and geography however dictate what is possible here. China might not be happy about buying Australian ore, but its need dictates its actions, and it continues to spend vast amounts of money to secure it. A similar situation occurs for meat (another large increase for Australian exports in 2021), and other agricultural products. It is also a big importer of cars and integrated circuits from South Korea, Japan and Germany. China is a huge country (the world's third largest in terms of territory) but its supply of agricultural land is limited, it has a massive population to feed and provide for, one which is becoming increasingly prosperous and wanting more goods and services. This large population is an asset in terms of being a source of growth that the rest of the world should be interested in and want to engage with – but a burden, because it means that China cannot disengage or walk away from a world where it needs such fundamentally important things to keep the desires of that population satisfied. The Enlightenment West should take heart. It might not see an easy way to divorce itself from China, but the feeling is mutual – China has no easy way to disengage from it. They are caught up in a tight embrace of mutual, increasingly reluctant dependence.

Assertive Wants

If the Enlightenment West and powers similar in mindset to it want a China that is more aligned to them in terms of values and respect for norms, China wants a world that abides by what it regards as its core interests. Over the years, these have gradually come into sight. They were first properly articulated by the State Councillor Dai Bingguo, the chief person responsible for foreign affairs in the Hu era. In 2009, he stated that these interests were 'to maintain [China's] fundamental system and state security; next is state sovereignty and territorial integrity; and third is the continued stable development of the economy and society.'[11] These are broad aims. The first relates to the insistence by the Communist Party that its legitimacy is respected by all who engage with it and that there are no moves to provoke regime change. The second relates to its continuing claims on the South and East China Sea and on Taiwan. Under this umbrella it also insists on the right to conduct matters as it best sees fit in Hong Kong, Macau, Tibet, Xinjiang, and other border areas. The final one is an allusion to what some have called the performative legitimacy of the Party State – its need to deliver economic growth to strengthen and stabilize China's global role and thereby justify the continuing monopoly on power the Communists have.

All of these core aims are to some extent outward facing, even where they refer to domestic issues. In stating them, China clearly wants the world to take these seriously. The difference in recent years is that it has become more confident about policing discussions and activities related to these beyond its borders. The three Ts – Taiwan, Tibet and Tiananmen, the latter a reference to the 1989 uprising and the deep international concern about this – have been joined in 2020 as the next chapter will discuss by another initial – X for Xinjiang. But there are a range of actions and accompanying responses by China that relate to each of these that have become more apparent as the years have gone on.

China definitely wants, for instance, heads of foreign governments to not meet the representatives of the Tibetan government in exile, or the Tibetan religious leader the Dalai Lama. In the past, when meetings between European leaders and the Dalai Lama happened on the grounds of his importance as a religious leader (this was the pretext used by whichever government head was meeting him, in order to blunt Chinese claims of recognition of Tibetan independence) the punishment was mostly in the form of words. Chinese officials would complain about offence caused to Chinese people, hurting their feelings. By 2011, when British prime minister David Cameron decided to meet the Dalai Lama in the undercroft of St Paul's Cathedral, London, during a religious service, the response was far more muscular. For over a year, no significant UK–China bilateral meetings occurred. The usually busy British embassy in Beijing became much quieter as VIPs stayed away. After this icy period, when the thaw came it was delivered, somewhat ironically, by a royal visit, that ultimate symbol of British imperialism and old-style patronage. Since then, no leader of a major European country has met the Dalai Lama. This is true for most of the rest of the world. The exception is the US, where at least Obama met the Dalai Lama in 2016 at the White House. China's response remained more muted in this case for the very good reason that even it baulked at a complete freeze of dialogue with its largest geopolitical partner.

On issues like Tibet, China has in recent years moved from not just defending its position, but (with very mixed results) on enforcing silence. The latter has involved far more offensive rather than simply defensive work. For this reason, this is where the real contention starts. The Enlightenment West has many dislikes, but one of the most serious is to be told to shut up. Overt, or covert (the latter perhaps even worse for the way it preys on the West's latent but recently rising paranoia) any signs of the Chinese government placing pressure on groups, individuals, businesses or the media to try to either present its line on the key sensitive issues that matter to it favourably, or to shut discussion down when critical issues arise, creates immense anger and pushback. This often is seen as a key piece of evidence giving credence to the claims about Chinese aggressive and forceful intentions discussed in earlier chapters. In this case, those claims are real.

A common theme of this book has been the need to see accurately these attempts from China to express its powers in the outside world proportionately and assess them accurately. China's Tibet lobbying has been consistent, irritating and often played into the hands of its critics. An example concerns students from the Durham University Union debating club in 2017 receiving a reportedly stern warning from the Chinese embassy in London saying that an event they were planning to run had best not go ahead illustrates this well. Part of the cause of the embassy complaint was about the participation of Anastasia Lin, a former Canadian beauty queen originally from China, who had become a vocal critic of China's human rights record, particularly relating to Falungong and Tibet. Following the law of unintended consequences, as with the heavy-handed removal of Taiwan-related material from the conference programme at an event in Portugal in 2015 mentioned earlier, the net result of this protest was to succeed in raising the profile of what would, in the normal course of things, have most probably been just one of a series of debates held by the student society that term which raised no interest beyond the university. Highly visible events like that made the claim that Chinese were not just trying to influence this university but all universities. By 2021 this had become a particularly hot topic. Some other examples particularly of Chinese students being involved in protests about on-campus events concerning Xinjiang or Hong Kong received coverage. But how can we best see these sorts of occurrences. Are they best described as heavy handed and often ineffective lobbying, or part of a far broader set of actions, where the values and function of western institutes of learning were being successfully, systematically attacked by the totalitarians in Beijing?

If we take an evidence-led approach, I think we fall some way short of going to the stronger claim above. Once more, it is clear that on the spectrum of issues, there are some where China will assert its line now despite the irritation and anger this causes, even when, in fact, this behaviour is self-defeating. These cases mentioned above were unpleasant ones, but they were proportionately small. The people most effected were working in a specialist field where the warning signs were clear. On the larger claim that China wanted a far deeper control over universities and the work they did, things are less straightforward. Where these claims of Chinese influence over enforcing what it wanted in regard to sensitive issues became most confusing was through the phenomenon of pre-emptive censorship where the main agent directly was not the Chinese state as such, but people outside that assuming it would respond in certain ways and therefore tailoring their own words on that assumption. The accident (there was nothing very planned about this after all – it was the result of many hundreds of thousands of individual choices rather than some diktat from the Chinese state) of Chinese overseas students being so numerous and financially important in western universities created the motive for this. Western universities had, however unintentionally, a growing dependence on this cohort, and many believed that speaking in certain ways about the Chinese government risked impacting on this critical group. Pre-emptive censorship is almost impossible to prove. By definition, it occurs covertly, in the thought train in a person's head who is undertaking the censorship. Perhaps by surveys one could capture people admitting that they didn't talk about issues, or avoided talking about them in a certain way, in lectures, or their research, because of risks to themselves or their university arising from its dependence on Chinese student money. But it is highly unlikely that this would be very convincing to those most sure of China having this impact if a survey like this contradicted their beliefs, because they could very easily argue that the culprits are all just lying.

The Chinese government is in the business of lobbying, which in effect is what much of this behaviour constitutes. It has the motive, and the means to do this. Lobbying, trying to persuade, promoting particular lines to defend themselves and pushing out favourable messages is the business of governments, corporates and organizations, even down to individuals the world over. It would be very strange if a state as huge and economically important as China therefore were not to be trying to get its way on matters that it regards as linked to its own national interest. And despite China's lack of transparency, the things that matter to it are not hard to spot. Addressing human rights, Tibet, Taiwan, Xinjiang, Hong Kong and China's domestic politics are clearly demarcated issues.

Once one leaves this territory, China is largely silent. It has little interest, and sometimes displays an attitude verging on indifference, to domestic issues in other countries. Disinformation to influence elections was laid largely at the door of Russians during the 2016 American election. China seemed to be mostly absent. That China is lobbying is indisputable. How effective and deep that lobbying is is much more open to question. Once more, we cannot get very far with this issue without far greater precision than occurs in current public debates. That relies on a much better consensus over what China is aiming for, and better knowledge about how it does this.

Power without Responsibility

Surely, of all the things China wants, power is the key. China in this context is a US in waiting, a new global policeperson ready to replace the current superpower. This is the guise the country appears in the more anxious speculations of commentators in the US and Europe. That China has consistently and often vehemently insisted that this is not a role it wants is only taken as even firmer proof that this is precisely therefore what it is aiming for. But against this idea are the clear signs that China is a power that dislikes taking responsibility for others and resists the model of the US with its involvement in security provision globally. It thinks these responsibilities pin it down, reduce its options and cramp its flexibility. It has an almost sociopathological mindset. The undercurrent of its diplomacy is like the Fortune's 1960s song, 'You've Got Your Troubles, I've Got Mine'. If China and other countries can find some happy mutual benefit, that's fine. But its record is largely to do all it can to avoid more direct and heavy involvement, even when presented with compelling humanitarian reasons to do so. Beijing's painful and contorted fence-sitting concerning the appalling invasion of Ukraine by Russia in early 2022 was a case in point – an opportunity for China to burnish its global credentials by using its unique leverage on both sides to get support for mediation which Beijing showed zero interest in pursuing. The only exception to proactive external involvement about issues that don't immediately relate to this is when it acts through bodies like the UN peacekeeping missions.

Part of this unwillingness to be more engaged is the result of historical trends. A brief phase of trying to export what Julia Lovell has called international Maoism in the 1960s and 1970s did not go well.[12] Maoism was either misunderstand, expensive to promote, or ineffective when adopted. On the diplomatic front, things are even worse. China's aid and assistance to Vietnam is a good example. Huge amounts of military kit and help were given to the Communist North Vietnamese during their decade long war with the Americans and the South. But this ended up with a unified country that was both ungrateful, and eventually an adversary for Beijing. The immense sacrifices made for the North Koreans in the 1950–3 war, one in which Mao Zedong's own son died, and which as John Garver argued in a history of Chinese foreign relations from 1949 effectively put an end to the People's Republic's one decent chance to invade Taiwan island, has also resulted badly.[13] The DPRK is a partner that has nuclearized against China's wishes, and has proved adept at blackmailing and pressuring the People's Republic to do things in its own interests, rather than its massive neighbour's. These and other examples give good reasons as to why China might be wary about being sucked into the problems of others.

Nor does it look on the record of the US and its interventions as a happy one. The Afghanistan war from 2001 to 2021 is a classic example – a bottomless pit for American money, vastly consuming in terms of political and diplomatic effort, and ending with an outcome which was diametrically opposite to what the US intended – the swift victory of the Taliban, who had been booted out of office right at the start. China regarded the US's endless interventions in the Middle East through the 2000s as events where the one good outcome was the distraction they provided while it got on with its key work without being too impeded by unwelcome American attention. This was the 'strategic opportunity' referred to above that Jiang Zemin referred to prophetically in 2002. China could only look on with perhaps a wry sense of *Schadenfreude* when it saw the high-minded American attempts to involve itself in the Arab world's affairs during and after the Arab Spring around 2010 end up in chaotic and unwanted outcomes, and a situation in Syria which remains perpetually broken and destabilizing.

China is a highly risk averse and cautious actor on the issue of getting enmeshed in the affairs of others. This ill suits the idea of a global policeperson. It understands that this is a game that it is new to, and one where it is surrounded by uncertainty and threat. Pakistan is a good example, a neighbour whose warm words of eternal friendship are often followed by demands for vast amounts of aid, investment and finance. The country as already mentioned has also had to deal with seeing itself manipulated in the same way as the US and other powers in internal conflicts in Africa and across the Asia Pacific. It clearly regards this kind of acknowledgement of its potential power and influence as unwelcome.

China might want the admiration and respect that the US often achieved in the latter part of the twentieth century, but it puts on a very convincing show of not wanting any kind of highly codified set of responsibilities that might go with that. Of the negative wants that China has therefore, that of not being regarded as some supplier of global security in the way the US often is ranks amongst the most important.

It is holding this attitude that prompts the claim that China is a free-rider. In its own region, it has, since 1980, enjoyed a largely benign and stable security environment that has been underwritten by the public goods supplied by the US. It is the US Seventh Fleet that has largely policed the vast waters of the Pacific, ensuring that partners with a long and lamentable history of conflict and tension between each other, like Japan, South Korea, Vietnam, Indonesia, Singapore and Malaysia, at least focus their energies on improving their economies and putting all their competitive aspirations there. US troops, as stated earlier, are stationed across the region. The security alliances that America has with partners like Japan, the Philippines, South Korea and Australia, and the cooperation it has with places like Singapore and Taiwan, mean that there is a level of predictability, something that China contests, but ironically has enjoyed the clarity that comes from. Instability and war disrupt supply routes, and impact on markets. They create high levels of uncertainty. China with its many domestic issues is averse to this. Implicit rather than explicit, and counterintuitive, but China has historically been a silent supporter of the American led order in the Asia Pacific region, except in areas which regards as its core strategic interests – Taiwan, and the South and East China Sea.

Were we looking at a static situation, no doubt this tension between a China that enjoys benefits from a rules-based order which it also at the same time contests would have some level of sustainability. Issues would always simmer without ever coming to the boil. It would be a world of complaints and grumbles, but not dramatic and upsetting surprises. China could therefore maintain its non-committal stance and avoid anything but economic involvements beyond its borders. There are two great pressures that are now causing this benign albeit imperfect situation to change. The first is that an economically more powerful and larger China defines the space for its strategic interest as being far wider than before. It is growing out of its older space, as its investment, trade and resource globally increase. Once it barely spoke of the South China Sea except as a territory it was interested in and staked an historic claim to. Today, it has the capacity and the geopolitical will to go for something much more ambitious. Accompanying this is the irritation by the US that it has commitments and responsibilities in a region that seems, on the surface, far from its main field of interest. The US is increasingly less interested in being responsible for others. It has its own domestic issues, with a deeply divided population and a political system that is clearly groaning at the seams. Trump was not the first to ask why it was that the US was underwriting in material and in money the security of people across much of the rest of the world. But he was the first to do this as president. However crude and simplistic the terms he used to ask the question, the question itself is a valid one. America's answer will have immense implications for China, whether it likes this or not.

This is because diplomacy like nature abhors a vacuum. The quandary for China is what to do as the world of US hegemony it has berated and moaned about for so long actually starts to crumble around it. The BRI is Xi Jinping's great foreign policy framework. But it is more a hegemony of words and soft expectations, of vague aspirations and win-win daydreaming, rather than hard, concrete action. It does all it can to avoid sharper security issues. In the economics realm, China and its regional neighbours do find some degree of harmony, even though that is sometimes beset by misunderstanding and misapprehension. But in the security realm, everyone has different interests and goes their own way. To the simple question of in what way China, India, Vietnam, Japan and South Korea's security priorities are the same, there could be as many answers as there are countries listed here. India fixates on Pakistan, one of China's most stalwart and dependable allies. Vietnam fears China's intentions towards it, suspicious that it is trying to hedge it in once more to a vassal relationship. Japan harbours its own larger regional ambitions, and keeps close to its own alliances with the US and the West, a country in Asia, but in many ways not of it, with its desire to stand somehow apart and aside from the region it is located in. South Korea is forever having to keep an eye on its northern neighbour, dealing with Pyongyang's mercurial and threatening nature. Where are the common threads that can join all these separate issues together? No wonder it was an outsider – the US – that since 1945 has supplied at least some refereeing role that prevented a major implosion. Even that, as the Vietnam war and the instability in Indo-China over this era showed, was not easy and sometimes came perilously close to breaking down.

These days China's desire to occupy a position of power but no responsibility, repeating its mantra of non-interference and respect for the sovereignty of others, is becoming less and less fit for purpose. The

US's declining interest, and declining economic capacity to fund the public goods it supplies through the Asia Pacific region, is any many ways something that is not in China's interests. It is opening up spaces that are tempting, and perilous. The Afghan debacle in 2021 is an excellent illustration of this. A country with a modern history of almost perpetual conflict and turmoil, it shares a short border with the sensitive northwest part of China, beside Xinjiang. Beijing's fixation with the security threat that might come from Islamic fundamentalist terrorists from Central Asia is one of the rationales behind its draconian clampdown in the Xinjiang region since 2017. It was also a key justification for China to sign up to the War Against Terror of the Bush years, convincing the Bush administration that there were Uyghur-related networks that should be added to the list of recognized terrorist groups. There was much scepticism about these claims. Even so, from China's side it revealed a deepening worry almost verging on obsessions about the threat from its western flank. Academics like Wang Jisi of Beijing university only reinforced this anxiety by arguing that China could not shift all its energies and focus onto its great maritime eastern interests but do something to shore up its land borders and unlock economic cooperation and collaborations into Central and Southeast Asia. He was speaking in the context of the Opening Up the West policy launched by the Jiang administration in 1999 which tried to do something about the imbalances between the eastern and developed part of the country, and the huge, more sparsely populated, less integrated western regions. Tibet, Xinjiang, Gansu, Qinghai, Sichuan, Yunnan – these kinds of autonomous regions or provinces had distinctive, complex and very different histories. They were potential locations of social discontent, but also targets of external meddling. In many ways, the BRI is the outward facing accompaniment to the Opening up the West policy. The two go hand in hand.

With Afghanistan, however, America's abrupt and complete withdrawal in September 2021 after two decades of conflict and involvement, resulting in the swift victory of the Taliban, was a nightmare as much for Beijing as for Washington, though for very different reasons. America had to worry about its international prestige and its reputation as a dependable partner. It also had the humanitarian crisis to deal with. For China, the void opening up in this vast, strategically important country was far more vexing. Unlike the US, it could not put together an international alliance of fellow powers and place a multinational military force in Kabul. The notion of the PLA mounting operations beyond its borders remains farfetched, not least because, even if the Chinese were to explain that they were operating for humanitarian or security reasons, that would never be believed, such are the levels of suspicion towards them. The symbolism of China being militarily engaged abroad on its own operations would be the first piece of decisive evidence its many critics and enemies ranged around the world would need that the country was in fact, as they had suspected all along, an aggressor, an aspiring US, coming to enforce, as the US did, its values with armaments, weapons and bullets.

In this context, Beijing's options are diplomatic, economic and symbolic. But the lack of any viable hard means of influencing the situation in Afghanistan is a huge disadvantage. The Taliban may well have sent personnel to have a friendly chat in the summer of 2021 with the Chinese foreign minister Wang Yi in Tianjin. But it is most unlikely that the Communist Party with its atheism and recent severe domestic campaigns against Islamic groups and the Islamic religion has any deep-seated affinity with the current leaders of Afghanistan. And it is hard to see how the Taliban view the crushing actions against their own fellow believers in Xinjiang in anything but a negative light. Afghanistan could one day be a breeding ground for the kinds of terrorist actions and campaigns that Beijing fears most. The People's Republic is a country where a rampaging knife attack that killed thirty-five in Kunming in 2014, a single incident however terrible that incident was, was the major event that accelerated the series of security campaigns and events that have happened subsequently. One has to imagine what a terrorist attack of the severity and sophistication for instance of the 11 September 2001 ones in the US, or the Paris attacks in 2015, might have on domestic Chinese politics. At the very least, it would be regarded as a major failing by Xi, and proof that the pre-emptive security campaign in Xinjiang had been a failure even in pure security terms, let alone the dreadful human costs that have resulted from it.

China does not want a void of the kind that Afghanistan presents. And yet it has no easy solution to defend its own interests in a situation like this. This kind of example shows that ways in which, just as the Enlightenment West want contradictory things from China, so China wants contradictory things back. It wants to be a great power, able to prosecute its own core interests and needs, enjoying a stable, predictable world around it while it continues to develop its own economy and capacity. And yet these are often things that are supplied by the partners like the US and the international system that China most dislikes and complains about. It presents the classic case of a power that wants its cake but also wants to eat it. Trying to operate with two almost wholly contradictory ideas in its head, it is not surprising that this generates feelings of deep unease and frustration by the outside world. China is a power that enjoys the benefits of the international order, and yet complains about them, and does not have a constructive or positive alternative vision of what might be able to replace them. It is a country that dislikes strategic or diplomatic voids, and yet has nothing to do about these when they appear. In the end, for its critics at least, China criticizes the global order currently, one it has done extremely well in, but either refuses to put forward another version that might work better, or when it does, presents something that would probably work far worse. China's desire for power but no responsibility is a significant geopolitical quandary, for it, and for the rest of the world.

Status

This relates to something that China also wants badly – and that is status. In a study of the geopolitics of emotion, Dominque Moisi wrote of how there is a new hunger in the world – that of being recognized, validated, and perceived as being as important as one feels one is.[14] In academic Richard Ned Lebow's cultural theory of international relations, he writes of the way that the quest for honour, admiration and high status are the main drivers of diplomacy.[15] These are ones that are so powerful that they often override more rational considerations such as managing military threat or securing economic gain. Ned Lebow returned to this theme in a recent book co-authored with a Chinese scholar where he identified the egotism and hunger to be admired as the common points between the US and China, and the real source of the tensions between them. In this regard, the problem is that they are so similar to each other rather than dissimilar.[16]

The performative nature of Chinese diplomacy is very striking. It has long been accepted that the notion of a Chinese 'face', a kind of social reputation that needs to be defended and guarded, and that can easily be besmirched and undermined, plays an important role in the country's diplomacy. This has been labelled 'emotional' diplomacy by some scholars.[17] It manifests itself when Chinese leaders complain of their people being 'hurt' by the actions or words of others. Britain often got this when it did things on Hong Kong before 1997 which were seen as against Chinese interests. Hurting the feelings of the Chinese has increasingly high costs. Companies like Zara were found guilty by online nationalists of speaking up on the Xinjiang issue in 2021 and had their products boycotted. So did those who were accused of doing advertising campaigns that were considered offensive to Chinese people. This resulted in steep declines in a company's business, demonstrating the power of the Chinese new consumer. It showed too the perils of taking the Chinese love of status and respect lightly.

Everyone likes to be liked. But there is a particular intensity for the Chinese version of this. Within it lurk issues of cultural pride and a sense of an unjust modern history that was undeserved and now makes the moment of deliverance even sweeter. Here, China, the Middle Country, returns to the key global position it believes it once had and deserves to occupy once more. This was Liu Xiaobo's point when he said that the desire of modern Chinese leaders was simply to lead their country back to where they thought they belonged, 'the center of all under heaven'.[18] This was a grand, startling claim. It was also one that indicated not just confidence by China, but a measure of condescension towards everyone else. This dynamic is crucial to note, because status is not just about claims a nation makes about its own greatness, but about the attitude others have towards it. There is no point being on a pedestal unless others see you there. In the Xi era, China can indeed dare to dream about its role in the world in ways that in the previous period it never did. But it also has to manage with the other side of this – the fact that for its desire to have recognition, it needs others to do the recognizing, and do that in the right way.

China is certainly in the business of being admired. Its landscape is often presented to those visiting it for the first time as one immense advert for what the country has achieved since the late 1970s. When one looks over the Pudong area of Shanghai today and regards pictures of it only forty years before as simply fields and shacks, one can understand why Chinese people regard the vast array of skyscrapers, one of them the second highest in the world, with something more than just pride. This is a monument to their achievement. It shows how their dream to be respected and looked up to is backed up by real evidence. The problem is when this thirst for the validation of outsiders becomes close to an addiction.

China's hunger for recognition is an interesting phenomenon. For all the confidence in the tone and posture of the Xi era, this desire for praise and recognition by outsiders is never far from the surface to the extent that it is almost pathological. The novelist Anthony Powell wrote once that flattering an egotist never worked. They were too busy luxuriating in their own high self-regard to bother hearing anyone else validate it. The US often seemed in the past like this to outsiders – happy enough if people express admiration for it, but largely indifferent to their positive or negative views for the simple fact that it itself is assured of being number one. For China, the national self-image is clearly more fragile. It not just wants to be admired and liked but needs this. That accounts for the huge amount of effort expended on soft power in the 2000s. It accounts for why the 2008 Olympics was such a harsh moment for China – with the tens of billions of investment and the high levels of razzmatazz getting in return a qualified to largely negative response from the outside world. Since then, this sense of victimization and being unfairly treated has intensified as China has failed to receive the admiration and status it feels it deserves.

When this comes to getting at least some recognition from the US, this reaches its acme. As Europe has historically had an ambivalent attitude towards China, half idealizing, half demonizing, so China has a split view of the US. Its whole mindset and world view has been framed by the relationship with the US for almost all of the post-world war period. America either dominated by being not present, during the Cold War era when it refused to recognize the People's Republic, or by being almost ubiquitous as is the case today. America's military power, its economic reach, its soft power and the way it created alliances around it, have impressed and angered Chinese more than the actions of any other player. This is not just about geopolitics. Chinese have voted with their feet, consuming American films when the censors let them through, adoring American baseball, loving American brands, sending the largest number of its young who go abroad to study to the US – including many of the children of the current political elite. Some years ago, a Chinese academic – one of the best known in China in their discipline – looked with pained sympathy at a student I knew at a conference we were attending in China where they had just said they were heading to the UK to study. 'Why go there?' they airily declared. 'America is the only place that matters for studying.' Ironically, this was the same place they had written scathing attacks on in their work.

China is not alone in being fascinated with the US. But in the post-Mao era America has clearly been the model for so much of what China has done, despite any attempts to say otherwise. China has in some ways tried to counterfeit the US, at times almost losing itself in the process. Perhaps this was the reason that the country's most important contemporary ideologue Wang Huning's message in the 1990s about reasserting and reclaiming a sense of Chinese cultural and intellectual autonomy in the face of this obsessive interest in America resonated so much. This caught the attention of central political leaders in Beijing.

Wang soon went to join them and work for them. He has been promoting the same basic idea ever since, albeit with rising levels of intensity.

Xi Jinping is the first modern Chinese leader who has not shared this love of the US. He has steered clear of giving any sense of feeling beholden to the world's current sole superpower. This is a sensible posture. Communists and the most archetypal capitalists were never going to make easy bedfellows, even if one subscribes to the philosophy that opposites attract. In the era since WTO entry, as the US moved from a more abstract, remote influence in Chinese daily lives and their imagination to something very present, accessible to tourists and students, and highly visible, a lot of the idealism has vanished. But the memory of that old passion lingers. This feeling is made more piquant by the fact that China's great love for the US went unrequited. Now it seeks through the BRI a publicity roadshow rather than an investment vehicle, for a world of admirers, finding them in Pakistan, Africa, Latin America, and in parts of the region around it. The one partner that is never seen there is that which China most yearns to hear validation from, but almost certainly never will. It's rarely viewed this way, but beyond international relations theory and high-level geopolitics, the US–China relations is best seen as a love story where the scorned party is now out to prove themselves.

Mirroring Each Other

Place two mirrors directly facing each other and you can stare from one side to the other into what seems like an eternally recurring image of the world you are in. For all their cultural, political, social and intellectual differences, China and the Enlightenment West enjoy a relationship where their mutual wants are often the same – investment, trade, technology, cooperation on shared challenges, recognition and acceptance from each other – and yet their frustration is perpetual and getting worse because of the way they frame and see these.

In terms of culture, history and identity there is a profound difference between China and the West. And yet, in terms of their wants and aspirations, the problem is not so much how much they differ, but how oddly close they are. They are both in the business of seeking tangible things that work for their self-interest. They both want affirmation and validation of their status. They want some level of predictability and stability. Their greatest challenges are not each other, but a set of existential threats to humanity where the critical issue is to cooperate and collaborate. This list of mutual desires is rational, and easy to understand. And yet, despite this, they are caught in a seemingly never-ending spiral of antipathy, suspicion, and a conviction that at some point they will experience a clash. It is not the things they want for themselves that is the issue here – it is what they want others to be. Europe's problem is not so much that it does not have, and does not know, it needs things from China. It is that the thing it most wants – China to be other than it is – is impossible. Exactly the same could be said of China – that it seeks in the West affirmation and validation it will never receive. With this diagnostic, perhaps we are now in a position to set China's relations with the world in a more realistic, more stable and more enduring framework.

Chapter Six

THE DARK SIDE OF CHINESE POWER

Beyond the often abstract-sounding, deeply politicized issues of human rights, conveyed through the torturous dialogues between China and the outside world, are very concrete matters of injustice and suffering involving individual people and families. In recent years, of all of these, those involved with Xinjiang, the co-called autonomous region that takes up almost a fifth of China's current landmass in the northwest of the country, occupy a particular position. By 2020, to China's many critics, Xinjiang's plight stands as a monument to all that is reprehensible and abhorrent about the reality of the country's current political system. The most passionate of these describe the management of this region as one akin to genocide, involving fundamental human right's abuses that are eradicating the dignity and identity of a specific ethnic group. This, they claim, is aimed at the Uyghur ethnic group who today compose half of the local population, and who are markedly different from the Han dominated population of the rest of the country in terms of their ancestral roots – primarily of Turkik origins – and their religious and cultural adherence to Islam. In the language of the critics, this place offers the starkest possible warning to the rest of the world of what the reality of Chinese power looks like. Their conclusion is powerful and direct: this is what is coming for us if we don't oppose and revolt against Chinese influence now.

For those writing about, working on or seeking to understand China as it now is, Xinjiang is the most challenging and difficult issue. It brings together problems over radical Islam, terrorism, China's need for natural resources and their sustainability, Chinese Han chauvinism, and colonization. The Xinjiang area has always been a complex one. Called by American scholar James Millward the Eurasian crossroads, it is a place where powers have brushed against each other deep in the heart of inner Asia for centuries. This history shapes its current status – somewhere that combines the seeming opposites of being peripheral, and yet at the same time of central strategic importance. I will not dispute that Xinjiang is a problem or deny the seriousness of abuses there. Scholars like Darren Byler in his powerful and moving 'Terror Capitalism' have given accounts of the ways in which relentless, invasive security measures targeting Uyghur people in the region have destroyed families, communities, and individuals. One of the most poignant aspects of Byler's work is how, towards the end, the network of friends he had made during his stay in Xinjiang gradually started disappearing into the 're-education' camps.[1] Instead, my aim in this chapter is to show the real limits of seeking to influence Chinese power, and how in a case like this, choices about approaches to finding this influence in the outside world are complex, and can sometimes have utterly unintended, and unwelcome, consequences. In essence, the issue of Xinjiang presents a quandary – how do you seek leverage over a power that is economically, geopolitically, and militarily unavailable for the kinds of pressures used on more modest powers. This chapter will show that with China, there are no easy answers, and that while it is fine to condemn, what one actually does about a situation to positively change it is an entirely different matter.

I have spent time in Xinjiang, so have some direct experience. But it was many years ago. My first visit to the area was over the summer of 1995. Back then, the three-day train journey from Beijing to the local capital of Urumqi covered only half the distance necessary to really penetrate this vast space. Once off the train, and slowly getting used to a world without the persistent sound of wheels clattering on iron tracks, the next stage was the far less comfortable bus journey to Kashgar. An oasis visited by such celebrated figures as Peter Fleming, brother of James Bond creator Ian, in the 1930s, this settlement right on the edges of the current People's Republic was accessible at that time either by Russian-built local airplanes for those with money, or sleeper buses for budget travellers like me. The latter continued night and day. Once you got on them, apart from meal breaks at roadside places almost invariably selling Lanzhou Noodles, there was no way of getting off. Finally, when I thought the journey would never end, the bus wended its way into its destination – the centre of the old town, close to the Pakistan border.

When I first visited, despite the vast statue of Mao Zedong standing pointing his outstretched hands from the central square, the place looked like somewhere in the Middle East. My abiding memory was of huge mosques, street markets with piles of raisins for sale, the amazingly tasty lamb kebabs in the darkened restaurants with their Persian rugs to sit on, and the ice cream sold for next to nothing from vendors. This was a paradise for drifters, dreamers and the romantics, so utterly unlike anywhere else in China to such an extent that it did not seem to be part of the country at all. In hindsight, that sense of being apartness was a problem. This was why, the moment they could, the central authorities wanted to make sure Kashgar became far more assimilated. Even then, and without anyone there knowing, its days as a remote, almost half-forgotten haven, were numbered. Old buildings were brought down. New housing put in place. Modernization started to transform the landscape in complex and sometimes destructive ways.

In the 1990s, there were also social and political tensions. There had been protests in the early part of the decade. A few weeks before my own visit, a friend who was based in the town teaching in a university told me of how a local figure accused of being a radical Islamist was sentenced before the huge Iqbal Mosque. He had gone down defiant, shaking his fist at the watching crowd before being bundled away to be executed. Describing it like a city under occupation was not an exaggeration. Those that looked Han Chinese were barely 10 per cent of the local population. The government buildings were heavily fortified and seemed like they were under siege. Everything I saw made me think I was back in the Arab quarter of Jerusalem, with its tiny streets smelling of spices. But all of this trouble figured as constant, barely discernible background noise. There had been nothing like the upsurge of protests in 1987 or 1989 in Tibet, yet.

Despite these darker murmurings, it is hard now not to view that period a little nostalgically, because at least parts of Xinjiang had preserved some of their remoteness from the centre in Beijing. Difficulties with logistics, communication and transport all happily conspired to maintain the area's uniqueness. It was like retreating from the rest of China to a forgotten world. Unfortunately, as the years afterwards proved, it was not forgotten enough. Back in the great hub of Urumqi, quickly tiring of the more standard urban sprawl I decided to take refuge in the beautiful settlement of Turpan nearby, a place where grape vines draped along trellises hung over the walkways underneath. It is also amongst the hottest places in the whole country. The ancient water irrigation works were visible, still working after almost two thousand years. Close by were the Flaming Mountains, sand ridges that had figured in the great classic Ming era novel 'Journey to the West' about the monk Xuanzang's epic journey to bring Buddhism to China a millennium and a half before. This was a reminder that at that time this had been the limits not only of the China that existed then, but of pretty much the known world for it. The only links with what lay beyond was through the trade routes traversing this region, subsequently romanticized as the silk roads.

This was and remains a complicated place with a troubled past. The area broadly covered by the so-called autonomous region today did not enjoy a seamless, peaceful connection with the different Imperial Chinese entities that had existed over the area east to it in the centuries before. That it was currently part of the modern People's Republic of China had an almost provisional, accidental feel about it. It could have easily been part of the USSR, and, for a brief point after the Second World War as Stalin's hand hovered over the territory, very nearly went that way. Such trauma reached far back. The deserted cities that lay a little into the desert near Turpan were haunting remnants of this sometimes tumultuous past – ruined since the Mongolian armies swept through on their way to wreak even greater havoc in Central Asia and Europe 800 years ago. All of this contributed to a sense this area was significant as much as a place of transition as one of settlement. It was an environment pervaded by a feeling of transience. Perhaps that was what made the current Beijing overlords so nervous – an awareness that like all the others who had come here, they too, one day, would move away, leaving nothing but traces on the sandscape.

Even as a someone just passing through, there were voices I could clearly here back then, messages encoded in the language of those looking after me while I was there, which portended more ominous developments in the future. Complaints about the excessive force used by police, a constant sense of wariness and the need to be on guard against speaking too freely and openly about political matters. One student I got to know, trusting me no doubt as a total outsider, complained about how the worst people were the collaborators, those from within the Uyghur community who gave information about activists trying to create a stronger sense of culture and identity for locals. Byler's work, already cited, shows the terrible pressures put on people to compromise in this way simply for survival. One scholar around this time had tried to issue a book detailing the history of the region and been silenced in the process. Another referred to the experience of the Cultural Revolution from 1966 for a decade, with the closing of mosques, the enforced eating of pork for local Muslims and the imposition of social, political and cultural norms that were aimed directly at eradicating Islam as a force in the area. In Urumqi when I got back there after my excursions, it was easier to see it now as a city divided into two almost wholly different communities, the Han, and the Uyghur, existing with other groups like Kazakhs in between, in an uneasy and sometimes mutually uncomprehending truce. The question was whether this was sustainable.

Over the years before my next visit, Xinjiang figured in the press from time to time. Reports of a bomb explosion launched in Beijing by a local radical group which wanted separation from China in 1997 around the time of the death of the paramount leader, Deng Xiaoping was one such occasion. This was something that ruffled the usually placid atmosphere at the centre, and prompted one of the earliest of what became, a decade later, an almost continuous series of large-scale clampdowns. By the time I came back to the area in 2002 I was a diplomat. My visit was only to the city, and only to attend a large conference, with all the paraphernalia that involved. It was during the World Cup. England were into the quarter finals. Things were looking OK. We were allowed out of the conference to watch the deciding match, returning crestfallen to our deliberations once the competition ended in the English team's defeat. The presiding Communist Party Secretary at the time, Wang Lequan, graced the event with a short speech, descending on us amid huge security, and alerting me to just how tight the leash was that this place was being kept on. By this time, China had managed to persuade the US to place two of the local groups agitating for independence on a list of recognized terrorist organizations. The terrifying attacks in America on 11 September the year before had transformed the geopolitical environment in ways unfavourable for Xinjiang. For a period in the early 2000s, though it often gets forgotten today, the US and China were allies in this struggle, and their list of targets partly a shared one. With the ongoing war just across the border in Afghanistan against the Taliban as its priority, Washington was happy for China to keep the situation in its own part of Central Asia stable. Around this time, the central government put huge resources into building infrastructure. It was then that Kashgar was connected by train to Urumqi, reducing the gruelling three-day bus journey to a few hours on a comfortable carriage – and bringing the oasis much more within the central government's reach. Airport construction and urbanization continued across the whole area. With abundant natural resources, including oil, Xinjiang became wealthy on the back of the hunger by the rest of China for energy as the country entered its era of stratospheric post-WTO entry fuelled growth. The question increasingly became, however, to whom this wealth was going. Plenty from the Uyghur community in the area felt it wasn't them. On top of this, they were seeing different parts of their identity and heritage slowly taken away – rights to use their language in universities, rights to having their mosques and other ancient buildings maintained, rights to publish certain things and say certain statements. In various edicts and policy documents, from the most senior political leadership in Beijing downwards, the message went out: Xinjiang was only ever going to develop through becoming economically better off, and the central and local government were making massive investments in these areas. It was all about the economy, and about forging forward with a form of modernization which saw religion, and localism, as impediments, not assets. It was to this phenomenon that Byler applied the term 'terror capitalism'.

The Lull Before the Storm

Despite all this, in the 2000s, Xinjiang did not attract the world's attention in the way Tibet always had. One of the big disadvantages Uyghur activists had was that there was no recognized leader for their movement. The businesswoman Rebiya Kadeer was perhaps the closest the area came to a spokesperson. A successful figure through the 1990s, seemingly trusted by the government, she dramatically fell out of favour because of her refusal to denounce her husband, Sidiq Rouzi, for his work in the US for Radio Free Asia. As a result, she was imprisoned on the grounds of claims she had leaked him confidential material (the definitions under Chinese regulations of this term is infamously broad). Only after pressure from the US and others was she finally released to go to the US in 2005. She subsequently become something approaching a mouthpiece for the Uyghur movement.

But compared to the Dalai Lama, whose role for the Tibetan cause has been so critical for maintaining awareness and profile in the rest of the world, Kadeer is not that well known. Nor is her leadership recognized by many in the Uyghur movement, even abroad. Xinjiang has had no one with the Dalai Lama's standing and charisma. Domestically, the most prominent figure, the scholar Ilham Tohti, was, despite the most moderate pronouncements, silenced by being jailed for life in 2014. Indeed, for much of the last quarter of a century, in terms of sympathy and understanding, and despite a steady, albeit small, stream of material about concerns and abuses in the area, Xinjiang has often seemed to be Tibet's poorer relative. There may have been more worrying reasons for this. As a colleague dealing with human rights issues pointedly stated when I joined the Foreign Office China Section in the late 1990s, 'if there is any news about Tibet on television, we get a sack full of post from the public asking what we are doing. If it is about Xinjiang, we get just a card or two.' They paused, as though pondering something, and then said, 'I wonder if it's because they see Tibetans as friendly, harmless Buddhists, and people in Xinjiang as Muslims, so don't feel much sympathy for them?'

This issue occurred again in the 2008–9 period. The uprising in Tibet in 2008 just before the Beijing Olympics aroused a chorus of international condemnation. It nearly led to the boycott of the August games by some. But the deadly mass riots in Urumqi in July the following year, caused by the mistreatment and then murder of two Uyghur migrant workers in Southern China, which led to over 200 deaths, got a more complex response. Perhaps this was because it had mostly been Han Chinese who had died in the events at the hands of protesting Uyghurs and others. The horror of what had happened got brief attention in the international press. The aftermath of the Great Financial Crisis pushed it quickly down the news agenda. In the following years, this is where it stayed. The Xinjiang issue remained almost under the radar, perpetually of concern, but seemingly being addressed by large-scale investments and central government involvement. Only from time to time were there jolting reminders that this was not an area to remain complacent about. The worst was the horrifying Kunming Railway attack in 2014. There were other events too – a suicide bomb in Tiananmen Square, Beijing in 2013, along with incidents more locally like attacks on police stations. Beijing made it clear over this era that as a result of these it believed it was dealing with terrorists, and that it had the right to do whatever it needed to ensure stability. But despite all of this, nothing was to prepare for the raft of news that came from the area from 2018, which seemed to show that over a million residents of the region had been put in detention centres.

If there is cognitive dissonance between the West and China, the issue of Xinjiang has become the most dramatic example. Both sides increasingly speak and act as though they are addressing different things. One of the first problems with describing the events since 2018 is to find the right language. On the one side, Beijing insists that it is dealing with a terrorist threat, that it has established re-education centres, and that these have been part of a campaign to stabilize, pacify and modernize the area. Taking part in a seminar in Beijing in late 2018 where members of the Chinese government and military were present, I noticed how whenever someone from the non-Chinese side used the word 'concentration camps' they were immediately, and firmly, corrected. Deploying the language used in much of the rest of the world about the situation in the autonomous region (which is what its formal title is) elicits bafflement and confusion amongst those inside the Chinese system. The problem, as I will explain, is that this is not feigned. Chinese officials, and many Chinese people, are utterly convinced that their language is right, and that when the outside world talks of genocide, concentration camps, and human rights abuses, they are not only displaying political bias, but ignorance. This complete clash of mentalities means that even before talking about the issue of Xinjiang, there is a hefty argument about what language to use about it. Frequently, that is as far as the discussion gets.

When two sides have such wildly different perceptions of one reality, as they do in this case, then this is not a problem of one side deceiving or misleading the other. Were that to the case, at least we can say that the deceiver does know there is a singular truth, and that their objective is to conceal or obscure this. On the matter of Xinjiang, the stark reality is that officials there and in Beijing believe their language is truthful, that their assessment of what is going on is correct, and that their critics with their own assertion of a separate truth are simply wrong. Seen in this context, it becomes clear why Xinjiang matters so much. It is the single most powerful issue that shows a profound fault line of world views, underpinned by different philosophies and values and the way they shape understanding that world. The most vehement critics outside of China cite the issue of Xinjiang as proof of the evil intentions of the system and its malevolence. But the Chinese government feels it is acting morally, it is preserving stability, and that it is these people attacking it for what it does who are evil and have bad intent.

With this kind of clash, attempting to give an empirical, neutral description of what has happened in Xinjiang since 2018, one that everyone can agree on, is next to impossible. Work of scholars like Byler refers to very specific, empirical facts, and to the people at the centre of this issue – those living, experiencing, and trying to survive in Xinjiang itself. As he states, for Uyghurs as autonomous agents in contemporary Xinjiang, in external discourse they figure either as potential terrorists and resisters for the Chinese state, or objects of pity for outsiders. 'Of course, the Chinese state authorities,' Byler writes, 'and their proxies want to know everything about musapir (Uyghur travellers) lives in order to dominate them while liberal Western readers might hope to save them.'[2] Neither of these, for very different reasons, commits to wanting to know any independent truth about who Uyghurs are to themselves.

If we go from the many things the Chinese government has stated about its actions over this period in the region we know that it has been implementing measures it believes will de-radicalize religious elements in the local population, with the aim of preserving stability. From satellite images, from first-hand accounts by visitors and those who have come from the area, we know that in order to do this large facilities were built in 2018, and that these contained a significant number of people. We know that the overwhelming majority of those incarcerated were of Uyghur ethnicity, because in its news releases and guided 'information' tours for the few diplomats and journalists allowed into the area, this is what the Chinese government itself has admitted. We know that the work in these centres has involved a large amount directed at the religious beliefs of those inside – Islam, and in particular attempts to eradicate radical Islamist beliefs and behaviours. We know from documents that the *New York Times* and others obtained originating from the Chinese government that there has been meticulous planning over the establishment of these centres, and that they have been run at the same time as the imposition of an expensive grid security pattern covering most of the urban region. We know that a comprehensive network of security cameras and other surveillance methods have been accompanied by the deployment of Chinese officials to visit, and speak, often daily, to a group of families allocated to them.

That is a neutral presentation, mostly taken from Chinese official sources. But it is easy to transfer this to a different framework. Once we do that we might as well believe we have passed through the looking glass. In reports from human rights groups, Uyghur overseas communities, and the international press, evidence has been presented that upwards of a million people of Uyghur ethnicity have been taken to these centres where they have been forced to eat food they believe is unclean, men have had to shave off beards they may have grown, and everyone has undergone lengthy indoctrination sessions in which they have been told that their most intimate and precious beliefs are evil and wrong. Many have been taken from their families, unable to contact them, causing unbelievable emotional and psychological stress. There have been reports of physical and mental torture, and of a harsh daily regime of observation and labour, which brings to mind concentration camps. There have even been reports of forced sterilization and of torture and rape. People have been deprived of any sense of privacy, with their smartphones, computers and other forms of personal communication exposed to outside scrutiny. Even for those not in the camps, the most basic daily liberties in terms of movement and activity have been curtailed, with an overt and covert police presence everywhere. Xinjiang, on this interpretation, has become the world's largest and most advanced hi-tech surveillance society, with face recognition and other tools, and a formidable suite of artificial intelligence tools used to track and isolate people. While reports of actual deaths are largely absent from this story, spiritual and emotional deaths have been a metaphor deployed by many who either have experienced the system first hand, only to escape, or for those who have managed to get out information to the outside world via intermediaries. Language like 'genocide' has been deployed. The accusation is harsh, powerful and stark: a whole people and their culture is being systematically eradicated. This is stability at the cost of annihilation.

Xinjiang is clearly many things, but as these two descriptions of the same situation prove it is above all a monument to cognitive dissonance. To the Chinese government, they are engaged in an act of kind mercy to people who need to be delivered from the fetters of extremist religious belief and backwardness, because they are facing a terrorist threat of existential gravity. On the contrary, to the outside world it looks like a vast act of unjust punishment visited on a whole people. However one brokers between these seemingly irreconcilable viewpoints, there is at least one incontrovertible fact everyone can accept. The operation there from 2018 to 2020 has proved vastly expensive. Whatever the Chinese government did in the region, and whatever their reasons for doing this, by late 2019, the 're-education'/concentration camps started to be wound down because they were simply too expensive to be sustainable. This is one of the most little noticed but important solid facts that come from this issue. Xinjiang proves that repression this complete and this advanced, even for a political and economic system where so many resources and so much control is in the hands of the central state, is simply unsustainable. That, and perhaps that alone, is what made the current Chinese leadership scale back their plans. Like the best accountants in the West, the bottom line is the only significant line to them. That gives a clue to their mindset.

Xinjiang – Why It is So Hard to Find Common Ground

Xinjiang is clearly a serious problem. There is copious evidence of the abuses that have occurred there. The focus here however is to try to understand both what the meaning of this problem is – how representative of contemporary China as a whole, and how influential over other areas of engagement and dialogue – and what to do about it. If we do interpret what is happening in Xinjiang as being so serious that it is symptomatic of the wrongness of China's power per se, a clear sign of its malevolence and moral indefensibility, then that commits to a series of follow-up actions and responses that have profound implications far beyond Xinjiang, and China. In current debates about the nature of China's power, on the surface at least, that is precisely the position many have taken in the public debate. Xinjiang is often thrown at anyone who is seen to speak on behalf, or at least neutrally, about the country and its future role. 'Well, all this other stuff might be true,' they say, about the necessity of it working with the rest of the world on growth, climate change, and public health, 'but what about Xinjiang?' The plight of the region is presented as absolute irrefutable proof of China's unfitness for any international role, and its malign intent. Attempts to think a bit more about the implications of the stance and recognized at least a degree of complexity are closed down with shouts of 'apologist' or, when things get really heated, claims that one is similar to those who appeased Hitler's Germany in the 1930s. Feeling, and in particularly feeling angry, about Xinjiang is fine, and permissible. Thinking about the what the problem of Xinjiang is and what its implications are is all too frequently not.

Is there at least some space where the holders of the starkly competing views on what has happened in Xinjiang in recent years can at least stand, and hear each other out? This includes the people of Xinjiang, the Chinese government, and those who lobby passionately against repression in the region in the outside world. Are there some specific and concrete issues that might be used as a point of arbitration? Appeals to history, for instance, which might supply evidence of the existence of a place with strong identity, stability and integrity, which at least offers the notion that were the current order to disappear an alternative would immediately reassert itself in its place. Alas, it is hard to see this. The territory currently bearing the name Xinjiang does not have either a straightforward historic story nor a clear territorial identity which would support this idea. Unlike Tibet, or even Inner Mongolia for that matter, where there are other areas of overlap, its historical boundaries have dramatically shifted over the decades and centuries, meaning that in many ways Xinjiang operates simply as a name with no clear entity to refer to. Reading through authoritative histories such as that by James Millward in his excellent 'Eurasian Crossroads' makes this abundantly clear. 'The Xinjiang region,' he writes, 'was not an integrated political unit with its current boundaries until the eighteenth century.'[3] This is a reality that fits neither with the Chinese contemporary claims to the area stretching back to the Han era 2,000 years ago are, ('a distortion arising from later historians', as Millward describes this)[4] nor in favour of any other competing group. Many can claim part of today's Xinjiang. No one can clear claim all of it. Millward shows this by plotting a bewildering and often confusing patchwork of different groups and different territories, all of them controlling places that are in what is today's entity, and which could (and are) cited as support for different contesting groups today, but none of them dominant. Even recent history offers little help. One can cite the case of the Republic of East Turkestan, briefly in existence from 1933 to 1934, and then again from 1944 to 1949. But this covered only part of the current Xinjiang area. It is not easy to demand the re-imposition of an order there that never existed in the first place. This is not an issue which one can resolve by purely referring to anything in the past.

Nor is a direct appeal to morality a space where one can find common ground. Critics can say the actions in Xinjiang unequivocally prove the absolute wickedness and evil of the Communist Party. But the Beijing government disregards this and says that it is operating on its own moral terms. It castigates the West, saying they have double standards through their own murderous campaigns of war in the Middle East and Central Asia, also justified in recent years partly as being against terrorism. They go further and say that they have ethical rationale for what they are doing, one that is motivated by defence of majority rights – that while a minority may have suffered, the greater good was preserved. Stability was enforced. The vast mass of Chinese people's interests were safeguarded, even though this involved the sacrifice of a comparatively small number in this remote region. To the liberal entreaties that it needs to hold itself against the standard of how the worst off and the most marginalized are treated, Beijing can answer that its approach, looking after such a vast number of people, ensuring more and more are lifted out of poverty, has served to create greater happiness in the world than the approach of the West, where minorities and small groups all too often dictate standards and terms for everyone, leading to a general rise in discontent and fractiousness. Appeals to a commonly accepted morality therefore do not look promising.

Nor for that matter can the West easily stand as an arbiter here. The greatest problem is that the US, and Europe, in modern history right up to today, have in the name of preserving security and defending their values committed acts that Beijing at least sees as no different to its own in Xinjiang, or even worse. Examples are not hard to find. From 2001, the US, the UK and others, in their endless adventures in Iraq, so horribly and painfully exposed in the aftermath of the Second Gulf War from 2003; NATO in their involvement with Libya at the start of the Arab Spring, where their chief priority despite all the grand sounding words at the start was to get out as soon as they could after going in. A little further in the past things get even worst. Britain's colonial adventures, America's history of slavery and racial conflict, Australia's settlement by Europeans and their brutal treatment of aborigines all figure. The tragedy is that while the West largely makes the most passionate and powerful arguments about the wrongness of Xinjiang, it is in the worst place to do so through its own track record. And those who might be in a better position – Saudi Arabia, Iran, Pakistan, with their closer relations and lack of values clash with Beijing – remain silent about the abuses meted out to their brothers and sisters in Islam.

And to drive a further wedge between the West and China over this issue is the language used about it. In James Legges' great translation of Confucius' 'Analects' the Sage states: 'If names be not correct, language is not in accordance with the truth of things. If language be not in accordance with the truth of things, affairs cannot be carried on to success.'[5] With Xinjiang, there is not just lack of historic and moral common ground, but a wholly divided language by which to refer to what they see. The application of the word 'genocide' to the situation in the area has increased from 2020. The Uyghur Tribunal convened in London over this period which issued its deliberations in late 2021, spent considerable time defining what was meant in international law by the term, and why they felt that some events in Xinjiang justified the use of this. That the word conveys some of the anger, fury and revulsion of people about the situation is evident. And yet the term has triggered savage fury and objections in Beijing. It is a simple equation. If one uses this word, Beijing simply refuses to speak and engage on the issue.

Finally, there is the issue of how one interprets Xinjiang – as a sign of the Chinese government's terrifying powers and reach – or the precise opposite, that Chinese power has severe, clear limits. The management of Xinjiang has been a zone not of success, but of consistent failure, one where Beijing has been forced to use measures that are untried, untested, and fraught with very real long-term dangers. What Beijing has done in the area from 2018–19 has been consistent with this – a massive, high risk experiment, which for a risk-fearing entity is proof that it is the result of desperation, not of confidence. The paradox is that for all the lack of common ground and common language for the world to have a meaningful debate with China about this issue, Xinjiang presents challenges that are simply insoluble by the current Beijing state, and which it would be in its interests therefore to have greater global support to manage. Urging it to use successful ideas from the past management of problematic areas elsewhere like Aceh in Indonesia, or Northern Ireland in the UK, has fallen on deaf ears. It is a tragedy for Xinjiang, for the world, but also for China that those ears have become deaf either through mistrust, paranoia about foreign meddling dressed up as assistance, and through anger at the ways in which Xinjiang itself has figured as a point of attack against the current regime by some (I stress, some) whose key interest is not Xinjiang itself, but to undermine and end the government in Beijing.

The Xinjiang Quandary

For those in the outside world concerned about what is happening in Xinjiang there is a terrible quandary: the more one takes the line of moral fury and condemnation, and paints Beijing in the darkest colours, the less one is then able to exercise any influence over the decisions Beijing takes. Perhaps that is a desirable outcome for some. But it means that the main result is to criticize, condemn and denounce, with no attempt to commit to some way of making the situation in the region better. Xinjiang people, who sit at the heart of this and suffer the consequences, are simply passive objects as the geopolitical fight rages back and forth above their heads. Surely this too is morally problematic – to be engaged in the issue of Xinjiang, and not to think seriously about how to find at least some way of trying to improve the situation there, rather than make it a geopolitical battlefront.

One could argue that moral pressure, sanctions and political condemnation do make Beijing change. Were it to be able to operate in complete darkness with no outside scrutiny, things could be even worse. But the signs of Beijing listening much to the outside world on this issue, despite the evidence that its own policies have proved imperfect, is scant. Its commitment to a security and sovereignty outlook that resists compromises has, in fact, toughened over the years. One of the big changes is how much Beijing can call the West's bluff these days when pressure is brought to bear on it. When dependence lay more on China's side in the past, and when it needed the West, it was willing to make at least some compromises. But these days it can dismiss the threats of companies and governments who say they will delink from it by welcoming them to try doing so. Easy alternatives are hard to find. The stark truth is that, for reasons spelled out elsewhere in this book, co-dependence economically, and in facing global issues, is so deep that cutting off many links in protest is not only hard, but in some cases impossible.

That means that a language of pure fury and rage against China over an issue like Xinjiang risks ending up just as that – language, with no real impact beyond rhetoric. If the West feels the crimes it sees in modern China are so great that it cannot under any circumstances engage with such a partner, then it needs to contemplate cutting supply lines, trade links, all people-to-people contact, all environmental and pandemic cooperation, and putting up a real and virtual iron wall. The imposition of such a wall will have deep human and economic costs for both China and the outside world. It is hard to see any circumstances where a measure as extreme as this would be feasible. That makes contemplating travelling along this route meaningless.

Faced with that stark reality, the West needs to rethink urgently and profoundly how it does engage with China on these, the most difficult issues, to have impact, and to actually work for common good. It needs to stop indulging in the high-minded rhetoric of condemnation and denunciation, and throwing around the strongest possible words, and start to work out what it wants China to do, and why China might want to listen to it. We can either be realists about this and have some hope of seeing positive change in this lamentable situation – or we can idealize and continue to see things carry on as they are. Xinjiang is symbolic not just of the challenges Beijing itself faces in its ability to be a responsible, sustainable nation under its current model, but of the real sincerity and intentions behind western concern and worry about that China. Are we criticizing to see real, positive change – or are we just criticizing. There is a world of different between these two postures.

Chapter Seven

THE GREAT SEPARATION – PART ONE

When one tries to get a taxi in Beijing or Shanghai until COVID-19 largely stopped travel to China from the outside world, there was an immediate issue. Without a locally loaded hailing app, the chances of managing to get an available cab to slow down and pick you up of the street were low. When it rained, and during rush hour, they came close to nil. Those long-term visitors to China could think back nostalgically to the time in the 1990s and 2000s when a foreigner walking along the road was tailed by a fleet of empty taxis making noisy pleas for business. Without the Chinese version of Uber, in recent years a visitor is going to have to either throw themselves at the mercy of a local friend to use their app and get a car or take the subway.

The change is getting deeper. Up to around 2010, using anything but cash in country was next to impossible. Even in the 2000s, the number of places in cities where you could get out your credit card and pay for goods was limited to large shops and international hotels. In the last decade, the situation is precisely the opposite. With a group of high-level Australian officials on a study tour of China in 2018, I remember the amusing moment when we were buying coffees in a Starbucks in Hangzhou. The barista looked baffled when, instead of simply swiping their WePay function on their smart phone and paying electronically, this group of people came from a place evidently so undeveloped that they got out dirty, folded paper currency and settled their bills with that. The cashier took the notes like they had been handed unwanted litter. It had been a while since they had last seen this happen and they were evidently in mild shock.

A similar thing occurred when one engaged in the 'when was the last time you used an ATM cash dispenser to get out money' discussion. In response, most Chinese looked like they were deep in concentration, trying to summon up a memory from way back in their childhoods. ATMs on bank fronts became akin to museum pieces – ones almost only ever used by foreigners trying to get cash out to amuse local store owners.

These are just some examples of how China for visitors is more and more like another world. But these are also symbols of that great separation – of a deeper disconnect between the People's Republic and the outside world. For a brief period some years ago there was a hope that alignment would happen, and China was going to adopt many of the habits and customs of the developed outside world. But in the era of dual circulation under Xi Jinping where the domestic and external market are separated and with the continuing non-convertibility of the Chinese RMB currency this process is reversing. COVID-19 has made it worse, with the unique pursuit of a zero tolerance policy, causing draconian lockdowns more extreme than anywhere else. Before our eyes, China is becoming different. But this is not the difference of the past, where its lack of development and inability to modernize were the main sources of surprise. What we see now is definitely a form of modernity. China practices something that looks and feels and sounds modern. But it is very different to the modernity of elsewhere. The question is whether once more this is all a mirage, a counterfeit, or whether it has an authenticity and durability of its own.

One issue needs to be kept in mind at the start of this discussion. As China stands, it is in the business of either revising or completely undermining and forcing the rewrite of key narratives that emanated elsewhere. We can broadly call these the Enlightenment West's story of modernity. These laid down that this process has to happen in a certain way. This is not an optional, but a scientific fact. It was loudly and famously proclaimed originally in works like Francis Fukuyama's 1992 work 'The End of History and the Last Man'.[1] In a less sensational form, the idea went that once a population reached a specific economic level and per capita figures of GDP growth, then political reform had to follow. The roots of this idea went back to the Enlightenment idea of thinkers like Tom Paine who epigrammatically captured it by saying there was no taxation without representation. This idea showed that economic development had to end with a certain form of political outcome, and that the two were intimately connected. In his book 'China's Futures', American sinologist David Shambaugh stated 'China's future development is ... going to be *the test* of longstanding debates among social scientists over whether political democratization must accompany economic modernization.' (Italics in original).[2] This makes clear that how much China can develop but avoid fundamental political change involves more than just what happens in a single, however very important, country. If China succeeds in resisting this process, the vast edifice of assumptions, models, and predictions about the nature of modernity that many in universities, policy institutes, government and broader society have bought into over the post-Second World War period is thrown into question. It would offer a dramatic paradigm shift, on the model described in the 1960s by philosopher Thomas Kuhn. Ironically, it is here, in the most important area, that the People's Republic is in the business of creating something wholly new, rather than in the other areas talked about in this book – and that in a largely accidental way. Many in the intellectual establishment beyond those who focus purely on China have skin in this game. The People's Republic's act of dissent and its continuing practice of heretical difference is therefore more than a geopolitical issues. It offends against a whole world view and a conviction of how reality should be, one that felt triumphant and vindicated in the 1990s when the Soviet Union collapsed, and Fukuyama issued his declaration that liberal democracy was the tide history was now inevitably flowing in.

If China does prove that a one-party political system is sustainable, and that it can rule over a functioning, expanding economy, then we will need a new theory, or a major modification of what we currently have. Of course, there are many reasons to remain sceptical that China can achieve this. It may be that after this epic blip of the last four decades where it was able to achieve a great balancing act, the course to the hegemony of liberal democracy will continue. As so often predicted, Beijing will be forced to make changes and adopt a more pluralistic governance system. There is nothing to dislike about such a world if it could come into existence. But as of the time of writing in 2022, the confidence that this will be the way things turn out has to be much more tepid than it was even two decades ago. Sometime in the next decade, the odds are still on the world's largest economy being run by a Communist country where there is no competition for organized political power. For Fukuyama and his ilk, this was neither regarded as being a viable end of history, nor even a halfway station on the way there. It is in fact an abrupt disruption.

In contemplating that this might happen, we must stand apart from any emotional commitment we have to this narrative of history ending with the final liberal victory which once looked so certain. Instead, we have to adopt a position where we can observe what is happening dispassionately and figure out how best to adapt and change our views and theories to fit the new facts we are seeing. The philosopher Thomas Kuhn showed that throughout history theories and world views were never easy to move on from, even when empirical evidence was heaped against them, showing they had to be revised or even abandoned.

Paradigm changes are about more than just observing the evidence and mechanically changing ideas when necessary. Feelings, convictions, identities and sense of security are all wrapped up in a complex way to make this much harder.

China Explanation Number One: We are Right: China is Undertaking a Huge Con

For liberals, the situation in China today is confusing. If one sticks to one's guns as a true liberal believer and says that however late in the day, at some point economic development will have to bring about liberal political change, then the longer this doesn't happen the more pressure there is to say why not. The Soviet Union collapsed over three decades ago. How has the Communist Party of China bucked the trend so long since then? In answering this question, one can simply explain things by saying that in fact the liberal posture is right, and China is performing a vast con, one where it relies on luck, guile and mass brainwashing to keep it in power, while misleading the outside world by refusing to be open and transparent. It is a fake capitalist, using the guise of economic openness but in reality being a standard Communist actor. This trick has been done through vast expense and huge effort by the Party state and is not about serving the market but solely to maintain its own power interests. The attraction of this is that it proves that once one sees past appearances, western critiques are correct. It also underlines how China is only able to maintain this trick because as number two, it can evade responsibility and be dependent on others to prop up the global order it relies on so heavily. Once China is pushed into prime position and needs to take up many new responsibilities, the great moment of exposure will come. History has just taken a little longer to reach its conclusion than was originally expected, but it still triumphantly gets there.

The notion that what China is, and what it has achieved, is inauthentic and a mirage is a widely shared one – and not just by critics outside the country. The writer Yu Hua made 'bamboozle' one of his ten key words for the contemporary PRC. 'Huyou' (忽悠), the Chinese term for this, had, be said, become something akin to a national pastime in the reform era. It had 'already insinuated itself into every aspect of our lives. If a foreign leader visits China, people will say he's "come to bamboozle," and if a Chinese leader travels abroad, people will say he's "gone to bamboozle those foreigners."'[3] Perhaps a more poetic way to put this is contained in anthropologists Caroline Humphrey and Frank Bille's book about the Sino-Russian border from 2021. Comparing the cities of Hehe on the Chinese side, and Blagoveshchensk on the Russian side, the authors state that inhabitants of the latter see the very new skyscrapers and other symbols of development and wealth facing them in their neighbour as 'a glitzy façade of modernity, barely concealing poverty, dirt and a rural, uneducated population'.[4] This, the description continues, is tangled up in the end with the ways that Russians in the Siberian area also see the almost ostentatious visibility of Chinese material development as a trigger for their own failures and relative decline. Looking at photos of the two cities taken in the 1980s and today it is easy to see why, with the Russian side largely staying unchanged to the point of stagnation, and the Chinese side exploding from nothing to a huge, high-rise city.

The China built on a chimera, a huge empire of fantasy, a Ponzi scheme of the mind is a familiar theme. It recurs across the years when we hear about the imminent collapse of the property market in the country, or the implosion of Chinese growth, and the coming collapse of the whole system. Will Hutton, the British journalist, argued as early as 2007 that China's challenges were so vast and its economic model unsustainable that sooner or later it would go under. It was up to the world to somehow aid China to become better and more stable, so that it did not pull everyone down. In view of what happened merely a year later, with the US nearly imploding rather than anyone else, this proved to be an argument with a short shelf life.[5] British veteran economist George Magnus over a decade later also predicted that, under the very different leadership of Xi, the country was facing daunting challenges that meant it had to undertake comprehensive reforms to avoid a similar demise.[6] There was something spurious, inauthentic and fundamentally faulty about trying to build a hi-tech sector, viable property rights for an emerging middle class, and non-state companies to employ most people without somehow adopting the legal, political and regulatory models that had been used in the Enlightenment West for these arguments.

Chinese debt and loans were a particularly important area. Throughout the era from 1999 onwards these two issues in one way or another figured in news stories and analysis about the country. A problem of bad loans and how to manage them particularly in state enterprises figured in the late 1990s, associated with the Asian financial crisis that had just happened (but which China had managed to avoid) and the severe reforms that Zhu Rongji had just delivered for Chinese state-owned enterprises to make them more competitive and sustainable. Respected American economist Nicholas Lardy referred to the very high levels of non-performing loans at one of the state banks in 2001, stating that the situation was 'alarming' and that the government needed 'to accelerate the restructuring of its loss-making state-owned manufacturing companies – underlying cause of most of the non-performing loans in the banking system – and to develop a fully commercial credit culture in its state-owned banks. If it fails, it will find itself in a full-blown fiscal crisis.'[7] A little over a decade later, a Reuters report referred to the continuing bad debt problem, and how the 'broken system may soon come home to roost. The debt debris is growing as China's economy confronts its slowest growth in a decade.'[8] In 2021, with the problems around property company Evergrande, variations on the same story are still popular. A report from September 2021 stated that the Evergrande problem was the 'greatest test yet of President Xi Jinping's effort to reform the debt-ridden behemoth of the Chinese economy. It could also be the most significant test that China's financial system has faced in many years.' It went on: 'As angry protesters occupied the headquarters of the troubled property developer in recent weeks, some analysts have described the Evergrande crisis as "China's Lehman Brothers moment"', referring to the moment in 2007 when the legendary and long established US bank simply crashed, against everyone's expectations.[9]

Other reports akin to these are easy to find. For every year since the late 1990s, this particular issue of debt and economic unsustainability has been covered, in detail. In 2021, *Fortune, Quartz, Business Insider*, and *Forbes* all carried prominent stories of China's imminent economic demise. In 2013, author James Gorrie issued a book simply titled 'The China Crisis: How China's Economic Collapse Will Lead to a Global Depression.'[10] Somewhat earlier, in his 'The China Dream', Joe Studwell stated that 'history teaches that time and again China has failed to fulfil the promise that foreigners ascribe to her'.[11] He proceeds to list the huge contracts and Memorandum of Understanding that are signed when foreign dignitaries visit China, and then the underwhelming follow-up that proceeds from these. Once more, the sense is given of an edifice built on rhetoric, unfulfilled promises and daydreams.

And yet despite this, in the era from 1999 to 2021 the worst predictions did not come to pass. All the areas that Roger Irvine looked at in his study 'Forecasting China', from environmental to political, economics, were distinguished by 'constant underestimation'. Irvine went on: 'Even those who thought they were being optimistic often underestimated both the strength and durability of growth.'[12] That meant either that China was able to sustain one of the greatest mirages of all history, or that there was something real underneath the things that were regarded as inauthentic. This is not to deny that China's economy presented plenty of challenges and problems. But that it was systematically built on foundations that would one day cause it to be blown away in a puff of smoke or collapse in total chaos was a far stronger claim. In the end, the record so far has proved China was not a faker in all of this, even if it did some things in strange, unorthodox and puzzling ways. They were no fantasies that people were gazing at when they looked at Chinese skyscrapers, but real buildings which, if you kicked them, proved they had solidity and foundations. The con was mainly in the heads of those who even after kicking, still persisted in claiming that it was mirages standing before them.

Within the metanarrative of the Chinese mirage economy there were some amusing subsidiary stories. Ghost towns were a popular bandwagon from around 2010. It is true at this time that there was a haunting, empty quality as one drove around the periphery of even the better known, larger cities. Xian in late 2011, when I was being driven out of the city, seemed to fall from the brightly lit magnificence of its ancient centre into spooky darkness amongst the endless rows of newly constructed residential blocks marching out towards what was once the countryside. These were part of the 60 million or so empty apartments reportedly dotted across the country. Ordos was amongst the best known. ' In Inner Mongolia a new city stands largely empty,' the BBC reported in March 2012. 'This city, Ordos, suggests that the great Chinese building boom, which did so much to fuel the country's astonishing economic growth, is over.' Describing the vast newly erected urban landscape around them, the correspondent went on, ' [A statue of] Genghis Khan Plaza is flanked by huge and imposing buildings. Two giant horses from the steppes rise on their hind legs in the centre of the Plaza, statues which dwarf the great Khan himself. Only one element is missing from this vast ensemble – people.'[13] And yet, by 2016, another report, admitting that the myth of the perpetual empty cities like Ordos, 'built for nobody out in the middle of a desert' was 'a fascinating, chilling story' with one huge problem: 'It's simply not true.' They went on, 'The real story is perhaps more matter-of-fact, mundane, and less worthy of hype. It consists of a mining boomtown building a new district on a long-term timeline in a period when hundreds of other cities across the China were doing the same thing.'[14] The 'matter-of-fact' story of course would not get the click-through traffic on the internet that the ghost myth does. And yet, it seems that the 2016 Forbes report saying that the city now had 100,000 daytime residents, 80 per cent full time, was true. By 2021, another report said that demand for properties to live in was so high there were now new plots being built on in the city. As a neat metaphor of the illusory quality attributed to Chinese economic results anywhere, this would be hard to better – the ghost stories, and the phantom collapse, that were largely interpretations of a complex issue as a very specific time before the more complex reality indecorously interrupted things.

China Explanation Number Two: China Has to Democratize

That China had no choice but to adopt some form of democracy, for all the material results of its successes economically and developmentally in the first decades of the twenty-first century under one-party rule, is another theme that has also proved long lasting. It is one that has been exhaustively discussed. Larry Diamond has been amongst the most powerful and eloquent proponents of this idea. In 2012, months before Xi Jinping was made party head of the Communists in China, Diamond wrote an article in the *Atlantic* simply titled 'Why East Asia – Including China – Will Turn Democratic Within a Generation'. Following on from the wave of reforms that had happened in the Arab world from 2010, Diamond wrote that ' If there is going to be a big new lift to global democratic prospects in this decade, the region from which it will emanate is most likely to be East Asia.'[15] Referring to one of the more fanciful of geopolitical predictions made by Henry S. Rowan in 1996, which stated that the People's Republic would be a democracy by 2015,[16] Diamond stated that 'China cannot keep moving forward to the per capita income, educational, and informational levels of a middle-income country without experiencing the pressures for democratic change that Korea and Taiwan did more than two decades ago.'[17] Seven short years later, such sunny predictions had become decidedly cloudy. In a podcast in 2019, the same author argued that China's authoritarianism had become a threat to democracies in the rest of the world.[18]

I am not mocking those (and there were plenty of them – Bruce Gilley, for instance, a journalist turned academic is another good example, devoting a whole book to the subject of the inevitability of China's democratic future published in 2004[19]). There is a very good reason to not do this. I too believed strongly that as a middle class rose, as per capita GDP increased, and as people became consumers and citizens in China they would also be stakeholders. This need for participation in decision making would have to lead along a road of democratic change. In 'Ballot Box China', a work I produced in 2011, I drew on a journey I had made to research how foreign support for democratization was going in the People's Republic. Despite the significant setbacks experienced in the Hu era, and the brutal crackdown on the China Democracy Party a decade before in 1998, the raft of village elections that had occurred since the 1980s, and the township elections that began a decade later, along with rumours of even party positions being subject to multi-candidate competitions, I accepted with many others that at some point the ruling Communist Party would need to bite the bullet and do what it had been putting off for so long – hold meaningful multi-party elections. Taiwan was the model for this, moving from martial law in the 1980s to the embracing of political plurality and then, in 1996, the first ever open elections with universal adult franchise for the president.

At the back of my mind, however, was the idea of how difficult the road along which China had to travel to achieve this was, rather than whether it would be able to avoid doing it. My visit around China talking to different kinds of actors and officials in 2010 had been commissioned for the World Movement for Democracy. In the report I later submitted to them, I wrote that 'While willing to experiment in areas seen as largely non-problematic, the leadership of the Party is clearly very unwilling to be bolder and experiment more.'[20] My final words of the report were 'My strong impression is that in this area, the CCP, and only the CCP, can address its own problems, and it will only seek help and assistance if it feels it is strongly within its own interests.' Alas, that proved to be true. This in many ways is precisely what Xi Jinping's leadership chose to do two years later. In 2022, they have not changed their position.

That it is an *a priori* rule that a wealthy, developed country must, therefore, have a democratic system of governance is now looking less tenable than ever before. At most one can say that for a period over the decades after the Second World War, democracies were in the ascendent. Freedom House plots this. It also plots the decline in either the quality of that democracy in already extant ones, or the falling back into non-democracy of other places (Myanmar will be a sad addition in 2021, with its reversion to military rule earlier that year). Victory in the Cold War produced a conviction verging almost on fanaticism that there was only one path to go along. This then acquired an underpinning theoretical justification, meaning that language loaded with imperatives and quasi- scientific levels of certainty appeared. It is easy to understand why lobbyists and politicians would fall into this discourse. But for those whose business is to be professionally sceptical, there should have been more self-criticism and scrutiny. Were we believing what we wanted to believe, or what we should believe because we had good evidence and were interpreting it well? As of 2022, we are going to have to adopt a far more circumspect attitude. Xi Jinping's China may be swept away by immense instabilities and fractures tomorrow. Larry Diamond and others may be proved right. China in the end may only have one path it can go along politically. If there is political revolution and change, the Xi era will be seen as the last hurrah of a broken system. But at the moment one can be permitted for being unwilling to commit too deeply to this outcome. China will change because socially and economically it has been changing every day since the 1980s. But it is also likely that it will also come up with something very different than the kinds of futures predicted for it politically by the Enlightenment West's theorists. Many of the confident predictors in the recent past like myself will also have to search deep in their souls as time goes on and the big changes expected don't happen to admit that the evidence base they were making their assumptions from was very narrow, that they were operating with a self-created paradigm that was simply that – created by themselves, and therefore modifiable to the point of no longer having any meaning at all. There is more in Heaven and Hell that is dreamed of in our philosophies, as Shakespeare's Hamlet wistfully said. The same seems to be true of viable political models developed economies can run on. This is not a happy conclusion, nor a comfortable one. But as someone once quipped, the truth will make you free, but before that it will also make you deeply miserable. China's democratic future, and the notion that it must at some point change to become like the Enlightenment West has never looked more like a myth than it does in 2022.

Golden Rule of the Enlightenment West: Always Ten Years Too Late

The pushback against China under the Trump presidency from 2017 had some strategic sense. Vice President Mike Pence's statement to the Hudson Institute referred to before in 2018 contained a long list of grievances by the US against China, many of which held water: IP theft, unfair trade practices, cyber spying and other forms of espionage, refusal of China to open up its markets to western companies in the same way as it was able to enjoy their markets. The list went on. All of these were linked by one common characteristic: an underlying sense of lack of reciprocity between the West and China with things loaded in China's favour.

This lack of reciprocity has its own monument – the vast trade imbalances on China's balance sheet with the US, and most European countries. Economists can argue about what sort of meaning to impute to these figures. Who wants to be the world leaders in manufacturing small value, high volume, polluting and low technology products, as China sometimes was in the 2000s? Even so, as a tangible symbol of an imbalance that is perceived (and here perception is everything) as unfair, the vast figures in China's favour of greenbacks flowing into the Beijing central reserves arouses visceral levels of anger and frustration in Trump and his allies.

The new partial trade agreement between the US and China concluded just before the pandemic in early 2020 was heralded by Trump administration officials as being part of a grand new movement to rebalance things, and to stop what was claimed by the White House to be China's theft and trickery in the global system. In their view, engagement in the 1980s and 1990s was an act of faith, predicated on generosity from the US and others in terms of trade, exports, technology and other kinds of aid assistance, leading eventually to the political change discussed in the previous section. But by the 2010s, particularly once Xi Jinping came to power, all signs of this change happening disappeared. Engagement by that time looked like it had been a noble punt. But it had not been a successful one. Now it was time for the Leader of the Free World to organize his troops in a fightback. Closing down different parts of the West's economy to unfettered Chinese access and a more confrontational, hard-nosed approach to working with China ensued.

There is one huge problem with all of this however. Speaking at a conference in Europe I attended in 2018, a former high-level security analyst when addressing the challenges posed by Huawei and what the rest of the world needed to do to counter these, put the futility of trying to close the company down succinctly. 'We are a decade too late,' he said. 'We could have done something back in the late 2000s. But now it has so many other options. European and American markets are no longer central to its profit. Back then, they were. So was our technology. We had leverage. Now we don't.' If there has been a consistent golden rule over the last three decades of dealing with China that characterizes American and European behaviour, this has been it. In countering China, whether in the security, economic or diplomatic fields, the story is the same: we are always five to ten years too late. We are forever busy shutting the stable door and securing it with sturdy locks long after the horse has bolted.

One of the most important examples – perhaps the most important single example of the last half a century regarding the Enlightenment West and China – revolves around the opportunity offered by the Tiananmen Square unrest in 1989. If there was a moment when the US and its allies could come good on their commitment to seeing full political change in China and an ending of the Communist Party's monopoly, then this was it. If the language about the West wanting Communism to collapse and believing passionately in the preferability of democracy was true, then 1989 was a chance to show this. It was not an easy chance, and prosecuting it by supporting those who wanted the political system in China to change would have been vastly risky, and carried massive costs. But the depth of commitment to its convictions no matter what by the Enlightenment West was the issue here. If it had real confidence and sincere belief in the rightness of political change per se, then the costs would have been worth it, and the risks could have been borne.

What is striking however is that events in Washington and elsewhere in the Free World over that tumultuous summer proved the kind of fervent desire they had often expressed for political change in China had severe limits. There were clear parameters. The then president George H. W. Bush, only a matter of days after expressing the most powerful condemnation of the butchery the world witnessed in the early hours of 4 June in central Beijing sent out feelers to the Deng leadership. As Robert S. Ross showed, the priority was to maintain stability and to ensure that America's interests were preserved.[21] The same applied to the Europeans. One can never prove counterfactuals. But one of the more intriguing 'what ifs' of modern times would be about whether a concerted and powerful, unified pushback by the outside world would have created enough confidence in the more reformist arm of the Communist Party at that time, which, along with foreign support for the government's opponents would have seen the uprising spreading to the point that it became unstoppable. These are massive 'ifs'. What we do know from confidential material leaked and then published on afterwards is that the elite leadership were divided about how to deal with the protests, with some proposing a more conciliatory line.[22] There was also sympathy amongst parts of the armed forces. In this context, perhaps a sense that the outside world was on their side and would stand by them might have emboldened people who were agitating for change. It might have meant that the crackdown on 4 June when tanks rolled into the central square was followed by a far less systemic purging of the system, as different parts of it wobbled and questioned their allegiance. The vulnerability of the Deng core leadership was considerable. This was the one moment since 1949 when they were on the backfoot. But rather than act, the outside world simply watched. It did not prosecute any positive policy and set of accompanying actions that worked with those trying to achieve change within China. In the end, when the moment to display decisive commitment came, Chinese democracy activists could see that the US and its allies were more about talk than doing anything. And while in the months and years that followed many activists were able to get to the US, the subsequent careers of key rebellion leaders Chai Ling, Wuerkaixi and Wang Dang have not been particularly happy or successful ones, at least as far as promoting reform back in China. 1989 was an opportunity, albeit a very slender one. In the years that followed what it showed was that while the Enlightenment West had conflicted and often contradictory desires and views of China, if there was a default it was to support the economic and business opportunities, and the narrative of a country that was working for the West in terms of providing current or future material benefits. The loftier goal of sacrificing this for some more complex, political goal was easily sidelined, or even lost sight of. 1989 lamentably proves this.

This is a hard thing to admit today. We can only remember the brief exhilarating moments when the Goddess of Democracy, modelled on the US Statue of Liberty and created by students at an art college in Beijing, towered hauntingly over Tiananmen Square. We can remember too how that vast square was full of protesting Chinese people, and the tangible whiff of a real, historic change was in the air. Those images remain intoxicating to this day. In the decade that followed 1989, with US partnership and contribution, China finally recommitted to economic opening up and reform. That soon pulled its economy towards a path where it could placate at least most Chinese people with material benefits. The 1990s saw house ownership reform, the dismantling of most of the state-owned enterprise system, and incremental opening up to larger and larger amounts of foreign investment. While this was happening, Chinese leaders were able to observe, first with deep consternation, what happened in the USSR once the Communist system there was swept away. This, they could reflect, would have been China's fate if it had heeded the advice of the foreign advocates for its own liberal reform in 1989. The Russian state fragmented and its economy imploded. Western advisers came and sold reform ideas which helped to enrich foreign consultants, but resulted in the rise of the oligarchs, racing inequality, and the miserable side effects of collapsed male life expectancy rates and social issues like rampant alcoholism, increased poverty and ubiquitous corruption. Boris Yeltsin personified this deep malaise and rot: a leader whose brief moment of heroic purposefulness when the USSR actually fell apart soon degenerated into him becoming an international laughingstock, often so incoherent and drunk at summits and conferences that he was barely able to function. The tragedy of Russia in this period gave rise to the wry joke that the only thing worse than Communism was what came after it.

Over this period, in the Great Financial Crisis of 2008, and the COVID-19 chaos from 2020, the Chinese government has managed to reinforce its mindset that far from being on the 'wrong side of history', as President Clinton solemnly intoned during a visit to China in 1998, it has been right. The Enlightenment West's interference in Russia delivered poor advice, advice which was characterized by arrogance, self-interest and hypocrisy. Even liberals in the Chinese system had to undertake deep soul searching, and acknowledge that whatever path China was on, it was best to travel this on its own. The key activists from the democracy movement that did go abroad were often a sad advert for how incoherent and fractious they were in turning ideas into action. Once able to form pressure groups to try to lobby for change back home, they were riven by internal arguments, squabbling, personality clashes, and sometimes profound mutual antipathy. A few of the most prominent individuals maintained some levels of dignity. But the fact that on the whole they offered such negative role models was one of the reasons that Liu Xiaobo chose to stay in prison domestically, and maintain at least some moral standing, rather than take the option of being sent abroad into exile and irrelevance.

Dual Circulation – China says 'We Have Had Enough'

The Dual Circulation policy that appeared in 2020 was interpreted at the time that Xi Jinping launched it as being a counter-response to the closing down by the outside world towards it. Now finally there was a united front against China similar to the United Front that China had been working on in the outside world, restricting its space, frustrating its grand ambitions for dominance, cutting it down to size. COVID-19 was the great revelation – a stark illustration of the danger that the country posed, a crisis caused by its government's love of secrecy and lack of transparency. The world was now able to see it clearly for what it was – a threat, against the values and way of life of the Enlightenment West. Even the original agitator for Brexit, the political opportunist and populist rabblerouser Nigel Farage in the UK was able to declare that dealing with the threat of China now merited his serious attention. It had become the Next Big Thing.

We have heard plenty about the fury, frustration, disappointment, anger and dislike of actors from government to media to other areas in the Enlightenment West in particular. By 2020, the narrative of 'dealing with China' and standing up to it has become a well-developed one. If figures like American author and key Trump ally Michael Pillsbury and former US politician Newt Gingrich in the US start feeling that contributing their soothsaying wisdom to foreseeing the coming conflict with China, and how the West needs to win that, is worth their important time, then clearly something immensely important is happening. And yet, the other dimension to this is less noted – the fact that the party being spoken about is investing in greater separateness, and welcomes barriers coming up as much as those talking about erecting them. This is unlikely to be a popular observation to make while western political figures busily parade their newly acquired set of opinions about how China needs to be dealt with in public, but their frustration is fully reciprocated with a wholehearted weariness and impatience on the side of many Chinese. Wolf Warrior diplomacy has been interpreted as China showing its true, intemperate colours to the outside world as a bullying, domineering and arrogant player. In fact, this phenomenon equally well represents total frustration, and utter disillusionment at a series of partners who have gone beyond addressing it with any civility. Once more the West is being mirrored here – but seems to have lost sight of the idea that copying is a sincere form of flattery.

China has been growing increasingly upset for a while. What we see is a culmination. In the 2000s, nationalists wrote a book in Chinese, 'Unhappy China'.[23] There they described a country which was fed up with its position as the global whipping boy, always being consigned to a subsidiary position, producing the cheap products for a greedy, ungrateful mass of western consumers, and yet constantly blamed for everything from pollution in California to colonization in Africa. Over a decade later, China may or may not still be unhappy, but it is certainly more frustrated and irritated than ever before at the outside world. This has reached such a level of intensity that there has been a formal policy response: 'Dual Circulation' – a strategy in many Chinese people's eyes to simply get whingeing, moaning, sore losing Westerners with their toxic social media, their crazy political systems, their moralizing and ignorance and arrogance, off China's back.

'Dual Circulation' has two prongs. The technical, neutral description of these is to firstly rely more on domestic consumers and the second is to create larger amounts of China's own technology and make the country autonomous through innovation. For the first of these, the political reason is to aim for liberation from the reliance on fickle, and dwindling, western markets for Chinese goods. For the second, it is to remove, as soon as possible, dependence on western technology with all the hurt to China's self-esteem and the impact on its strategic flexibility that reliance brings. Dual circulation is a relatively neutral way of telling the West to push off. It places what is emerging as China's greatest new economic asset centre stage – its own middle class. These are the producers of something long heralded and hoped for: rising domestic consumption. Consumption levels in the People's Republic for much of the last four decades has stubbornly sat at a third of GNP, only half that of US levels. This are the most significant source of potential future GDP growth, but one which continuously frustrates the hopes to see this happen of not just the Chinese government, but companies in the outside world who want to sell to them. Napoleon reportedly said (though no one can find out where this actually was) that when China stood up, it would shake the world. This phrase can be updated. When Chinese consumers start spending, they can shake the world. Before the pandemic, they literally did – often constituting the key high spending purchasers in places like the boutiques of the *Champs Elysee* in Paris, or Oxford Street in London. The Chinese middle class are also service sector working, increasingly urbanized, and highly global. They are truly a giant which is slowly waking up. Their purchasing decisions can make companies like Apple whose products they have favoured in the last decade have a current worth of USD2.2 trillion, ranking it the world's sixth largest company in 2021 according to *Fortune*.[24] Of that, about 14 per cent of their income annually comes from the People's Republic, though historically this has been as much as 25 per cent in 2015.[25] Dual Circulation recognizes the core importance of this internal source of growth, but also how critical it will be to keep the profits and benefits as much as possible within the country. In the past, much growth was generated by using cheap labour to manufacture goods for sale to the consumers elsewhere – particularly in Europe and North America. But now, with sweet irony, the core challenge is for China to sell to itself.

That explains too why there is a premium on strengthening indigenous technology research and levels of innovation. Once more, the assumption by many was that the freedom of speech loving, critically enquiring Enlightenment West would continue to be the key player into the future in producing the greatest number of worthwhile, high value patents, and the largest number of Nobel Prizes. When Tu Youyou was awarded the Nobel Prize for Physiology and Medicine in 2015 for discovering a treatment for malaria, she was the first Chinese person still resident in the People's Republic to gain a science-focussed award from the Nobel committee. This is a disappointing performance, particularly in view of the effort and investment that the Chinese government has put in to getting validation from what is regarded as the ultimate western prize-giving body. It has served as an apt symbol of the country's knowledge deficit. With the 14th Five Year Plan from 2021, however, annual increases of at least 7 per cent of GNP until 2025 were promised in Research and Development (R and D) in order to address this. Bearing in mind that in 2020, according to Chinese government data, this amount was USD378 billion, that means the figure is likely to climb beyond USD400 billion very quickly.[26] Even before this commitment, China was second only to the US in how much it was spending on R and D. In 2019, it spent ten times the total for UK.[27] It is hard to imagine that this amount of investment will lead to no useful outcomes. At the very least, it shows the country's absolute commitment to bringing the day forward when they can use the words to the current technology leaders that Emperor Qianlong had said to Lord Macartney in his famous letter of 1793: 'We have no need of your ingenuous manufactures' – with the added clause 'because we have plenty of our own.'

A New Cold War?

In 2022, with the Clausewitz-like chaos of words and confusion of action and constant new developments occurring at high speed, we are in an era of rising contention. The threat of conflict seems real. But the greatest confusion reigns about what sort of description we can supply to this situation. Of those currently used, the notion that we are all in a 'new Cold War' is amongst the most common, and amongst the most pernicious and unhelpful. There are many reasons for this. Firstly, the idea of a Cold War comes laden with historic burdens. It refers back to the first play-off between the West and a Communist country, the USSR. In that sense, it places a binary struggle between two political ideologies to the fore, making it seem that this sort of Manichaean conflict is inevitable, and that it will always be a zero-sum game. This commitment to strict binaries is not helpful because China does not sit easily within such a framework. It is not easily seen as a communist country in the same way that the USSR was, for a start. It has a more complex, hybrid set of values, and has a form of communism that clearly allows it to engage with capitalist practices in ways far more unnerving and radical than anything the Soviet Union ever managed. Even for those who therefore subscribe to it being a threat and an ideological opponent, using the Cold War template paints China as a more straightforward opponent than it is. Wrongly assessing someone in this way creates many problems, not least that it means responses are often ineffective and unfit for purpose.

The Cold War 2 narrative misreads lots of other things that make China's global role very different to that of the USSR. The USSR was often keen to export the ideology of Marxism-Leninism in ways that China, I have argued before in this book, is not. Nor was the USSR ever into the business of integrating itself in finance, investment, trade and business flows in the way that China is. The USSR barely registered in the economic life of the West. Its ultimate collapse in 1991 witnessed an economy that was largely parallel to and unconnected to that of the America and Europe. The greatest headache for even the most zealous of those urging the world to take China on is what to do about these immense mutual dependencies across areas of manufacturing, economic benefit, and capital and investment flows. This means that were a conflict ever to occur, even one that ends in a form of defeat for China, this will dramatically and negatively impact on the rest of the world's economic wellbeing.

On top of this is the overall context. The USSR rose and fell in an era we can call the infancy of globalization. There was not the heightened awareness of issues like climate change, or even pandemics, and their worldwide impact as a constant backdrop. While the UN arranged important global meetings on environment in the 1970s, they had nothing like the urgency and specificity that, for instance, the 2021 COP26 held in Glasgow did. Globalization has clearly created at least awareness of a set of issues around sustainability and environmentalism that acknowledge they are either solved by everyone, or they will not be solved. The idea of a Cold War where there is a huge area of issues where one has to continue speaking is therefore not a Cold War along the lines we had before. It is a very different kind of conflict. We need a new term for it, and a new, nuanced way of understanding the kind of complex contention we are seeing.

Finally, the notion of a Cold War 2 is a fatally misleading one for the Enlightenment West because it sets up an underlying narrative of there being a win to go for, and of all that is happening today being a rematch of the previous epic struggle. Fed on thrillers and fantasies, supplemented by the baddies in blockbusters like James Bond films increasingly becoming not just Russians but Chinese the self-proclaimed free world can feel that it is taking part in a sequel where all out victory is where the story has to end. We must remember however that this is the real world, not some Hollywood story board. Cold War 1 is marked down as a victory in the West. But by the Russians that experienced the collapse of the USSR, and all the uncertainty that followed it, and who were able to witness with their own eyes the direct impact, the Cold War 'victory' has been mostly bitter. Cold War 2, the sequel, is a daydream by an Enlightenment West hoping to relive its greatest hits. And having watched the first series, China clearly has no intention of appearing in a sequel that trots out the same story line.

Chapter Eight

MAKING THE DUAL TRACK WORLD WORK

The pandemic offered a chance for the world to slow down. Flights could no longer be taken. Even the busiest people found themselves for the first time in their lives confined to a specific place, time rich as large parts of their diaries were freed up from cancelled journeys or lengthy daily commutes. In this highly unexpected and uncharacteristic stillness, everyone could start to notice things that had been right before their eyes but which had never before caught their attention. Some for the first time noticed nature around them, proclaiming their discovery of this like it was a remarkable epiphany. Others noticed that they liked, or, in some unfortunate cases, did not like the people they had been living with but never spent much time with before, simply because of the restlessness and itinerant nature of their lives. Others through Teams and Zoom discovered that they hardly really knew the organizations they worked for, having happily absented themselves from most of the daily meetings they were too busy to attend, but now having no excuses were being forced to participate online in. Over the period from 2020 there was something akin to the Great Learning spoken of in ancient Chinese philosophy.

In this moment where so much action was arrested or slowed down, it was as though China and the US were two people who, after years of complex bickering and tension, sighed deeply and came to terms with the fact that, for very different reasons, they really didn't like each other. Perhaps they never had liked each other. As Albert Camus presciently said, in love there are two great deceptions – falling for someone that never really exists at the start, and then, when disillusionment sets in, ending up despising someone who never existed either. Of course, China and the US are vast countries, not single people. But the depths of their antipathy towards each other went beyond simple cold, realistic mutual disregard. They realized they couldn't stand each other. That there were once ideals and expectations they had held towards each other only gave their new animosity added bite and depth. This was no momentary whim, but a deeply considered, decisive moment, the culmination of years of simmering spats and disagreements. They had both had enough of each other and wanted to pack up and move out. The only problem was that there was nowhere else for them to go. They were stuck in the same world, in the same shared space, in the same environment.

Let's be clear. The relationship between the US and China and their feelings towards each other are the predominant problems. The rest of the world has to slip into the context they have created. As argued many times in this book, Europe has been enjoying a practiced, knowing ambiguity towards China for hundreds of years. Asia has as part of its regional identity an inbuilt memory of how to get through life with a China that was half admired, half feared. And for Africa and Latin America, they were able to enjoy a position of neutrality, watching for the first time two immense powers slogging it out for the chance to gain their affections and allegiance. But the US has the most issues with China for a very simple reason – that it is the current incumbent of the number one position and so has most to lose if and when that changes. To add to this, it also has the most zealously proselytizing attitude towards spreading its own values and the most capacity to do this, along with a relatively brief history of dealing with China (for the very prosaic fact that as a nation state it arrived on the scene later than Europe). In terms of diplomatic behaviour, geopolitical expectations and general world view, China and the US may as well be on different planets. Perhaps in the hope that one day this might be possible, both have been energetically exploring outer space in the last decade or so. China or the US decamping en masse to Mars might be a fantasy, but it is one that both powers use to alleviate their current deep frustration.

In this situation, we can daydream about one of them annihilating the other – until we recognize that as vast nuclear powers, that would stand a good chance of destroying the rest of the world in the process. We can hope that the Chinese undergo some Damascene conversion and magically change their minds about adopting a political system more conducive to the West – until we realize that if China ended up wholly upending the universal creed of Marxism, whatever democracy it devises is unlikely to be easily recognizable. Maybe the two can just cut their losses, take a deep breath, accept their incongruities, and live in a world where they operate around and past each other, without having much direct interaction. But that would ignore the towering issues of climate change, pandemics and other common challenges that operate above and beyond country boundaries and which they urgently and immediately have to cooperate with each other on.

In discussions over many years about China both in a government, business, academic or other context, I have often been struck by this phenomenon of overestimating our own impact as outsiders. It is like the story always ends up being somehow about us. A good example of this is the notion that it was the Enlightenment West's benevolent charity in kindly reaching out to China and engaging with it that unleashed many of the changes that have happened since the early 1980s. This idea was behind the words former US Secretary of State Mike Pompeo used when speaking at the Nixon Library in June 2020, where he stated that 'The kind of engagement we have been pursuing has not brought the kind of change in China that President Nixon hoped to induce . . . The truth is that our policies – and those of other free nations – resurrected China's failing economy, only to see Beijing bite the international hands that fed it.'[1] This idea of rapprochement being a magnificent gift that the US and its allies handed to China runs along the lines of the anthropologist Marcel Mauss who created the concept of 'gift debt'. Gifts, he stated, are objects which 'are never completely separated from the men who exchange them'.[2] They carry obligations and duties the moment they are handed from the giver. China may not have known it, but that day in 1972 when Nixon visited Beijing it was being delivered a responsibility to one day change. That what happened subsequently did not follow along that expected track should give us pause to reflect. Have we not learned since then to scale back our role in this story, and to be modest in the claims we make not only for what we have done, but what we might be able to do?

On top of this, however, we also grant ourselves the illusion of choice. We tell ourselves that in fact we didn't have to engage with China in the past, and that we could have simply ignored it, and that, today, we can shut it out of the global system, and impose sanctions on it that will enforce change we want to see. But did we ever really have much choice about what happened? Wasn't more than half this China story in the hands of the real key players – the Chinese? Did we have much say about how they started to run with economic reforms, and then succeeded at them, creating opportunities we then had to engage with because the costs of ignoring them and opting out were already too great?

China was never a passive entity in all of this, acted on rather than acting. Historians know that even in the period traditionally regarded as when it was most separate and disengaged from the outside world, the country in the later 1960s proactively sought out opportunities to speak to the West. They know that it made a fuss of journalist Edgard

Snow in his visit to the country in 1970, allowing him a prominent position on the podium in Tiananmen Square during a national day celebration, because it wanted to send a message to Washington that it was ready to talk after almost two decades of ignoring each other. Nor should this have been a surprise, bearing in mind the geopolitical and domestic challenges both were facing at the time, many deriving from a common enemy, the USSR. Neither China *nor* the US had much space for choice in finally working with each other. Both had no viable alternative counterweight to the Soviets than each other. Both were facing divided, contentious domestic politics, even though China's was at the time the more dramatic (Watergate versus the Cultural Revolution and the fleeing of Lin Biao, Mao's chosen successor, and his death in September 1971). Both would no doubt have preferred having other options if they had existed. But in terms of size, importance and capacity, the world only has so many powers like the US, USSR/Russia or China. Perhaps the only other comparable one would be Europe – but in 1970, no EU existed (just the far smaller European Economic Community), and the continent was divided by the Iron Curtain. There were no better options to protecting their self-interest than that which happened. The miracle is not that the US and China spoke to each other. It is more that they managed to avoid this for so long before Nixon touched down in Beijing.

The idea of rapprochement and all that flowed from it by the US being some gift that has never been properly acknowledged too is spurious. The US had clear interests, and pursued opportunities that came up with energy and commitment. Its companies were in China from the start of the reform era – Coca Cola was the first joint venture in 1979 between a foreign and Chinese company under the new model with a bottling plant for the drink in Tianjin. Ford and Proctor and Gamble, along with Kentucky Fried Chicken and McDonalds, spread across the country in the 1980s and into the 1990s. These were not charitable, benign, altruistic actions. They were guided by business imperatives and the hunt for financial gain. The problem was not that the US engaged with pure desires and lack of self-interested motives, but more that in the end its endeavours did not generate the kinds of profits and scale of return that had been expected. It is an interesting thought experiment – but if the US enjoyed massive trade surpluses with China in 2020 rather than the other way around – if the tables were reversed as it were – would Pompeo have been so damning on the situation, even if political reform had not happened and the security situation remained the same? The issue is not that China is a failure for democracy that has most hit home, but that it is a success as a capitalist. These are very different sources of resentment. The former is a damage to one's strategy. The second is hurtful to one's pride and therefore far more upsetting.

If we set aside this notion that it was a mistake in the past to choose to engage with China on the part of the Enlightened West, and accept that there was no real choice about dealing with a country that constituted a fifth of humanity (just as Nixon himself accepted in 1968 before becoming president), had nuclear weapons, and occupied one of the key strategic areas on the planet, then we can at least rid ourselves of some torturing remorse that this situation could all have been different. History shows that Chinese dynasties deep into the past had immense impact on the world – either economically, or through their relationships in the region and, at times, further afield. It is hard to see how the processes of modern globalization could have happened with China not playing a role in these in the last four decades. Its absence and non-participation would have posed even larger problems. The issue has always been what kind of role China plays in the world – not that it should or should not have a role in the first place. On that question, there was never any choice.

Once we accept the great constraints that were in place and reject most of the illusory choices we think might have been possible but in fact were not, then we are in a good position to take our bearings. The philosopher Thomas Nagel pithily defined truth as something that is the case regardless of whether the person knowing likes it or not. Whether we embrace or have distaste towards China as it is politically today, we have no choice but to recognize that it is there and that it is as it is. Denying this means we are engaging in solipsism. We will not all wake up tomorrow, like protagonists in some fantasy film, and find China is no longer there, or that it has magically transformed to become somewhere we actually like and feel close to. We can console ourselves with the associated thought that exactly the same in reverse applies to China. They too will not wake up to a world without the US or its allies in it busying themselves by trying to constrain, thwart and interfere. We all have to just deal with this rather than wishing the issue away.

This brings us to the second key thing that needs to be accepted. If there is one conclusion from the lamentable record of predictions and expectations about China, particularly in the last half a century, it is that whoever is brave enough now to say what might happen next needs to be modest and humble, both in what they say and how they say it. Bold declarations of China's global dominance, or its catastrophic collapse, are for the ill-informed, or the underoccupied. If anything, predictions in some areas have erred towards the pessimistic. It is likely that China, at least on this track record, will do better than is usually thought, simply going from the past. But that is a slender empirical basis to try to do much on. China has always been offering surprises – that alone remains consistently true.

The third key issue is the all-important one of narratives. This is not so much about the narratives themselves, as where these came from, who created them, why they did so, and whether the entities they were about ever had much say in the stories being told about them. No one ever sat Chinese leaders down in the 1970s and 1980s as engagement became more intense and said that all of this was predicated on them ultimately doing certain things and ending up behaving in certain ways. The narrative of economic reform leading to political reform, and of that political reform being in a democratic direction, was one that came from the Enlightenment West and served its interests. There was no consultation with China about this story line that was consciously and unconsciously being written for it. In fact, at many occasions Chinese leaders made it explicitly clear they did not buy into this. That today we are not in the place we expected this story to take us is more the fault of the story and the teller rather than of the subject the story was about.

One thing we can do to learn from this experience is to improve our narratives immediately by jettisoning any neat, binary model of good and bad, right and wrong, that we want to inject into them. The two dominant narratives publicly on China in most mainstream western media referred to before – of the place which is a human rights hell, or that which is an economic behemoth that is going to be a source of enrichment for whoever cracks its market, need to go. To have such limited, and limiting, narratives is not only a source of endless misunderstanding and frustration. It is also the main reason why China's complexity continues to irritate, evade and unsettle many in the outside world. We have been using Stone Age tools to address a space age problem. Getting rid of the 'evil/good' dichotomy is a great place to start addressing this.

Finally, there is the fundamental division within the mindsets of many of the elites and wider publics in the Enlightenment West about what kind of problem China is. To see it as an existential opponent, a partner that is looking for not just domination but annexation of the rest of the world, changing the values and beliefs of others so they chime with its own is one kind of problem. A country that is exceptionalist, dissents from the idea of universal global values, does not object to others holding these, but does not subscribe to them itself, and seeks a unique, exclusive space is clearly another. In this latter reading, China is a threat because it is doing what many thought couldn't be done. More negatively, it is a threat because it practices a profoundly self-interested and self-motivated, ultra-realistic diplomacy. But that doesn't mean it wants to annex and obliterate others. It just means it's a problem because it dissents.

Taking all of these factors into account, one thing stands out – the complexity of the issues that China poses, just being itself, and doing the kinds of things it does as an actor of its size and reach. Complexity alone is a vast problem, and one the Enlightenment West in particular, with its love of orderly frameworks and all-embracing, tidy theories clearly abhors. China upsets the epistemology of the West – it violates notions of universalism being universal. This means that even in just being itself, China has committed the original sin of causing disruptions and challenges. It offends against the notion of a global order built on shared ideas of how reality either is or is constructed. China's hybridity and identity is the greatest challenge it poses.

These are not shallow problems. They cannot be dealt with by a few policy changes and some deft diplomatic intervention. The lofty tone of one politician I encountered in 2020 who said that the UK's policy towards China was to be one of engagement, but with frank statements of disagreement when it was felt China was in the wrong is like attempting a schoolroom chastisement towards an adult well into their maturity. The impact of taking this line is almost certainly going to be counterproductive. It typifies the maintenance of a mindset that has simply failed to understand either the scale, or the depth, of the challenge China poses. Underneath it is the assumption that in the long term, the Enlightenment West will be proved right, and China will need to become something different from what it is. Apart from playing to a certain nationalistic and nostalgic sector of the public in the UK, it is hard to see what effectiveness such an approach would have with a government that, like that of the UK, expects to be treated with an equality of seriousness and respect, and not patronized and scolded like a child. This is especially the case after the great levelling experienced during the pandemic where governance everywhere was shown lacking. One could say the same about any other European or North American country.

Policy is often as much about setting out the limits of what is possible, saying where things cannot be done as much as busily plotting out possible interventions. There is an important economy of effort here. Spending much time trying to convince Americans of the merits of one-party systems makes about as much sense as trying to persuade British not just to say they will pay more tax for better public services in surveys, but to actually vote for this when the chance comes (something they have never done). In the end, certain things just are as they are. It is clear in the discussion in this book that the long, often serious, and no doubt sincere debates about how to help China with its legal and political reforms in the past have received a clear response from the Xi administration: they are not welcome, and they are no longer needed. The Chinese want cooperation, but one with their full input. The issue now is that there are many areas where they can name their terms as never before. Pragmatic acceptance of the closing down of these spaces which once looked promising means that we can focus on others that might lead somewhere.

For all the grand sense of responsibility felt by many in the West about the imperative to 'save' China, I have often wondered what really drove this large-hearted selflessness. Was China that interested in saving us? Clearly not, if one took its non-intervention stance seriously. But underneath this missionary zeal, there was always a sense that such a generous desire was in reality highly controlling and built on a colossal sense of cultural superiority. This book has referred to the British views in the nineteenth century which figured China as some ancient, crumbling, ruined edifice that had miraculously survived into the modern age. In the 1990s, a family friend who had been to Hong Kong four decades before, when I told him of my interest in studying Chinese, simply laughed and commented that his stay there only made him wonder how 'far they had fallen behind'. Observing myself, and people from outside of China accompanying me around the country when I lived there between 2000 and 2003, I became aware of what could almost be called a pornography of pity – looking at the clapped-out cars on the streets, seeing rundown buildings, people who dressed and looked poorly, and markets and public places that were chaotic and dirty in the way a third world place was meant to be. It was all somehow entertaining, almost comforting. This place was always going to struggle, it was never going to really make it. Gerald Segal in the 1990s simply used the phrase de Gaulle had deployed about Brazil: it was a country that had a lot of potential, and always would.[3]

Not before so long however, China stopped looking like this poor place. Visitors had to deal with cities that had better infrastructure, better facilities, grander hotels and vaster skyscrapers than their own developed countries. The 'saving Chinese' narrative needed to be updated. It became about the hidden hell these poor people were in behind these mirages, trapped in this phoney, predatory capitalism their leaders had cynically drugged them with. The business of saving China could therefore still go on. And yet, in the period after 2008, it became hugely complicated by the totally unscripted new plot line where the Enlightened West needed to start saving itself before being the saviour of others. Part of that meant getting help from China, not giving it. The sight of the European Stability Mechanism head Klaus Regling going to Beijing in 2009 seeking to secure funds to shore up Europe's financial system was one of the strangest, and most indicative of this new situation. This proved to be no blip. After the storming of the US Congress by protesters refusing to accept the outcome of the November 2020 US elections in January 2021, and the deep divisions in Europe from 2015 around the time of the UK's vote for Brexit, it is now unequivocally clear: the Enlightenment West can put its shining armour away and attend more urgently to its own business. The 'aid' of face masks given by China to Italians and others in 2020 was an event with a particular symbolic edginess in view of this history of Europeans wanting to save China. Who was the giver of aid now? And how did Europeans feel about that? Josep Borrell, the EU's High Representative for Foreign Affairs warned that the 'politics of generosity' concealed 'a geo-political component including a struggle for influence'. China, he added, 'is aggressively pushing the message that, unlike the U.S., it is a responsible and reliable partner ... Armed with facts, we need to defend Europe against its detractors.'[4] So much for accepting a gift with good grace.

Moving from the Bungalow

The geopolitical shift we are seeing is an historically significant one. For the first time in modern history, the world's largest economy could well be an Asian country under a Communist government. This may happen well before 2030. This is not the end of history as it was predicted in the 1990s when Communist systems were largely regarded as being well on their way to being relegated to the dustbins of history.

Even were China to have the same cultural and political characteristics as the US, a transition would have proved challenging. But very unfortunately, it is as though China had been designed in this scenario by a malevolent deity to be the absolute antithesis. Not only is it politically dissimilar but it is also that ultimate trigger to the US – a communist country. Since the 1940s, this is the political ideology the freedom-loving American's historically most despise. To add to the pain, it is also an atheist power. And finally, is a place with few strong common points socially and culturally. In view of this formidable list of issues, the wonder is not that the US and China get on so badly, but that they are all on speaking terms at all.

We also have to factor in the importance of ego and emotion here. For the US, it will remain the per capita superior to China long into the future. The average American is materially much better off, and will continue to be so for a long time, than the average Chinese. But this won't compensate for loss of that hugely important symbolic slot as the global economic number one, at least in gross terms. In 1985, according to CNBC, China's GDP in US dollars was 0.3 trillion, compared to 4.3 trillion for the US. In 2020, the figures were 14.7 and 20.9 respectively. China has gone from being 14 per cent of the American economy's size to almost three-quarters. This is one of the great catch ups of history.[5] The US has good cause to look nervously over its shoulder.

This potential change is more symbolic than anything else. But to human beings, symbols matter. At the moment, if and when China edges ahead of the US, the period of unipolar dominance America has enjoyed since the fall of the Soviet Union will come to an end. We will live in a multipolar world again. We will, in effect, be moving from a bungalow, to a two, three, or multilevel building – one with plenty of stairs from one storey to the next, and plenty of opportunity therefore to experience accidents and mishaps.

On the positive side, as this happens this world will be one of potentially huge creative dynamism. It will be one where the vision of a uniform, global set of norms and practices is no longer applicable. We will have different options, and different potential standards to choose between. This will be a world of radical diversity. Surely, for the pluralistic loving Enlightenment West this is a good thing? It will also be a world where the vast populations of China and India, constituting over a third of humanity, will be experiencing better living conditions than ever before. It will be a world where the limiting Second World War settlement of a tight group of victorious nations will have largely faded into the background, and a new more representative order appear in its place. It's also a world where the forever fretting, anxiety ridden West, always worrying about how to help and look after others, will be liberated by the fact that it can now attend to its own urgent issues. The rest of the world has a chance of looking after themselves just fine.

On the negative side, this is a world for which the Enlightenment West are ill prepared, and unlikely to feel comfortable in. It is one where their own norms and rules are likely to be ignored, sidelined, or contested. Fundamental areas of their thinking and huge numbers of assumptions they have made will need to be jettisoned. Modernization theory for a start will need a huge rethink. Political science will need to be rewritten too. Many will need to admit they were wrong – never an easy thing to do on a large scale. This is going to be a painful paradigm shift. The West are likely to prove sore losers, even if the situation is spun to them as an ultimate win. The multilevel world is one of where the possibility of trouble and potential instability is ever present. The neatness of the unipolar order where the only phone numbers that mattered to sort big issues had Washington dial codes will be gone. Now there will be a larger number of equally important voices. Agreement between them will be hard to achieve. Intervention in Syria in 2011 proved that, with Russia and China dissenting at the UN over what to do when the civil war broke out vetoed any multilateral action. This world will usher in a golden age for diplomats, because never before have there been issues of such scale and frequency and intensity that need dialogue and negotiation rather than assertion and force to resolve. No one will be able to impose solutions unilaterally. This is going to be a world where there is a lot of talk – and where that talk is necessary.

The multilayer world with the US on the first floor will have China on the second. That means that for China too, with its dislike of wider responsibilities, and its narrow definition of its national interests and the need to defend those, things will not be easy. It will be one in which frequently, over issues it does not regard itself as experienced about or ready to take a large role in, the fact that no one else will want to step in will necessitate its proactive response. It will experience the constant complaints, criticisms and demands of others the way that the US has had to do since 1945. Expectations towards it will often be too high. It will not have the capacity to do what is wanted of it, but nor will it have the option of doing nothing. As with its own people, in many ways it is not fears from others that it should most worry about, but their hopes towards it.

This will not be an easy world. China poses as many problems to itself as to others. But it will, at very least, be a possible world. The Enlightenment West will need to think in a different way. It will need to be constantly alert to the importance of reciprocity, balance, the kind of sources of harmony that Chinese often speak about as key to their own world view. This is a world where complexity is at least acknowledged by recognizing that there are some issues occupying common space, and others where fences and barriers of varying permeability are constructed.

There will need to be plenty of signs saying 'Keep Out' or 'Stay Away'. Some of these will need to be constructed in the virtual world. But this at least will be a world that can work up to a point. The only issue is just how much the Enlightenment West is willing to put away its beloved Ideals in order to head towards this new reality. China, however, is already well on the way there. Once more, we are playing catch up. But this time, we have no other option than to hurry – there is no other direction we can go in that does not lead to chaos, destruction and calamity.

NOTES

Introduction

1. Walter Russell Mead, 'Is China the Real Sick Man of Asia', *Wall Street Journal*, 3 February 2020. https://www.wsj.com/articles/china-is-the-real-sick-man-of-asia-11580773677

2. 'Greater China' here refers to The People's Republic of China, Hong Kong and Macau Special Administrative Regions, and Taiwan – though the latter as the Republic of China enjoys de facto independence. This term is therefore a geographical one, and carries no connotations of political unity.

3. Jamil Anderlini, 'Xi Jinping Faces China's Chernobyl Moment', *Financial Times*, 10 February 2020, https://www.ft.com/content/6f7fdbae-4b3b-11ea-95a0-43d18ec715f5

4. Clive Hamilton and Mereike Ohlberg. *Hidden Hand: Exposing How the Chinese Communist Party is Reshaping the World.* One World: London. 2020.

5. Kerry Brown. 'Why the West Needs to Stop its Moralising Against China.' E-International Website, 10 August 2020, https://www.e-ir.info/2020/08/10/why-the-west-needs-to-stop-its-moralising-against-china/

6. In the second week of January 2022, for instance, there are two excellent examples. The *Spectator* ran an astonishing piece by former US government official Dan Negrea, simply called 'China is the New Evil Empire' (https://spectatorworld.com/topic/china-new-evil-empire/). The same day, Li Yuan in the *New York Times* suggested that the draconian lockdowns in Xian were akin to the Holocaust of the Second World War (https://www.nytimes.com/2022/01/12/business/china-zero-covid-policy-xian.html). Both articles were full of hyperbole and attempted parallels between China and examples in the past like Nazi Germany which have been judged as evil. Both articles were typical of a huge amount of other material produced elsewhere.

7. For one example – there are many of these – see *The Times*, Roger Boyes, 'Xi Jinping Policy Reveals His Sinister Goals', 21 August 2021, https://www.thetimes.co.uk/article/xi-s-child-policy-reveals-his-sinister-goals-kpncdgdtm

Chapter 1

1. John Barrow. *Travels in China.* London: Cadell and Davies. 1804.

2. Kenneth Pomeranz. *The Great Divergence: China, Europe, and the Making*

of the Modern World Economy. Princeton University Press: Princeton and Oxford. 2000.

3   Angus Maddison, 'Monitoring the World Economy, 1820-1992', Organisation for Economic Cooperation and Development: Paris 1995. 30. See https://www.mtholyoke.edu/acad/intrel/ipe/topten.htm

4   Gordon Chang. *The Coming Collapse of China.* Random House: New York. 2001.

5   David Shambaugh, 'The Coming Chinese Crack Up', *Wall Street Journal,* 6 March 2015, https://www.wsj.com/articles/the-coming-chinese-crack-up-1425659198

6   Roger Irvine. *Forecasting China's Future: Dominance of Collapse.* Routledge: London. London and New York. 2016.

7   Mark Moore, 'China's President Xi Jinping Warns Bullies will "Face Broken Heads and Bloodshed"', *New York Post,* 1 July 2021, https://nypost. com/2021/07/01/chinas-xi-warns-bullies-will-face-broken-heads-and-bloodshed/

8   Françoise Jullien, trans. Janet Lloyd. *A Treatise on Efficacy.* University of Hawaii Press: Honolulu. 2004.

9   But for an excellent riposte to this and how effective it was in the twentieth century, see Wang Fanxi, trans. Gregor Benton. *On Mao Zedong Thought.* Haymarket Books: London. 2021.

10 Bernard Williams. *Truth and Truthfulness.* Princeton University Press: Princeton. 2002.

11 In his great *Imperial China: 900-1800/* Harvard University Press: Camb., Mass. 2003.

12 Yan Xuetong. *Ancient Chinese Thought. Modern Chinese Power.* Princeton University Press: Princeton. 2011.

Chapter 2

1   Ewan MacAskill, 'WikiLeaks: Hillary Clinton's Question: How Can We Stand up to Beijing?', Observer, 4 December 2010, https://www. theguardian.com/world/2010/dec/04/wikileaks-cables-hillary-clinton-beijing

2   It is hard to find the source for these words, however. At best, they are now so closely associated with Deng that they haven on a posthumous authority.

3   For at least one example of this kind of claim, see Rush Doshi, 'The Long Game: China's Grand Strategy to Replace American Order', *Brookings,* August 2021, https://www.brookings.edu/essay/the-long-game-chinas-grand-strategy-to-displace-american-order/

4   He is reported to have said that they 'Apparently appeared out of nowhere'. See B Li, 'Retrospect and Prospect of TVEs during the Fifteen Years of Reform and Opening Up,' *Management World,* No.5, 156–65, 1993.

5 Victor Nee and Sonja Opper. *Capitalism from Below: Markets and Institutional Change in China*. Harvard University Press: Camb., Mass., and London. 2012.

6 FBI Website, 'The China Threat', https://www.fbi.gov/investigate/counterintelligence/the-china-threat

7 Clifford Coonan, 'China Holds Military Parade to Commemorate End of WWII', *The Irish Times*, 3 September 2015, https://www.irishtimes.com/news/world/asia-pacific/china-holds-military-parade-to-commemorate-end-of-wwii-1.2338706

8 Helen Davidson and Julian Borger, 'China Could Mount Full-Scale Invasion by 2025, Taiwan Defence Minister Says', *Guardian*, 6 October 2021, https://www.theguardian.com/world/2021/oct/06/biden-says-he-and-chinas-xi-have-agreed-to-abide-by-taiwan-agreement

9 For an account of this, see Michael Schoenhals. *Spying for the People: Mao's Secret Agents 1949-1967*. Cambridge University Press, Cambridge. 2013.

10 In Fei Xiaotong, trans. Gary Hamilton and Wang Zheng. *From the Soil*. University of California Press: Irvine. 1992.

11 Liu Xiaobo, 'The Internet is God's Present to the Chinese', *The Times*, 28 April 2009, https://www.thetimes.co.uk/article/the-internet-is-gods-present-to-china-dtlnjwgxd2k

12 David Graeber and David Wengrow. *The Dawn of Everything: A New History of Humanity*. Allen Lane: London. 2021.

13 'Resisting Chinese Government Efforts to Undermine Academic Freedom Abroad A Code of Conduct for Colleges, Universities, and Academic Institutions Worldwide,' Human Rights Watch 2019. https://www.hrw.org/sites/default/files/media_2020/09/190321_china_academic_freedom_coc.pdf

14 Shih Hsiu-chan, 'EACS to Protest Hanban's Academic Meddling,' *Taipei Times*, 31 July 2014, https://www.taipeitimes.com/News/taiwan/archives/2014/07/31/2003596335

15 See John Garnaut, 'Chinese Spies at Sydney University', *Sydney Morning Herald*, 21 April 2014, https://www.smh.com.au/national/chinese-spies-at-sydney-university-20140420-36ywk.html

16 Daniel Hurst, 'Nearly one in five Chinese-Australians threatened or attacked in past year, survey finds', *Guardian*, 2 March 2021, https://www.theguardian.com/australia-news/2021/mar/03/nearly-one-in-five-chinese-australians-threatened-or-attacked-in-past-year-survey-finds

17 Peter J. Buckley, L. Jeremy Clegg, Adam R. Cross, Xin Liu, Hinrich Voss and Ping Zheng, 'The Determinants of Chinese Outward Foreign Direct Investment', *Journal of International Business Studies*, 2007, Vol 38, no 4, pp 499–518.

18 See, for instance, Theresa Fallon, 'The New Silk Road: Xi Jinping's Grand Strategy for Eurasia', *American Foreign Policy Interests*, 37(3), 140–7, May 2015. https://app.dimensions.ai/details/publication/pub.1022083070. For an excellent riposte to this, see Lee Jones and Shahar Hameiri. *Fractured*

China: State Transformation and Rising Powers. Cambridge: Cambridge University Press. 2021.

19 Samanth Subramanian, 'The rich vs the very, very rich: the Wentworth golf club rebellion', *Guardian*, 2 March 2021, https://www.theguardian.com/news/2021/mar/02/wentworth-golf-club-reignwood-yan-bin

20 See the list sourced from the CIA Factbook, available at https://en.wikipedia.org/wiki/List_of_countries_by_FDI_abroad, with data up to 2017. China comes twentieth in this list – below Ireland and Canada.

21 Maria Abi-Habib, 'How China Got Sri Lanka to Cough Up a Port', *New York Times*, 25 June 2018, https://www.nytimes.com/2018/06/25/world/asia/china-sri-lanka-port.html

22 Eleni Varvitsioti, 'Piraeus port deal intensifies Greece's unease over China links', *Financial Times*, 19 October 2021, https://www.ft.com/content/3e91c6d2-c3ff-496a-91e8-b9c81aed6eb8

23 https://www.theguardian.com/world/2017/jun/18/greece-eu-criticism-un-china-human-rights-record

24 John Hursh, 'A Bump in the Belt and Road: Tanzania Pushes Back Against Chinese Port Project', Center for International Maritime Security, 2 December 2019,https://cimsec.org/a-bump-in-the-belt-and-road-tanzania-pushes-back-against-chinese-port-project/

25 Eyck Freyman. *One Belt One Road: Where Chinese Power Meets the World.* Harvard University Press, Camb., Mass. 2021.

26 Tania Branigan and Justin McCurry, 'Japan releases Chinese fishing boat captain', *Guardian*, 24 September 2010, https://www.theguardian.com/world/2010/sep/24/japan-free-chinese-boat-captain

27 Caroline Humphrey and Frank Bille, *Along the Border.* Harvard University Press: Camb., Mass. 2021.

28 Henry Kissinger. *On China.* Penguin Press: New York. 2011.

29 Jullien, *A Treatise on Efficacy*, 32–33.

30 'National Intelligence Law of the PRC', China Law Translate, 27 June 2017, https://www.chinalawtranslate.com/en/national-intelligence-law-of-the-p-r-c-2017/

31 Michael, Smith, 'Spy Chiefs Fear Chinese Cyber Attack', *Sunday Times*, 29 March 2009, https://www.thetimes.co.uk/article/spy-chiefs-fear-chinese-cyber-attack-3z9vqhslsnt

32 Daniele Lepido, 'Vodafone Found Hidden Backdoors in Huawei Equipment'. Bloomberg, 30 April 2019. https://www.bloomberg.com/news/articles/2019-04-30/vodafone-found-hidden-backdoors-in-huawei-equipment

Chapter 3

1 François Jullien trans. Michael Richardson and Krzysztof Fijalkowski, *On the Universal: The Uniform, the Common, and Dialogue Between Cultures.* Polity: Cambridge. 2014.

2 For a selection of his views, see Kerry Brown and Chenger Deng. *China Through European Eyes*. World Scientific: Singapore. 2022. 74–90.

3 T. H. Barrett gives an eloquent account of this, at least from the case study of the UK, *in Singular Listlessness: Short History of Chinese Books and British Scholars*. Wellsweep Press: London. 1989.

4 Robert Cooper, 'The New Liberal Imperialism', *Guardian*, 7 April 2002, https://www.theguardian.com/world/2002/apr/07/1

5 For one more recent example, see Robin Emmott and Angeliki Koutantou, 'Greece blocks EU statement on China human rights at UN'. Reuters, 18 June 2017, https://www.reuters.com/article/us-eu-un-rights-idUSKBN1990FP

6 Xi Jinping, 'President Xi's speech at the College of Europe', China.org.cn, 1 April 2014, http://www.china.org.cn/world/2014-04/04/content_32004856.htm

7 Martin Jacques deploys this term in *When China Rules the World*. Allen Lane: London and New York. 2008.

8 European Commission: Closer Partners, Growing Responsibilities A policy paper on EU-China trade and investment: Competition and Partnership. 2006. https://eur-lex.europa.eu/legal-content/EN/TXT/?uri=celex%3A52006DC0632

9 Foreign and Commonwealth Office, 'The UK and China: A Framework for Engagement', 2009, This is, ironically, no longer available on the website of the Foreign and Development Office, but via other sites. https://www.yumpu.com/en/document/read/46582234/the-uk-and-china-a-framework-for-engagement

10 European Commission, 'Joint Communication to the European Parliament and the Council: Elements for a new EU strategy on China,' 22 June 2016, https://eeas.europa.eu/archives/docs/china/docs/joint_communication_to_the_european_parliament_and_the_council_-_elements_for_a_new_eu_strategy_on_china.pdf

11 European Commission and HR/VP contribution to the European Council, 'EU-China – A strategic outlook,' March 2019, https://ec.europa.eu/info/sites/default/files/communication-eu-china-a-strategic-outlook.pdf

12 State Council of the People's Republic of China: 'China's Policy Paper on the European Union', 18 December 2018, http://english.www.gov.cn/archive/ministrydocument/201812/18/content_WS5d3ae98cc6d08408f5022944.html

13 Fei Xiaotong, trans. Gary Hamilton and Wang Zheng. *From the Soil*. University of California Press: Irvine. 1992.

14 Jonathan Spence. *The Memory Palace of Matteo Ricci*. Viking: New York. 1984.

15 Matteo Ricci, trans. Douglas Lancashire and Peter Hu Kuo-chen. *The True Meaning of the Lord of Heaven*. Institut Ricci, Ricci Institute, Paris, London and Hong Kong. 1985. 97.

16 Ibid., 99.

17 Ibid., 175.

18 Simon Leys, *The Hall of Uselessness*. Black Inc: Collingwood, Australia. 2011, 260: 'Cultural initiation involves metamorphosis, and we cannot learn any foreign values if we do not accept the risk of being transformed by what we learn.'
19 Christine Gross-Loh and Michael J. Puett. *The Path: What Chinese Philosophers Can Teach Us About the Good Life*. Simon and Schuster: London and New York. 2016. Roel Sterkxx. *Chinese Thought: From Confucius to Cook Ding*. Pelican: London. 2019.

Chapter 4

1   United States Census, 'Trade in Goods with China', 2021, https://www.census.gov/foreign-trade/balance/c5700.html
2   Eurostat, 'China-EU – International Trade in Goods Statistics,' March 2021, https://ec.europa.eu/eurostat/statistics-explained/index.php?title=China-EU_-_international_trade_in_goods_statistics
3   Matthew Ward, 'Statistics on UK Trade with China,' UK Parliament, 14 July 2020, https://commonslibrary.parliament.uk/research-briefings/cbp-7379/
4   Imam Ghosh, 'How China Overtook the U.S. as the World's Major Trading Partner,' *Visual Capitalist*, 22 January 2020, https://www.visualcapitalist.com/china-u-s-worlds-trading-partner/
5   Weizhen Tan, 'Australia's Exports to China are Jumping Despite their Trade Fight,' CNBC, 27 October 2021, https://www.cnbc.com/2021/10/28/australias-exports-to-china-are-jumping-despite-their-trade-fight.html
6   Mark Jahn, 'Which Country is the Largest Exporter of Goods in the World,' Investopedia, 21 July 2021, https://www.investopedia.com/ask/answers/011915/what-country-worlds-largest-exporter-goods.asp and 'Is China the World's Top Trader?' China Power, 2021, https://chinapower.csis.org/trade-partner/
7   CNN Newsource, 'Tariffs with China will Cause Walmart to Raise Prices, Company Says,' 16 May 2019, https://www.10news.com/news/national/walmart-says-it-will-raise-prices-because-of-tariffs
8   Carl Crow. *400 Million Customers*. Earnshaw Books: Shanghai. 2008.
9   Full Text of Clinton's Speech on China Trade Bill, *New York Times*, 9 March 2000, https://archive.nytimes.com/www.nytimes.com/library/world/asia/030900clinton-china-text.html?source=post_page
10 'President Bush Speaks at Tsinghua University, Tsinghua University,' 22 February 2002, https://georgewbush-whitehouse.archives.gov/news/releases/2002/02/20020222.html
11 Remarks by President Obama and President Xi of the People's Republic of China in Joint Press Conference, 25 September 2015, https://obamawhitehouse.archives.gov/the-press-office/2015/09/25/remarks-president-obama-and-president-xi-peoples-republic-china-joint
12 'Remarks by Vice President Pence on the Administration's Policy Toward China,' Hudson Institute, 4 October 2018. https://trumpwhitehouse.

archives.gov/briefings-statements/remarks-vice-president-pence-administrations-policy-toward-china/

13 William J. Broad and David E. Sanger, 'Flexing Muscle, China Destroys Satellite in Test', 19 January 2007, https://www.nytimes.com/2007/01/19/world/asia/19china.html

14 Andrews Scobell, 'The J-20 Episode and Civil-Military Relations in China', Rand Corporation, March 2011, https://www.rand.org/content/dam/rand/pubs/testimonies/2011/RAND_CT357.pdf

15 Demetri Sevastopulo and Kathrin Hille, 'China tests new space capability with hypersonic missile', *Financial Times*, 16 October 2021, https://www.ft.com/content/ba0a3cde-719b-4040-93cb-a486e1f843fb

16 See for instance, Andrew J. Bacevich. *The Limits of Power: The End of American Exceptionalism*. Metropolitan Books: New York. 2008.

17 James Randerson and Mark Tran, 'China Accuses US of Double Standards Over Satellite Strike', *Guardian*, 21 February 2008, https://www.theguardian.com/science/2008/feb/21/spaceexploration.usa

18 Yasheng Huang. *Capitalism with Chinese Characteristics*. Cambridge University Press: Cambridge. 2008.

19 See https://www.hurun.net/en-US/Home/Index

20 Helene Cooper, 'China Could Have 1,000 Nuclear Warheads by 2030, Pentagon Says', *New York Times*, 3 November 2021, https://www.nytimes.com/2021/11/03/us/politics/china-military-nuclear.html

21 'World Nuclear Weapon Stockpile,' Ploughshares Fund , quoting the 'Bulletin of the Atomic Scientists' Nuclear Notebook', 15 June 2021, https://ploughshares.org/world-nuclear-stockpile-report

22 Rone Tempest, 'Barbie and the World Economy', *Los Angeles Times*, 22 September 1996, https://www.latimes.com/archives/la-xpm-1996-09-22-mn-46610-story.html

Chapter 5

1 Former president of Senegal, Abdoulaye Wade, referred approvingly as early as 2008 that 'I achieved more in my one hour meeting with President Hu Jintao in an executive suite at my hotel in Berlin during the recent G8 meeting in Heiligendamm than I did during the entire, orchestrated meeting of world leaders at the summit,' Wade, 'Time for the West to Practice what it Preaches', *Financial Times*, 23 January 2008, https://www.ft.com/content/5d347f88-c897-11dc-94a6-0000779fd2ac

2 The word 'caricature' is used carefully here, because there are many questions by, amongst others, John Wills about whether in fact historic Chinese dynasties did adopt this kind of posture towards others. See John E. Wills. *Past and Present in China's Foreign Policy: From 'Tribute System' to 'Peaceful Rise'*. Portland, ME: MerwinAsia. 2010.

3 Xi Jinping, 'Full Text of Xi Jinping keynote at the World Economic Forum', CGTN America, 17 January 2017, https://america.cgtn.com/2017/01/17/full-text-of-xi-jinping-keynote-at-the-world-economic-forum

4 Jiang Zemin, 'Full Text of Jiang Zemin's Speech to the 16th Party Congress', 2002, at http://www.china.org.cn/english/2002/Nov/49107.htm

5 Dong, K.Y., Sun, R.J., Li, H. et al. 'A Review of China's Energy Consumption Structure and Outlook Based on a Long-Range Energy Alternatives Modeling Tool', *Pet. Sci.* 14, 214–227, 2017. https://link.springer.com/article/10.1007/s12182-016-0

6 BP, 'Energy Outlook', 2019, https://www.bp.com/content/dam/bp/business-sites/en/global/corporate/pdfs/energy-economics/energy-outlook/bp-energy-outlook-2019-country-insight-china.pdf

7 'How is China's Energy Footprint Changing,' China Energy, 2021 CSIS, https://chinapower.csis.org/energy-footprint/

8 International Atomic Energy Agency, Country Nuclear Power Profiles 2020, https://cnpp.iaea.org/countryprofiles/China/China.htm

9 Import value of iron ore to China in 2020, by country of origin, *Statista*, 2021, https://www.statista.com/statistics/1070171/china-iron-ore-import-share-by-country/

10 'China's Iron Ore Imports Hit Record in Boost to Australia,' *Bloomberg News*, 13 September 2021, https://www.bloomberg.com/professional/blog/chinas-iron-ore-imports-hit-record-in-boost-to-australia/

11 Dai Bingguo quoted in *China Digital Times*, 7 August 2009, https://chinadigitaltimes.net/2009/08/dai-bingguo-%E6%88%B4%E7%A7%89%E5%9B%BD-the-core-interests-of-the-prc/

12 Julia Lovell. *Maoism: A Global History.* Bodley Head: London. 2020.

13 John Garver. *China's Quest.* Oxford University Press: Oxford. 2015.

14 Dominique Moisi. *The Geopolitics of Emotion.* Anchor: New York. 2010.

15 Richard New Lebow. *A Cultural Theory of International Relations.* Cambridge University Press: Cambridge. 2008.

16 Richard Ned Lebow and Feng Zhang. *Taming Sino-American Rivalry.* Oxford University Press: Oxford. 2020.

17 Todd H. Hall. *Emotional Diplomacy: Official Emotion on the International Stage.* Cornell University Press: New York. 2015.

18 Liu Xiaobo, edited Perry Link, Tienchi Martin-Liao and Liu Xia. *No Enemies, No Hatred.* The Bellknap Press of Harvard University Press: Cambridge, Mass. 2012. 233.

Chapter 6

1 Darren Byler. *Terror Capitalism: Uyghur Dispossession and Masculinity in a Chinese City.* Duke University Press: Durham, North Carolina. 2021.

2 Byler, 218.

3 James Millward. *Eurasian Crossroads: A History of Xinjiang*. Columbia University Press: New York. 2009. 4.
4 Ibid., 25.
5 Confucius, trans. Arthur Walley, *Analects, Book XIII*, Chapter 3, verses 4–7.

Chapter 7

1 Francis Fukayama. *The End of History and the Last Man*. Free Press: New York. 1992.
2 David Shambaugh. *China's Future*. Polity Press: Cambridge. 2016. xiii.
3 Yu Hua trans. Allan H Barr. *China in Ten Words*. Pantheon Books: New York. 2011. 219.
4 Caroline Humphrey and Frank Bille, *On the Edge: Life Along the Russia China Border*. Harvard University Press: Cambridge, Mass. 2021. 240.
5 Will Hutton. *The Writing on the Wall*. Simon and Schuster: New York. 2007.
6 George Magnus. *Red Flags: Why Xi Jinping's China is in Jeopardy*. Yale University Press: London and Yale. 2018.
7 Nicholas Lardy, 'China's Worsening Debts', Brookings Institute, Washington DC, 22 June 2001, https://www.brookings.edu/opinions/chinas-worsening-debts/
8 Koh Gui Qing. 'China's Ailing Bad Debt Market Cries for Change.' Reuters, 26 April 2012. https://www.reuters.com/article/china-economy-banks-idINDEE83P03I20120426
9 Martin Farrer and Vincent Ni. 'China's Lehman Brothers moment?: Evergrande crisis rattles economy', *Guardian*, 17 September 2021. https://www.theguardian.com/world/2021/sep/17/chinas-lehman-brothers-moment-evergrande-crisis-rattles-economy
10 James Gorrie. *The China Crisis: How China's Economic Collapse Will Lead to a Global Depression*. Wiley: Singapore. 2013.
11 Joe Studwell. *The China Dream: The Elusive Quest for the Greatest Untapped Market on the Earth*. Profile Books, London. 2002. X.
12 Roger Irvine. *Forecasting China's Future: Dominance of Collapse*. Routledge, London. London and New York, 2016. 99.
13 Peter Day, 'Ordos: The biggest ghost town in China', BBC, 17 March 2012, https://www.bbc.co.uk/news/magazine-17390729
14 Wade Shepard, 'An Update On China's Largest Ghost City – What Ordos Kangbashi Is Like Today', Forbes, 16 April 2016, https://www.forbes.com/sites/wadeshepard/2016/04/19/an-update-on-chinas-largest-ghost-city-what-ordos-kangbashi-is-like-today/?sh=5f0816862327
15 Larry Diamond, 'Why East Asia – Including China – Will Turn Democratic Within a Generation', *The Atlantic*, 24 January 2012, https://www.theatlantic.com/international/archive/2012/01/why-east-asia-including-china-will-turn-democratic-within-a-generation/251824/

16 Henry S Rosen, 'The Short March: China's Road to Democracy', *The National Interest*, 1 September 1996, https://nationalinterest.org/article/the-short-march-chinas-road-to-democracy-416

17 Diamond, ibid.

18 China's Threat To Democracies Around The World , Democracy Works, 16 September 2019, https://www.democracyworkspodcast.com/china/

19 Bruce Gilley. *China's Democratic Future: How it Will Happen and Where It Will Lead.* Columbia University Press: New York. 2004. The book once more reads somewhat differently in 2021 than it must have when it came out. 'In our age, in which democratic norms are universally accepted and authoritarian regimes struggle unsuccessfully to disempower societies strengthened by globalisation' (xi) had a particularly hubristic quality, and sounds, at least to a British person, like fellow nationals celebrating going one goal up in a World Cup football final, and thinking the whole event is now over!

20 Kerry Brown, 'Assessing Democracy Assistance', Fride, May 2010, https://www.kerry-brown.co.uk/wp-content/uploads/2020/01/website-7.pdf

21 Robert S Ross. *Chinese Security Policy: Structure, Power, and Politics.* Routledge: London. 2009.

22 Zhang Liang (ed.), Andrew J. Nathan and Perry Link. *The Tiananmen Papers.* Public Affairs: New York. 2001.

23 Song Qiang, Huang Jisu, Song Xiaojun, Wang Xiaodong and Liu Yang. *Unhappy China: The Great Time, Grand Vision and Our Challenges.* 2009.

24 Fortune 500 Top Companies 2021, *Fortune Magazine*, https://fortune.com/global500/?utm_content=invest&tpcc=gfortune500&gclid=Cj0KCQiA47GNBhDrARIsAKfZ2rCIDTm3o6m3x4l3NCisJq2Z1Sf3bs8DFaLi_3sXRYpeYr06VT66ejoaAglxEALw_wcB

25 Felix Richter, 'The Size of Apple's China Business', *Statista*, 18 February 2020, https://www.statista.com/chart/13246/apple-china-revenue/

26 Arjun Kharpul, 'China Spending on Research and Development to Rise 7% Per Year in Push for Major Tech Breakthroughs', CNBC, 5 March 2021, https://www.cnbc.com/2021/03/05/china-to-boost-research-and-development-spend-in-push-for-tech-breakthroughs.html

27 OECD Data, 'Gross Domestic Spending on R and D', 2020, https://data.oecd.org/rd/gross-domestic-spending-on-r-d.htm

Chapter 8

1 Matthew Lee, 'At Nixon Library, Pompeo Declares China Engagement a Failure', AP News, 23 July 2020, https://apnews.com/article/ca-state-wire-tx-state-wire-richard-nixon-foreign-policy-politics-052b38be7c16782dfc0409c452a18468

2 Marcel Maus. *The Gift: Forms and Functions of Exchange in Archaic Societies.* Cohen and West: London. 1966.

3   Gerald Segal, 'Does China Matter?', *Foreign Affairs*, September/October 1999, https://www.foreignaffairs.com/articles/asia/1999-09-01/does-china-matter

4   Charlie Campbell, 'China's "Mask Diplomacy" Is Faltering. But the U.S. Isn't Doing Any Better,' *Time Magazine*, 3 April 2020, https://time.com/5814940/china-mask-diplomacy-falters/

5   Evelyn Cheng and Van Lee Nee, 'New Chart Shows China Could Overtake the U.S. as the World's Largest Economy Earlier than Expected', CNBC, 31 January 2021, https://www.cnbc.com/2021/02/01/new-chart-shows-china-gdp-could-overtake-us-sooner-as-covid-took-its-toll.html

SUGGESTED FURTHER READING

The literature on China and its place in the world is truly voluminous, and would take several life times to read. The following suggestions are either for works that I personally found stimulating when preparing to write this book, or are from more recent works that present some fresh or updated insights.

I have been indebted here and elsewhere to the work of François Jullien in particular for larger framing issues. Thinking about comparisons between different cultures involves acts of faith around deciding in the first place how coherent the notion of a culture is, how best to define it, and in what ways one might select characteristics that can then be meaningfully compared between them. Discussing huge and contentious terms like the West, China, Asia, the Far East, has produced some wild and unruly work. But that doesn't mean that this labour shouldn't be done, and that we have to necessarily refrain from to trying to do it. Jullien's *A Treatise on Efficacy* (trans. Janet Lloyd, University of Hawaii Press: Honolulu. 2004) will no doubt enrage the purists and those that like their ideas small and under control, but I found his engagement with how to try to describe (and justify these descriptions) different Chinese and western world views immensely helpful. His work has stayed with me since I read it at the encouragement of a fellow participant at a conference in Beijing in 2017.

On the perennial issue of China's relations with the United States of America, Feng Zhang and Richard Ned Lebow, *Taming Sino-America Rivalry* (Oxford University Press, 2020) is a striking approach. It describes both as egotistical nations, ones which are largely concerned with their own notions of status and power, and have made multiple mistakes in their approach and relationship to each other over the last thirty years because of this underlying self-centredness. The book's third and fourth chapters in particular are an excellent and sobering diagnosis of American mistakes towards China and Chinese mistakes towards America in the period after 2006. The book is dismissive of power transition theory, and of ideas about deterrence, and proposes a much more hybrid and consensual framework for future relations – one that in my view may well be idealistic, but which is well argued and worth considering. This at least strives to show how a two track world might work. It has the added bonus of being by both an American and a Chinese author.

Grappling with similarly elemental issues, Shanghai-based historian Ge Zhaoguang's approach uses an historian's lens. His *What is China?: Territory, Ethnicity, Culture and History* (trans. Michael Gibbs Hill, Harvard University Press, Cambridge, Mass., 2018,) confronts the great issues lying at the heart of modern Chinese identity. His views might not be to everyone's taste (he makes few concessions on the issue of there being a coherent, unified sense of Chinese identity) but he backs them up with formidable scholarship. Yan Xuetong of Tsinghua University in Beijing is amongst the most influential of contemporary

China's thinkers and presents a more indigenous view of what the People's Republic's role in the world might be. Representative of his more recent work is 'Become Strong: The New Chinese Foreign Policy' in *Foreign Affairs* July/August 2021, https://www.foreignaffairs.com/articles/united-states/2021-06-22/becoming-strong. If there is an intellectual case within China for its current global posture then Yan is the person who makes it with most commitment and eloquence.

Lee Jones and Shahar Hameiri, *Fractured China: How State Transformation is Shaping China's Rise* (Cambridge University Press, 2021) look less outwardly, and more within the Chinese state. It argues that China's current state despite its external image as highly centralized and unified is in fact driven by multiple different power centres and many layers of policy considerations. They describe this as a regulatory state model, and argue that the interpretations of China's assertiveness are in fact only of partial elements of its behaviour. On the South China Sea issue, for instance, they state that China's approach has been contradictory, lacking in strategic clarity, and often reactive, rather than the more streamlined, aggressive posture credited to it in some commentary. The also show China as a more reactive than an assertive power in its relations with partners involved in the Belt and Road Initiative, such as Cambodia and Myanmar. While their model is not perhaps as novel as they say, because fragmentation has been a well understood feature of China's state behaviour for a long time, their argument that the reason Chinese diplomatic behaviour has proved so hard to properly describe is not so much due to its own strategic creativity, but because of the poverty of external conceptualizations of it, is well made.

The American international relations scholar, Brantly Womack, *Asymmetry and International Relations* (Cambridge University Press, 2016) is an excellent and intelligent account of how power is never as it seems, and how even between totally unequal partners it operates. This has helped in my own treatment of relationships and the power embodied with them I have used in this book. Initially a discussion of how the relations between larger and more powerful countries with ones smaller and weaker than them in fact involve far more complex dynamics, he uses the case of the DPRK and China well. Here he shows that despite vast disparities between the two, the DPRK often is able to achieve its goals because it has narrower and more focussed interests, and has less options to choose from, making life simpler and showing the strategic advantage, however paradoxical, of being small! Womack sets out a good theoretical model at the start of his book, which argues that the default in asymmetry is often not domination by the more powerful over the weaker, but stalemate. On this account, a world dominated by China is therefore not even theoretically that possible, because domination as it is portrayed by its main proponents has never really existed the way they suppose.

Values and the way they sit at the heart of debates with China about issues like human rights, is a thorny and complex area. Oxford academic, Rosemary Foot, in her *Rights Beyond Borders: The Global Community and the Struggle*

Over Human Rights in China (Oxford University Press, 2000) gives a characteristically lucid and cogent account of this area. An older book, it showed what the thinking was in the decade after the Tiananmen Square massacre in 1989 about how to conduct the values dialogue between China and the US/West and the balance between economic and other interests when there was at least some hope that eventually a global consensus on values and rights would prevail. If there was a case to be made, at a time it needed to be made, for enlightenment values, this was the book that best espoused this.

Similar to rights issues, the debate on highly contentious issues around China's behaviour and governance within itself best reaches its greatest intensity in recent years over the issue of Xinjiang. American expert Darren Byler's *Terror Capitalism: Uyghur Dispossession and Masculinity in a Chinese City* (Duke University Press, 2022) shines light in a dark place. This book is striking because it frames the region in terms of capital flows and interest, and the ways that these are linked to businesses in surveillance and face recognition technology, along with the apparatus of state repression. A hugely impressive work, based on detailed in-country field research, sophisticated in the framing of this issue, and one that places individual Uyghurs at the heart of the understanding and conceptualization of what is happening in contemporary Xinjiang.

INDEX